PREFACE

Developmental Mathematics: A Modular Curriculum for North Carolina is a fully integrated learning system that has been aligned to the redesigned curriculum established by the North Carolina Developmental Math Redesign Task Force. With the helpful input from instructors across the state, we have put together a program that presents problems in a meaningful context and explains the "why" behind problem solving in order to promote conceptual and sound mathematical learning. This is one of eight modules for the DMA curriculum, and is supported by a highly customizable online homework system that includes assessment tools, personalized study plans, and algorithmically generated problems to reinforce learning.

One central goal of the North Carolina Redesign Task Force was to create a curriculum with streamlined content in a modular format that could be completed in one academic year. Students can purchase only the modules needed for their developmental math requirements, and can work at a pace that is appropriate for their needs. Instructors can easily use this content with different classroom delivery methods, including self-paced Emporium labs, seated courses, and online or hybrid settings.

Another principle of the new curriculum is to develop students' conceptual understanding of mathematics through the use of contextually based problems. To that end, we have added the following features:

- New **Applied Introductions** have been written to introduce sections that are more applications-driven.
- Within the *Study Sets*, **Applications** problems and examples have been added and written to align with the NCCCS learning outcomes.
- **Concept Extensions** have been written and added to the *Study Sets* to ensure that key concepts meet the NCCCS curriculum.

In addition to new conceptual features that we have written specifically for North Carolina, we have added the following features to help guide students toward mastery of each module:

- **Course Information Sheets** start each module. These offer an explanation of the NCCCS process and ask questions that guide students to the practical knowledge that they will need in order to complete the program.
- **Are You Ready?** quizzes have been added to the beginning of each section to test students on the basic skills they will need in order to be successful with that section.
- **Module Tests**, appearing at the end of each module, have been carefully constructed to include the NCCCS learning outcomes required to pass the mastery test.

All content in these modules is supported by a corresponding prebuilt course in Enhanced WebAssign®, Cengage Learning's powerful online homework solution. Enhanced WebAssign® (EWA) engages students with immediate feedback on algorithmically generated versions of problems for unlimited practice. The *Show My Work* feature allows students to upload a file with the problem worked out, or to use a simple math palette to show their steps–helping you assess whether they understand the steps to solving a problem. The North Carolina EWA course has been prebuilt with a Personalized Study Plan, assignments, homework, and a Pre and Post Test for every module. Instructors can use the prebuilt course as is, or can customize or add material with ease.

A corresponding and fully interactive eBook, the Cengage YouBook, is integrated into the Enhanced WebAssign® course, and offers students convenient access to all module content. This powerful eBook lets you tailor the content to fit your course and provide your students with the ultimate learning experience with note-taking, highlighting, book-marking and search capabilities. Link students to your lecture notes, audio summaries, and engage them through conceptual tutorial videos as well as YouTube clips.

Cengage Learning is committed to providing unparallel service and training for faculty.

- **TeamUP Faculty Programs** help you reach and engage students by offering peer-to-peer consulting on curriculum and assessment, workshops, and professional development conferences.

TeamUP Faculty Program Consultants are a team of educators who understand your challenges whether your classroom is on-ground, online, or both.

Cengage Learning's team of **Faculty Advisors** are full-time educators and expert teachers in a diverse range of subject areas. They are available to share their experience on using Cengage Learning solutions and instructional best practices developed in their own classroom.

Explore all the ways TeamUP Faculty Programs can help you launch a new program or support your continuous improvement efforts. http://www.cengage.com/teamup/programs/ offers service and support from a dedicated team of experts to ensure your success using Enhanced WebAssign, including help with course set up, and more. http://www.cengage.com/coursecare/

TRUSTED FEATURES

- **Study Sets** found in each section offer a multifaceted approach to practicing and reinforcing the concepts taught in each section. They are designed for students to methodically build their knowledge of the section concepts, from basic recall to increasingly complex problem solving, through reading, writing, and thinking mathematically.

  Vocabulary—Each *Study Set* begins with the important *Vocabulary* discussed in that section. The fill-in-the-blank vocabulary problems emphasize the main concepts taught in the chapter and provide the foundation for learning and communicating the language of algebra.

  Concepts—In *Concepts,* students are asked about the specific subskills and procedures necessary to successfully complete the *Guided Practice* and *Try It Yourself* problems that follow.

  Notation—In *Notation,* the students review the new symbols introduced in a section. Often, they are asked to fill in steps of a sample solution. This strengthens their ability to read and write mathematics and prepares them for the *Guided Practice* problems by modeling solution formats.

  Guided Practice—The problems in *Guided Practice* are linked to an associated worked example or objective from that section. This feature promotes student success by referring them to the proper examples if they encounter difficulties solving homework problems.

  Try It Yourself—To promote problem recognition, the *Try It Yourself* problems are thoroughly mixed and are *not* linked to worked examples, giving students an opportunity to practice decision-making and strategy selection as they would when taking a test or quiz.

Developmental Mathematics:

A Modular Curriculum for North Carolina
Second Printing

FRACTIONS AND DECIMALS
DMA 020

ALAN S. TUSSY
CITRUS COLLEGE

R. DAVID GUSTAFSON
ROCK VALLEY COLLEGE

DIANE R. KOENIG
ROCK VALLEY COLLEGE

BROOKS/COLE
CENGAGE Learning

Brazil • Japan • Korea • Mexico • Singapore • Spain • United Kingdom • United States

BROOKS/COLE
CENGAGE Learning®

Developmental Mathematics: A Modular Curriculum for North Carolina, Second Printing: Fractions and Decimals
Alan S. Tussy, R. David Gustafson, Diane R. Koenig

Publisher: Charlie Van Wagner

Senior Developmental Editor: Danielle Derbenti

Senior Development Editor for Market Strategies: Rita Lombard

Assistant Editor: Stefanie Beeck

Editorial Assistant: Jennifer Cordoba

Media Editor: Heleny Wong

Marketing Manager: Gordon Lee

Marketing Assistant: Angela Kim

Marketing Communications Manager: Katy Malatesta

Content Project Manager: Jennifer Risden

Creative Director: Rob Hugel

Art Director: Vernon Boes

Print Buyer: Linda Hsu

Rights Acquisitions Account Manager, Text: Mardell Glinksi-Schultz

Rights Acquisitions Account Manager, Image: Don Schlotman

Text Designer: Diane Beasley

Photo Researcher: Bill Smith Group

Illustrators: Lori Heckelman; Graphic World Inc; Integra Software Services

Cover Designers: Ryan and Susan Stranz

Cover Image: Background: © Hemera/Thinkstock. © iStockphoto/Thinkstock.

Compositor: Integra Software Services

For product information and technology assistance, contact us at **Cengage Learning Customer & Sales Support, 1-800-354-9706**

For permission to use material from this text or product, submit all requests online at **www.cengage.com/permissions**

Further permissions questions can be e-mailed to **permissionrequest@cengage.com**

ISBN-13: 978-1-285-13309-6

ISBN-10: 1-285-13309-9

Brooks/Cole
20 Davis Drive
Belmont, CA 94002-3098
USA

Cengage Learning is a leading provider of customized learning solutions with office locations around the globe, including Singapore, the United Kingdom, Australia, Mexico, Brazil, and Japan. Locate your local office at **www.cengage.com/global**

Cengage Learning products are represented in Canada by Nelson Education, Ltd.

To learn more about Brooks/Cole, visit **www.cengage.com/brookscole**

Purchase any of our products at your local college store or at our preferred online store **www.CengageBrain.com**

Printed in the United States of America
1 2 3 4 5 6 7 14 13 12 11 10

To my lovely wife, Liz,
thank you for your insight and encouragement
ALAN S. TUSSY

▪

To my grandchildren:
Daniel, Tyler, Spencer, Skyler, Garrett, and Jake Gustafson
R. DAVID GUSTAFSON

▪

To my husband and my best friend, Brian Koenig
DIANE R. KOENIG

▪

Applications—The *Applications* provide students the opportunity to apply their newly acquired algebraic skills to relevant and interesting real-life situations.

Writing—The *Writing* problems help students build mathematical communication skills.

Review—The *Review* problems consist of randomly selected problems from previous chapters. These problems are designed to keep students' successfully mastered skills up-to-date before they move on to the next section.

- **Detailed Author Notes** that guide students along in a step-by-step process appear in the solutions to every worked example.

- **Think It Through** features make the connection between mathematics and student life. These relevant topics often require algebra skills from the chapter to be applied to a real-life situation. Topics include tuition costs, student enrollment, job opportunities, credit cards, and many more.

- **Using Your Calculator** is an optional feature that is designed for instructors who wish to use calculators as part of the instruction in this course. This feature introduces keystrokes and shows how scientific and graphing calculators can be used to solve problems. In the *Study Sets,* icons are used to denote problems that may be solved using a calculator.

ACKNOWLEDGMENTS

We want to express our gratitude to all those who helped with this project: Steve Odrich, Mary Lou Wogan, Paul McCombs, Maria H. Andersen, Sheila Pisa, Laurie McManus, Alexander Lee, Ed Kavanaugh, Karl Hunsicker, Cathy Gong, Dave Ryba, Terry Damron, Marion Hammond, Lin Humphrey, Doug Keebaugh, Robin Carter, Tanja Rinkel, Bob Billups, Jeff Cleveland, Jo Morrison, Sheila White, Jim McClain, Paul Swatzel, Matt Stevenson, Carole Carney, Joyce Low, Rob Everest, David Casey, Heddy Paek, Ralph Tippins, Mo Trad, Eagle Zhuang, and the Citrus College library staff (including Barbara Rugeley) for their help with this project. Your encouragement, suggestions, and insight have been invaluable to us.

We would also like to express our thanks to the Cengage Learning editorial, marketing, production, and design staff for helping us craft this new edition: Danielle Derbenti, Michael Stranz, Kim Fry, Heleny Wong, Charlie Van Wagner, Jill Staut, Liz Kendall, Marc Bove, Gordon Lee, Rita Lombard, Angela Hodge, Angela Kim, Maureen Ross, Jennifer Risden, Vernon Boes, Diane Beasley, Carol O'Connell, Graphic World and Integra Software Services.

Additionally, we would like to say that authoring a textbook is a tremendous undertaking. Producing a product of this scale that is customized to match a brand new curriculum would not have been possible without the thoughtful feedback and support from the following colleagues from throughout North Carolina listed below. Their contributions to this edition have shaped the creation of this book in countless ways.

A special acknowledgment is due to Lisa Key Brown, of Central Carolina Community College. Lisa's experience in the Developmental Math classroom, detailed knowledge of the new North Carolina curriculum, and expertise in using Enhanced WebAssign has been invaluable to us as we have prepared this developmental math program.

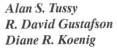

Alan S. Tussy
R. David Gustafson
Diane R. Koenig

Patricia C. Rome, *Delgado Community College*
Patricia B. Roux, *Delgado Community College*
Rebecca Rozario, *Brookdale Community College*
John Squires, *Cleveland State Community College*
Sharon Testone, *Onondaga Community College*
Bill Thompson, *Red Rocks Community College*
Barbara Tozzi, *Brookdale Community College*
Donna Tupper, *Community College of Baltimore County–Essex*
Andreana Walker, *Calhoun Community College*
Jane Wampler, *Housatonic Community College*
Arminda Wey, *Brookdale Community College*
Mary Lou Wogan, *Klamath Community College*
Valerie Wright, *Central Piedmont Community College*
Kevin Yokoyama, *College of the Redwoods*
Mary Young, *Brookdale Community College*

ABOUT THE AUTHORS

Alan S. Tussy

Alan Tussy teaches all levels of developmental mathematics at Citrus College in Glendora, California. He has written nine math books—a paperback series and a hardcover series. A meticulous, creative, and visionary teacher who maintains a keen focus on his students' greatest challenges, Alan Tussy is an extraordinary author, dedicated to his students' success. Alan received his Bachelor of Science degree in Mathematics from the University of Redlands and his Master of Science degree in Applied Mathematics from California State University, Los Angeles. He has taught up and down the curriculum from Prealgebra to Differential Equations. He is currently focusing on the developmental math courses. Professor Tussy is a member of the American Mathematical Association of Two-Year Colleges.

R. David Gustafson

R. David Gustafson is Professor Emeritus of Mathematics at Rock Valley College in Illinois and coauthor of several best-selling math texts, including Gustafson/Frisk's *Beginning Algebra, Intermediate Algebra, Beginning and Intermediate Algebra: A Combined Approach, College Algebra,* and the Tussy/Gustafson developmental mathematics series. His numerous professional honors include Rock Valley Teacher of the Year and Rockford's Outstanding Educator of the Year. He earned a Master of Arts from Rockford College in Illinois, as well as a Master of Science from Northern Illinois University.

Diane R. Koenig

Diane Koenig received a Bachelor of Science degree in Secondary Math Education from Illinois State University in 1980. She began her career at Rock Valley College in 1981, when she became the Math Supervisor for the newly formed Personalized Learning Center. Earning her Master's Degree in Applied Mathematics from Northern Illinois University, Ms. Koenig in 1984 had the distinction of becoming the first full-time woman mathematics faculty member at Rock Valley College. In addition to being nominated for AMATYC's Excellence in Teaching Award, Diane Koenig was chosen as the Rock Valley College Faculty of the Year by her peers in 2005, and, in 2006, she was awarded the NISOD Teaching Excellence Award as well as the Illinois Mathematics Association of Community Colleges Award for Teaching Excellence. In addition to her teaching, Ms. Koenig has been an active member of the Illinois Mathematics Association of Community Colleges (IMACC). As a member, she has served on the board of directors, on a state-level task force rewriting the course outlines for the developmental mathematics courses, and as the association's newsletter editor.

Module 2: Fractions and Decimals

iStockphoto.com/Monkeybusinessimages

from *Campus to Careers*

School Guidance Counselor

School guidance counselors plan academic programs and help students choose the best courses to take to achieve their educational goals. Counselors often meet with students to discuss the life skills needed for personal and social growth. To prepare for this career, guidance counselors take classes in an area of mathematics called *statistics*, where they learn how to collect, analyze, explain, and present data.

In **Problem 109** of **Study Set 2.4,** you will see how a counselor must be able to add fractions to better understand a graph that shows students' study habits.

JOB TITLE: School Guidance Counselor

EDUCATION: A master's degree is usually required to be licensed as a counselor. However, some schools accept a bachelor's degree with the appropriate counseling courses.

JOB OUTLOOK: A growth rate of about 20% from 2010 to 2020.

ANNUAL EARNINGS: The average (median) salary in 2010 was $53,380.

FOR MORE INFORMATION: www.bls.gov/oco/ocos067.htm

Course Information Sheet

Overview

Module 2: Fractions and Decimals is one of the eight modules that make up the North Carolina Community College System Developmental Math Program. This program is for students who want to meet the prerequisites for the math requirements for their two year degree, or for those who are planning to transfer to a college or university. It is designed to allow you to complete the required developmental math courses at a pace that is appropriate to your needs and knowledge.

Placement

The diagnostic test that you took to enter the NCCCS Developmental Math Program has indentified your mathematical strengths and weaknesses. The test results that you received indicate which of the eight modules you are required to complete before you can enroll in more advanced mathematics courses, such as Precalculus and Statistics. It is important to note that any modules you are required to take must be taken in numerical order. For example, if the diagnostic test indicated that you need to take Modules 2 and 3, you must successfully complete Module 2 before you can register for Module 3.

Mastery

A core principle of the NCCCS Developmental Math Program is the concept of mastery of the material. To show mastery, students need to successfully complete all coursework in a module, as well as pass a final assessment exam.

Getting started

Starting a new course can be exciting, but it might also make you a bit nervous. In order to be successful, you need a plan. Here are some suggestions: Make time for the course, know what is expected, build a support system. You can begin to form your personal plan for success by answering questions on the next page.

©iStockphoto/Thinkstock

1. What is your instructor's name? What is his/her phone number and email address?

2. When and where does your class meet?

3. What are the days and times of your instructor's office hours? Where does he/she hold office hours?

4. Does your campus have a math tutoring center? If so, where is it located and what are its hours of operation? Is the tutoring free? Do you need your instructor to sign a form before you begin at the tutoring center?

5. What other ways are there for you to receive additional help with this module?

6. What are the names, phone numbers, and email addresses of three students in your class that you can contact for help if you have missed class, want to form a study group, or have questions regarding a homework assignment?

7. How many hours does your instructor feel you should expect to spend on this course each week?

8. Did you write down your WebAssign user id and password in a safe place where you can find it should you forget?

9. On what day and at what time is the final module assessment exam?

10. What percent correct is needed to pass the final module assessment exam? How many times can the final assessment exam be taken?

SECTION 2.1

Applications Introduction: Fractions

The **whole numbers** are 0, 1, 2, 3, 4, 5, 6, 7, 8, 9, 10, 11, 12, … . They are often used to answer questions such as: *How many? How fast?*, and *How far?*

- The University of North Carolina Tar Heels have won 5 NCAA men's basketball tournament championships.

- The top speed of a NASCAR car on the Talladega Superspeedway is 212 miles per hour.

- The sun is at an average distance of about 93,000,000 miles away from Earth.

Fractions are used to answer similar questions, but they are needed when the answer is *more* than or *less* than a whole number. In general, a **fraction** describes the number of equal parts of a whole. For example, consider the figure below with 5 of the 6 equal parts colored red. We say that $\frac{5}{6}$ (five-sixths) of the figure is shaded.

In a fraction, the number above the **fraction bar** is called the **numerator**, and the number below is called the **denominator.**

Fractions in action   Fractions are everywhere! We see them while shopping at the mall, driving on the freeway, and cooking in the kitchen. They are also widely used in construction, music, sports, and gardening. In each statement, circle any words that describe fractions. Then write the fractions in numerical form. Number 1 is done for you.

1. ***Government.*** To approve an amendment to the United States Constitution, it takes the approval of three-fourths of the state legislatures.

2. ***Oceanography.*** Nine-tenths of an iceberg is below water. Only one-tenth is above water.

3. ***Gardening.*** The average inside diameter of a vinyl garden hose is five-eighths of an inch.

4. ***Transportation.*** In Philadelphia, the fare for a taxi is an initial charge of $2.70, and 30¢ for each additional one-seventh mile.

5. ***Music.*** The symbol ♪ represents a musical note that is to be played for one-eighth the length of a whole note.

6. ***Drag racing.*** The most common length of a drag racing track is one-quarter of a mile.

7. ***Horse racing.*** The Breeders' Cup Filly & Mare Sprint is a race for thoroughbred fillies and mares three years old and up. It is a distance of 7 furlongs, which is seven-eighths of a mile.

8. ***Law.*** The phrase "possession is nine-tenths of the law" is from English common law of the 1500's. It means that if you actually possess something, you

have a stronger legal claim to owning it than someone who merely says it belongs to him or her. This concept is not valid in today's legal system.

9. *Hair styling.* Curling irons come as small as three-eighths inch in diameter.

10. *Tires.* A brand new tire has a tread of about thirteen thirty-seconds of an inch. A tire is worn out when the tread reaches two thirty-seconds of an inch, or less.

11. *Anatomy.* On average, a human eye takes between three-tenths and four-tenths of a second to blink.

12. *Soft drinks.* There is about one-fifth cup of sugar in a 12-ounce can of Coke.

13. *Native Americans.* According to the Cherokee Nation's Department of Registration, 21% of the tribe has one-sixteenth to one sixty-fourth degree of Cherokee blood. This means that person has at least one Cherokee great-great-great-great grandparent.

14. *NBA records.* The most points scored in the first quarter by two teams of an NBA game was a total 91 by the Utah Jazz (50 points) verses the Denver Nuggets(41 points), on April 10, 1982.

15. *Tornados.* A monster tornado killed at least 116 people in Joplin, Missouri, when it tore through the heart of the city in the late afternoon of Sunday, May 22, 2011. Its path was nearly six miles long and about three-fourths of a mile wide.

16. *Swimming.* Michael Phelps won his seventh gold medal at the 2008 Summer Olympic games in the 100-meter butterfly by only one one-hundredth of a second.

17. *Geography.* The land area of North Carolina is about seven five-hundredths of the land area of the entire United States.

18. *Telling time.* Instead of saying, "It's 1:45 pm," we can say, "It's a quarter 'til 2."

19. *Circles.* π (pi) represents the quotient of the circumference of a circle and its diameter. Twenty-two sevenths is a good approximation of π. However, three hundred fifty-five one hundred-thirteenths is an even better approximation.

20. *Changing tires.* Lug nuts are used to secure wheels to automobiles. Two of the most common socket sizes for wrenches that are used to loosen and tighten lug nuts are three-sixteenths of an inch and seven-eighths of an inch.

21. *US Coins.* The *half cent* is the smallest denomination of United States coin ever minted. It was produced from 1793-1857 and was 100% copper. It was valued at one two-hundredths of a dollar.

22. *Shopping.* During Nordstrom's semi-annual sale, women's designer handbags are often marked one-third off.

23. *Fast food.* An internet site has a copycat recipe for making Wendy's famous chili. Some of the ingredients are one-half cup of celery and one-eighth teaspoon of cayenne pepper.

24. *Engineering.* The high-strength aluminum "skin" that covers the air frame of a Boeing 747 passenger jet is only one-fifth inch thick.

Objectives

1 Identify the numerator and denominator of a fraction.

2 Graph fractions on the number line.

3 Simplify special fraction forms.

4 Define equivalent fractions.

5 Build equivalent fractions.

6 Prime factor whole numbers.

7 Simplify fractions.

SECTION 2.1

An Introduction to Fractions

ARE YOU READY?

The following problems review some basic skills that are needed when working with fractions.

1. What is the value of $\frac{8}{8}$?

2. Multiply: $2 \cdot 3 \cdot 5 \cdot 5$

3. Is 42 divisible by 3?

4. Fill in the blanks.
   a. $16 = 2 \cdot 2 \cdot 2 \cdot$ ▓ **b.** $30 = 2 \cdot 3 \cdot$ ▓

5. Evaluate:
   a. $4 \cdot 1$ **b.** $12 \cdot 1$

6. Into how many equal parts has the circular region below been divided?

Whole numbers are used to count objects, such as CDs, stamps, eggs, and magazines. When we need to describe a part of a whole, such as one-half of a pie, three-quarters of an hour, or a one-third-pound burger, we can use *fractions*.

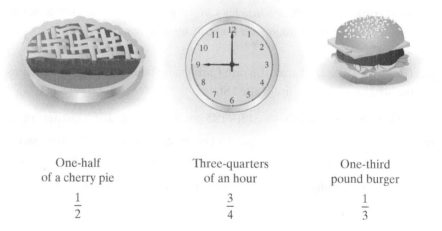

One-half of a cherry pie	Three-quarters of an hour	One-third pound burger
$\frac{1}{2}$	$\frac{3}{4}$	$\frac{1}{3}$

1 Identify the numerator and denominator of a fraction.

A **fraction** describes the number of equal parts of a whole. For example, consider the figure below with 5 of the 6 equal parts colored red. We say that $\frac{5}{6}$ (five-sixths) of the figure is shaded.

In a fraction, the number above the **fraction bar** is called the **numerator,** and the number below is called the **denominator.**

Fraction bar $\longrightarrow$ $\dfrac{5 \longleftarrow \text{ numerator}}{6 \longleftarrow \text{ denominator}}$

> ***The Language of Mathematics***   The word *fraction* comes from the Latin word *fractio* meaning "breaking in pieces."

EXAMPLE 1   Identify the numerator and denominator of each fraction:

a. $\frac{11}{12}$ **b.** $\frac{8}{3}$

Strategy We will find the number above the fraction bar and the number below it.

WHY The number above the fraction bar is the numerator, and the number below is the denominator.

Solution

a. $\frac{11}{12}$ ←— numerator
        ←— denominator

b. $\frac{8}{3}$ ←— numerator
       ←— denominator

Self Check 1

Identify the numerator and denominator of each fraction:

a. $\frac{7}{9}$

b. $\frac{21}{20}$

Now Try Problem 23

If the numerator of a fraction is less than its denominator, the fraction is called a **proper fraction.** A proper fraction is less than 1. If the numerator of a fraction is greater than or equal to its denominator, the fraction is called an **improper fraction.** An improper fraction is greater than or equal to 1.

Proper fractions

$\frac{1}{4}$, $\frac{2}{3}$, and $\frac{98}{99}$

Improper fractions

$\frac{7}{2}$, $\frac{98}{97}$, $\frac{16}{16}$, and $\frac{5}{1}$

> *The Language of Mathematics*   The phrase *improper fraction* is somewhat misleading. In algebra and other mathematics courses, we often use such fractions "properly" to solve many types of problems.

EXAMPLE 2   Write fractions that represent the shaded and unshaded portions of the figure below.

Strategy We will determine the number of equal parts into which the figure is divided. Then we will determine how many of those parts are shaded.

WHY The denominator of a fraction shows the number of equal parts in the whole. The numerator shows how many of those parts are being considered.

Solution
Since the figure is divided into 3 equal parts, the denominator of the fraction is 3. Since 2 of those parts are shaded, the numerator is 2, and we say that

$\frac{2}{3}$ of the figure is shaded.   Write: $\frac{number\ of\ parts\ shaded}{number\ of\ equal\ parts}$

Since 1 of the 3 equal parts of the figure is not shaded, the numerator is 1, and we say that

$\frac{1}{3}$ of the figure is not shaded.   Write: $\frac{number\ of\ parts\ not\ shaded}{number\ of\ equal\ parts}$

Self Check 2

Write fractions that represent the portion of the month that has passed and the portion that remains.

DECEMBER

X	X	X	X	X	X	X
X	X	X	X	12	13	14
15	16	17	18	19	20	21
22	23	24	25	26	27	28
29	30	31				

Now Try Problems 25 and 105

iStockphoto.com/Jamie VanBuskirk

There are times when a negative fraction is needed to describe a quantity. For example, if an earthquake causes a road to sink seven-eighths of an inch, the amount of downward movement can be represented by $-\frac{7}{8}$. Negative fractions can be written in three ways. The negative sign can appear in the numerator, in the denominator, or in front of the fraction.

$$\frac{-7}{8} = \frac{7}{-8} = -\frac{7}{8} \qquad \frac{-15}{4} = \frac{15}{-4} = -\frac{15}{4}$$

Notice that the examples above agree with the rule for dividing integers with different (unlike) signs: *the quotient of a negative integer and a positive integer is negative.*

2 Graph fractions on the number line.

Using a process called **graphing**, we can represent a single fraction or a set of fractions on a number line. **The graph of a fraction** is the point on the number line that corresponds to that fraction. To **graph** (or **plot**) a fraction means to locate its position on the number line and highlight it with a heavy dot.

Self Check 3

Graph $\frac{2}{5}$ and $-\frac{7}{8}$ on a number line.

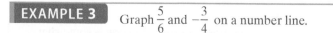

Now Try **Problem 29**

EXAMPLE 3   Graph $\frac{5}{6}$ and $-\frac{3}{4}$ on a number line.

Strategy We will think of the distance between 0 and 1 (and the distance between 0 and −1) on a number line as one whole. Then we will divide each distance into the proper number of equal parts.

WHY A fraction describes the numbers of equal parts of a whole.

Solution

The denominator of $\frac{5}{6}$ indicates that we should divide the distance between 0 and 1 on a number line into 6 equal parts. The numerator indicates that we should consider 5 of those parts. To graph $\frac{5}{6}$, we start at 0 and move to the right 5 parts. At that point, we draw a heavy dot and label the fraction.

Since $-\frac{3}{4}$ is negative, its graph lies to the left of 0. To graph it, we divide the distance between 0 and −1 into 4 equal parts, as indicated by the denominator 4. Then from 0, we move 3 parts to the left, as indicated by the numerator. At that point, we draw a heavy dot and label the fraction.

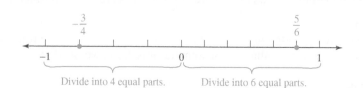

Success Tip The graph of any positive proper fraction is between 0 and 1 on the number line.

3 Simplify special fraction forms.

A fraction bar indicates division. This fact helps us simplify four special fraction forms.

- **Fractions that have the same numerator and denominator:** In this case, we have a number divided by itself. The result is 1 (provided the numerator and denominator are not 0). We call each of the following fractions a **form of 1.**

$$1 = \frac{1}{1} = \frac{2}{2} = \frac{3}{3} = \frac{4}{4} = \frac{5}{5} = \frac{6}{6} = \frac{7}{7} = \frac{8}{8} = \frac{9}{9} = \cdots$$

- **Fractions that have a denominator of 1:** In this case, we have a number divided by 1. The result is simply the numerator.

$$\frac{5}{1} = 5 \qquad \frac{24}{1} = 24 \qquad \frac{-7}{1} = -7$$

- **Fractions that have a numerator of 0:** In this case, we have division of 0. The result is 0 (provided the denominator is not 0).

$$\frac{0}{8} = 0 \qquad \frac{0}{56} = 0 \qquad \frac{0}{-11} = 0$$

- **Fractions that have a denominator of 0:** In this case, we have division by 0. The division is undefined.

$$\frac{7}{0} \text{ is undefined} \qquad \frac{-18}{0} \text{ is undefined}$$

> **The Language of Mathematics**   Perhaps you are wondering about the fraction form $\frac{0}{0}$. It is said to be *undetermined*. This form is important in advanced mathematics courses.

EXAMPLE 4   Simplify, if possible: **a.** $\frac{12}{12}$ **b.** $\frac{0}{24}$ **c.** $\frac{18}{0}$ **d.** $\frac{9}{1}$

Strategy To simplify each fraction, we will divide the numerator by the denominator, if possible.

WHY A fraction bar indicates division.

Solution

a. $\frac{12}{12} = 1$ This corresponds to dividing a quantity into 12 equal parts, and then considering all 12 of them. We would get 1 whole quantity.

b. $\frac{0}{24} = 0$ This corresponds to dividing a quantity into 24 equal parts, and then considering 0 (none) of them. We would get 0.

c. $\frac{18}{0}$ is undefined   This corresponds to dividing a quantity into 0 equal parts, and then considering 18 of them. That is not possible.

d. $\frac{9}{1} = 9$ This corresponds to "dividing" a quantity into 1 equal part, and then considering 9 of them. We would get 9 of those quantities.

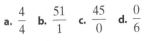

Self Check 4

Simplify, if possible:

a. $\frac{4}{4}$ **b.** $\frac{51}{1}$ **c.** $\frac{45}{0}$ **d.** $\frac{0}{6}$

Now Try Problem 31

The Language of Mathematics Fractions are often referred to as **rational numbers.** All integers are rational numbers, because every integer can be written as a fraction with a denominator of 1. For example,

$$2 = \frac{2}{1}, \quad -5 = \frac{-5}{1}, \quad \text{and} \quad 0 = \frac{0}{1}$$

4 Define equivalent fractions.

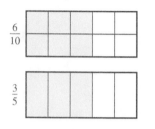

Fractions can look different but still represent the same part of a whole. To illustrate this, consider the identical rectangular regions on the right. The first one is divided into 10 equal parts. Since 6 of those parts are red, $\frac{6}{10}$ of the figure is shaded.

The second figure is divided into 5 equal parts. Since 3 of those parts are red, $\frac{3}{5}$ of the figure is shaded. We can conclude that $\frac{6}{10} = \frac{3}{5}$ because $\frac{6}{10}$ and $\frac{3}{5}$ represent the same shaded portion of the figure. We say that $\frac{6}{10}$ and $\frac{3}{5}$ are *equivalent fractions*.

> ### Equivalent Fractions
>
> Two fractions are **equivalent** if they represent the same number. **Equivalent fractions** represent the same portion of a whole.

5 Build equivalent fractions.

Writing a fraction as an equivalent fraction with a *larger* denominator is called **building** the fraction. To build a fraction, we use the following property.

> ### Multiplication Property of 1
>
> The product of any fraction and 1 is that fraction.

We use the following rule for multiplying fractions.

> ### Multiplying Fractions
>
> To multiply two fractions, multiply the numerators and multiply the denominators.

To build an equivalent fraction for $\frac{1}{2}$ with a denominator of 8, we first ask, "What number times 2 equals 8?" To answer that question we *divide* 8 by 2 to get 4. Since we need to multiply the denominator of $\frac{1}{2}$ by 4 to obtain a denominator of 8, it follows that $\frac{4}{4}$ should be the form of 1 that is used to build an equivalent fraction for $\frac{1}{2}$.

$$\frac{1}{2} = \frac{1}{2} \cdot \frac{4}{4} \qquad \text{Multiply } \tfrac{1}{2} \text{ by 1 in the form of } \tfrac{4}{4}. \text{ Note the form of 1 highlighted in red.}$$

$$= \frac{1 \cdot 4}{2 \cdot 4} \qquad \text{Use the rule for multiplying two fractions. Multiply the numerators. Multiply the denominators.}$$

$$= \frac{4}{8}$$

We have found that $\frac{4}{8}$ is equivalent to $\frac{1}{2}$. To build an equivalent fraction for $\frac{1}{2}$ with a denominator of 8, we *multiplied by a factor equal to 1* in the form of $\frac{4}{4}$. Multiplying $\frac{1}{2}$ by $\frac{4}{4}$ changes its appearance but does not change its value, because we are multiplying it by 1.

Building Fractions

To build a fraction, *multiply it by a factor of 1* in the form $\frac{2}{2}, \frac{3}{3}, \frac{4}{4}, \frac{5}{5}$, and so on.

The Language of Mathematics   Building an equivalent fraction with a larger denominator is also called *expressing a fraction in higher terms*.

EXAMPLE 5   Write $\frac{3}{5}$ as an equivalent fraction with a denominator of 35.

Strategy We will compare the given denominator to the required denominator and ask, "What number times 5 equals 35?"

WHY The answer to that question helps us determine the form of 1 to use to build an equivalent fraction.

Solution
To answer the question "What number times 5 equals 35?" we *divide* 35 by 5 to get 7. Since we need to multiply the denominator of $\frac{3}{5}$ by 7 to obtain a denominator of 35, it follows that $\frac{7}{7}$ should be the form of 1 that is used to build an equivalent fraction for $\frac{3}{5}$.

$$\frac{3}{5} = \frac{3}{5} \cdot \boxed{\frac{7}{7}} \qquad \text{Multiply } \tfrac{3}{5} \text{ by a form of 1: } \tfrac{7}{7} = 1.$$

$$= \frac{3 \cdot 7}{5 \cdot 7} \qquad \begin{array}{l} \text{Multiply the numerators.} \\ \text{Multiply the denominators.} \end{array}$$

$$= \frac{21}{35}$$

We have found that $\frac{21}{35}$ is equivalent to $\frac{3}{5}$.

Self Check 5
Write $\frac{5}{8}$ as an equivalent fraction with a denominator of 24.

Now Try Problems 33 and 45

Success Tip To build an equivalent fraction in Example 5, we multiplied $\frac{3}{5}$ by 1 in the form of $\frac{7}{7}$. As a result of that step, the numerator and the denominator of $\frac{3}{5}$ were multiplied by 7:

$$\frac{3 \cdot 7}{5 \cdot 7} \quad \begin{array}{l} \longleftarrow \text{ The numerator is multiplied by 7.} \\ \longleftarrow \text{ The denominator is multiplied by 7.} \end{array}$$

This process illustrates the following property of fractions.

The Fundamental Property of Fractions

If the numerator and denominator of a fraction are multiplied by the same nonzero number, the resulting fraction is equivalent to the original fraction.

Since multiplying the numerator and denominator of a fraction by the same nonzero number produces an equivalent fraction, your instructor may allow you to begin your solution to problems like Example 5 as shown in the Success Tip above.

Write 10 as an equivalent fraction with a denominator of 3.

Now Try **Problem 53**

EXAMPLE 6   Write 4 as an equivalent fraction with a denominator of 6.

Strategy We will express 4 as the fraction $\frac{4}{1}$ and build an equivalent fraction by multiplying it by $\frac{6}{6}$.

WHY Since we need to multiply the denominator of $\frac{4}{1}$ by 6 to obtain a denominator of 6, it follows that $\frac{6}{6}$ should be the form of 1 that is used to build an equivalent fraction for $\frac{4}{1}$.

Solution

$$4 = \frac{4}{1} \qquad \text{Write 4 as a fraction: } 4 = \frac{4}{1}.$$

$$= \frac{4}{1} \cdot \frac{6}{6} \qquad \text{Build an equivalent fraction by multiplying } \frac{4}{1} \text{ by a form of 1: } \frac{6}{6} = 1.$$

$$= \frac{4 \cdot 6}{1 \cdot 6} \qquad \begin{array}{l}\text{Multiply the numerators.}\\ \text{Multiply the denominators.}\end{array}$$

$$= \frac{24}{6}$$

6 Prime Factor Whole Numbers.

To work with fractions, we need to know how to *factor* whole numbers. To **factor** a number means to express it as a product of two or more numbers. For example, some ways to factor 8 are

$$1 \cdot 8, \quad 4 \cdot 2, \quad \text{and} \quad 2 \cdot 2 \cdot 2$$

The numbers 1, 2, 4, and 8 that were used to write the products are called *factors* of 8. In general, a **factor** is a number being multiplied.

Sometimes a number has only two factors, itself and 1. We call such numbers *prime numbers*.

Prime Numbers and Composite Numbers

A **prime number** is a whole number greater than 1 that has only itself and 1 as factors. The first ten prime numbers are 2, 3, 5, 7, 11, 13, 17, 19, 23, and 29.

A **composite number** is a whole number, greater than 1, that is not prime. The first ten composite numbers are 4, 6, 8, 9, 10, 12, 14, 15, 16, and 18.

Every composite number can be factored into the product of two or more prime numbers. This product of these prime numbers is called its **prime factorization**.

EXAMPLE 7   Find the prime factorization of 210.

Strategy We will use a series of steps to express 210 as a product of only prime numbers

WHY To *prime factor* a number means to write it as a product of prime numbers.

Solution

First, write 210 as the product of two whole numbers other than 1.

$$210 = 10 \cdot 21 \qquad \begin{array}{l}\text{The resulting prime factorization will be the same no matter which}\\ \text{two factors of 210 you begin with.}\end{array}$$

Neither 10 nor 21 are prime numbers, so we factor each of them.

$$210 = 2 \cdot 5 \cdot 3 \cdot 7 \qquad \text{Factor 10 as } 2 \cdot 5 \text{ and factor 21 as } 3 \cdot 7.$$

Writing the factors in order, from least to greatest, the **prime-factored form** of 210 is $2 \cdot 3 \cdot 5 \cdot 7$. Two other methods for prime factoring 210 are shown below.

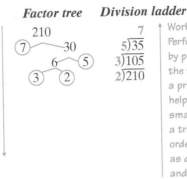

Factor tree   *Division ladder*

Work downward. Factor each number as a product of two numbers (other than 1 and itself) until all factors are prime. Circle prime numbers as they appear at the end of a branch.

Work upward. Perform repeated division by prime numbers until the final quotient is a prime number. It is helpful to start with the smallest prime, 2, as a trial divisor. Then, in order, try larger primes as divisors: 3, 5, 7, 11, and so on.

Either way, the factorization is $2 \cdot 3 \cdot 5 \cdot 7$. To check it, multiply the prime factors. The product should be 210.

> **Success Tip**   Some divisions end with a 0 remainder and others do not. We say that one number is **divisible** by another if, when dividing them, we get a remainder of 0.
> The following divisibility rules are helpful when prime factoring.
> A whole number is divisible by
>
> * 2 if it ends in 0, 2, 4, 6, or 8
> * 3 if the sum of the digits is divisible by 3
> * 5 if it ends in 0 or 5
> * 10 if it ends in 0

Self Check 7

Find the prime factorization of 189.

Now Try **Problem 57 and 63**

7   Simplify fractions.

Every fraction can be written in infinitely many equivalent forms. For example, some equivalent forms of $\frac{10}{15}$ are:

$$\frac{2}{3} = \frac{4}{6} = \frac{6}{9} = \frac{8}{12} = \frac{10}{15} = \frac{12}{18} = \frac{14}{21} = \frac{16}{24} = \frac{18}{27} = \frac{20}{30} = \cdots$$

Of all of the equivalent forms in which we can write a fraction, we often need to determine the one that is in *simplest form.*

> ### Simplest Form of a Fraction
>
> A fraction is in **simplest form,** or **lowest terms,** when the numerator and denominator have no common factors other than 1.

EXAMPLE 8   Are the following fractions in simplest form?   **a.** $\frac{12}{27}$ **b.** $\frac{5}{8}$

Strategy We will determine whether the numerator and denominator have any common factors other than 1.

WHY If the numerator and denominator have no common factors other than 1, the fraction is in simplest form.

Solution

a. The factors of the numerator, 12, are: **1**, 2, **3**, 4, 6, 12
The factors of the denominator, 27, are: **1**, **3**, 9, 27

Since the numerator and denominator have a common factor of 3, the fraction $\frac{12}{27}$ is *not* in simplest form.

Self Check 8

Are the following fractions in simplest form?

a. $\frac{4}{21}$

b. $\frac{6}{20}$

Now Try **Problem 67**

b. The factors of the numerator, 5, are: **1**, 5
   The factors of the denominator, 8, are: **1**, 2, 4, 8

Since the only common factor of the numerator and denominator is 1, the fraction $\frac{5}{8}$ is in simplest form.

To **simplify a fraction,** we write it in simplest form by *removing a factor equal to 1.* For example, to simplify $\frac{10}{15}$, we note that the greatest factor common to the numerator and denominator is 5 and proceed as follows:

$$\frac{10}{15} = \frac{2 \cdot 5}{3 \cdot 5} \qquad \text{Factor 10 and 15. Note the form of 1 highlighted in red.}$$

$$= \frac{2}{3} \cdot \frac{5}{5} \qquad \text{Use the rule for multiplying fractions in reverse:}$$
$$\text{write } \tfrac{2 \cdot 5}{3 \cdot 5} \text{ as the product of two fractions, } \tfrac{2}{3} \text{ and } \tfrac{5}{5}.$$

$$= \frac{2}{3} \cdot 1 \qquad \text{A number divided by itself is equal to 1: } \tfrac{5}{5} = 1.$$

$$= \frac{2}{3} \qquad \text{Use the multiplication property of 1: the product}$$
$$\text{of any fraction and 1 is that fraction.}$$

We have found that the simplified form of $\frac{10}{15}$ is $\frac{2}{3}$. To simplify $\frac{10}{15}$, we *removed a factor equal to 1* in the form of $\frac{5}{5}$. The result, $\frac{2}{3}$, is equivalent to $\frac{10}{15}$.

To streamline the simplifying process, we can replace pairs of factors common to the numerator and denominator with the equivalent fraction $\frac{1}{1}$.

Self Check 9

Simplify each fraction:

a. $\dfrac{10}{25}$

b. $\dfrac{3}{9}$

Now Try **Problems 69 and 73**

EXAMPLE 9   Simplify each fraction: **a.** $\dfrac{6}{10}$ **b.** $\dfrac{7}{21}$

Strategy We will factor the numerator and denominator. Then we will look for any factors common to the numerator and denominator and remove them.

WHY We need to make sure that the numerator and denominator have no common factors other than 1. If that is the case, then the fraction is in *simplest form.*

Solution

a. $\dfrac{6}{10} = \dfrac{2 \cdot 3}{2 \cdot 5}$ To prepare to simplify, factor 6 and 10. Note the form of 1 highlighted in red.

 $= \dfrac{\overset{1}{\cancel{2}} \cdot 3}{\underset{1}{\cancel{2}} \cdot 5}$ Simplify by removing the common factor of 2 from the numerator and denominator. A slash / and the 1's are used to show that $\frac{2}{2}$ is replaced by the equivalent fraction $\frac{1}{1}$. A factor equal to 1 in the form of $\frac{2}{2}$ was removed.

$= \dfrac{3}{5}$ Multiply the remaining factors in the numerator: $1 \cdot 3 = 3$. Multiply the remaining factors in the denominator: $1 \cdot 5 = 5$.

Since 3 and 5 have no common factors (other than 1), $\dfrac{3}{5}$ is in simplest form.

b. $\dfrac{7}{21} = \dfrac{7}{3 \cdot 7}$ To prepare to simplify, factor 21.

$= \dfrac{\overset{1}{\cancel{7}}}{3 \cdot \underset{1}{\cancel{7}}}$ Simplify by removing the common factor of 7 from the numerator and denominator.

$= \dfrac{1}{3}$ Multiply the remaining factors in the denominator: $1 \cdot 3 = 3$.

Caution! Don't forget to write the 1's when removing common factors of the numerator and the denominator. Failure to do so can lead to the common mistake shown below.

$$\frac{7}{21} = \frac{\cancel{7}}{3 \cdot \cancel{7}} = \frac{0}{3}$$

We can easily identify common factors of the numerator and the denominator of a fraction if we write them in prime-factored form.

EXAMPLE 10   Simplify each fraction, if possible: **a.** $\dfrac{90}{105}$ **b.** $\dfrac{25}{27}$

Strategy We begin by prime factoring the numerator, 90, and denominator, 105. We will use a **factor tree** to do this. Then we look for any factors common to the numerator and denominator and remove them.

WHY When the numerator and/or denominator of a fraction are large numbers, such as 90 and 105, writing their prime factorizations is helpful in identifying any common factors.

Solution

a. $\dfrac{90}{105} = \dfrac{2 \cdot 3 \cdot 3 \cdot 5}{3 \cdot 5 \cdot 7}$ To prepare to simplify, write 90 and 105 in prime-factored form.

$= \dfrac{2 \cdot \overset{1}{\cancel{3}} \cdot 3 \cdot \overset{1}{\cancel{5}}}{\underset{1}{\cancel{3}} \cdot \underset{1}{\cancel{5}} \cdot 7}$ Remove the common factors of 3 and 5 from the numerator and denominator. Slashes and 1's are used to show that $\frac{3}{3}$ and $\frac{5}{5}$ are replaced by the equivalent fraction $\frac{1}{1}$. A factor equal to 1 in the form of $\frac{3 \cdot 5}{3 \cdot 5} = \frac{15}{15}$ was removed.

$= \dfrac{6}{7}$ Multiply the remaining factors in the numerator: $2 \cdot 1 \cdot 3 \cdot 1 = 6$. Multiply the remaining factors in the denominator: $1 \cdot 1 \cdot 7 = 7$.

Since 6 and 7 have no common factors (other than 1), $\dfrac{6}{7}$ is in simplest form.

b. $\dfrac{25}{27} = \dfrac{5 \cdot 5}{3 \cdot 3 \cdot 3}$ Write 25 and 27 in prime-factored form.

Since 25 and 27 have no common factors, other than 1, the fraction $\dfrac{25}{27}$ is in simplest form.

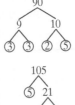

Self Check 10

Simplify each fraction, if possible:

a. $\dfrac{70}{126}$

b. $\dfrac{16}{81}$

Now Try Problems 81 and 85

EXAMPLE 11   Simplify: $\dfrac{63}{36}$

Strategy We will prime factor the numerator and denominator. We will use a **division ladder** to do this. Then we will look for any factors common to the numerator and denominator and remove them.

WHY We need to make sure that the numerator and denominator have no common factors other than 1. If that is the case, then the fraction is in *simplest form*.

Solution

$\dfrac{63}{36} = \dfrac{3 \cdot 3 \cdot 7}{2 \cdot 2 \cdot 3 \cdot 3}$ To prepare to simplify, write 63 and 36 in prime-factored form.

$= \dfrac{\overset{1}{\cancel{3}} \cdot \overset{1}{\cancel{3}} \cdot 7}{2 \cdot 2 \cdot \underset{1}{\cancel{3}} \cdot \underset{1}{\cancel{3}}}$ Simplify by removing the common factors of 3 from the numerator and denominator.

$= \dfrac{7}{4}$ Multiply the remaining factors in the numerator: $1 \cdot 1 \cdot 7 = 7$. Multiply the remaining factors in the denominator: $2 \cdot 2 \cdot 1 \cdot 1 = 4$.

$\begin{array}{ll} 3\underline{|63} & 2\underline{|36} \\ 3\underline{|21} & 2\underline{|18} \\ 7 & 3\underline{|9} \\ & 3 \end{array}$

Self Check 11

Simplify: $\dfrac{162}{72}$

Now Try Problem 91

Success Tip   If you recognized that 63 and 36 have a common factor of 9, you may remove that common factor from the numerator and denominator without writing the prime factorizations. However, make sure that the numerator and denominator of the resulting fraction do not have any common factors. If they do, continue to simplify.

$$\frac{63}{36} = \frac{7 \cdot \overset{1}{\cancel{9}}}{4 \cdot \underset{1}{\cancel{9}}} = \frac{7}{4}$$ Factor 63 as 7 · 9 and 36 as 4 · 9, and then remove the common factor of 9 from the numerator and denominator.

Use the following steps to simplify a fraction.

Simplifying Fractions

To simplify a fraction, *remove factors equal to 1* of the form $\frac{2}{2}, \frac{3}{3}, \frac{4}{4}, \frac{5}{5}$, and so on, using the following procedure:

1. Factor (or prime factor) the numerator and denominator to determine their common factors.

2. Remove factors equal to 1 by replacing each pair of factors common to the numerator and denominator with the equivalent fraction $\frac{1}{1}$.

3. Multiply the remaining factors in the numerator and in the denominator.

Negative fractions are simplified in the same way as positive fractions. Just remember to write a negative sign − in front of each step of the solution. For example, to simplify $-\frac{15}{33}$ we proceed as follows:

$$-\frac{15}{33} = -\frac{\overset{1}{\cancel{3}} \cdot 5}{\underset{1}{\cancel{3}} \cdot 11}$$

$$= -\frac{5}{11}$$

ANSWERS TO SELF CHECKS

1. a. numerator: 7; denominator: 9   **b.** numerator: 21; denominator: 20   **2. a.** $\frac{11}{31}$ **b.** $\frac{20}{31}$
3. $-\frac{7}{8}$ $\frac{2}{5}$ **4. a.** 1   **b.** 51   **c.** undefined   **d.** 0   **5.** $\frac{15}{24}$

6. $\frac{30}{7}$ **7.** $189 = 3 \cdot 3 \cdot 3 \cdot 7$ **8. a.** yes   **b.** no   **9. a.** $\frac{2}{5}$ **b.** $\frac{1}{3}$ **10. a.** $\frac{5}{9}$
b. in simplest form   **11.** $\frac{9}{4}$

SECTION 2.1   STUDY SET

VOCABULARY

Fill in the blanks.

1. A _____ describes the number of equal parts of a whole.

2. For the fraction $\frac{7}{8}$, the _____ is 7 and the _____ is 8.

3. If the numerator of a fraction is less than its denominator, the fraction is called a _____ fraction. If the numerator of a fraction is greater than or equal to its denominator it is called an _____ fraction.

4. Each of the following fractions is a form of ___.

$$\frac{1}{1} = \frac{2}{2} = \frac{3}{3} = \frac{4}{4} = \frac{5}{5} = \frac{6}{6} = \frac{7}{7} = \frac{8}{8} = \frac{9}{9} = \cdots$$

5. Using a process called *graphing*, we can represent whole numbers as points on a _____ line.

6. _____ fractions represent the same portion of a whole.

7. Writing a fraction as an equivalent fraction with a larger denominator is called _____ the fraction.

8. A fraction is in _____ form, or lowest terms, when the numerator and denominator have no common factors other than 1.

9. Whole numbers greater than 1 that have only 1 and themselves as factors, such as 23, 37, and 41, are called _____ numbers.

10. When we write 60 as $2 \cdot 2 \cdot 3 \cdot 5$, we say that we have written 60 in _____ form.

CONCEPTS

11. **a.** What two equivalent fractions are shown on the right?

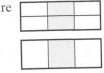

b. What two equivalent fractions are shown?

12. What concept studied in this section does the following statement illustrate?

$$\frac{1}{2} = \frac{2}{4} = \frac{3}{6} = \frac{4}{8} = \frac{5}{10} = \dots$$

13. Classify each fraction as a proper fraction or an improper fraction.

   a. $\frac{37}{24}$ **b.** $\frac{1}{3}$

   c. $\frac{71}{100}$ **d.** $\frac{9}{9}$

14. Remove the common factors of the numerator and denominator to simplify the fraction:

$$\frac{2 \cdot 3 \cdot 3 \cdot 5}{2 \cdot 3 \cdot 5 \cdot 7}$$

15. What common factor (other than 1) do the numerator and the denominator of the fraction $\frac{10}{15}$ have?

Fill in the blank.

16. Multiplication property of 1: The product of any fraction and 1 is that _____.

17. Multiplying fractions: To multiply two fractions, multiply the _____ and multiply the denominators.

18. **a.** Consider the following work: $\frac{2}{3} = \frac{2}{3} \cdot \boxed{}$

$$= \frac{8}{12}$$

To build an equivalent fraction for $\frac{2}{3}$ with a denominator of 12, _____ it by a factor equal to 1 in the form of ☐.

b. Consider the following work: $\dfrac{15}{27} = \dfrac{\overset{1}{\cancel{3}} \cdot 5}{\underset{1}{\cancel{3}} \cdot 9}$

$$= \frac{5}{9}$$

To simplify the fraction $\frac{15}{27}$, _____ a factor equal to 1 of the form ☐.

NOTATION

19. Write the fraction $\dfrac{7}{-8}$ in two other ways.

20. Write each integer as a fraction.

   a. 8   **b.** –25

Fill in the blanks to complete each step.

21. Build an equivalent fraction for $\dfrac{1}{6}$ with a denominator of 18.

$$\frac{1}{6} = \frac{1}{6} \cdot \frac{3}{\boxed{}}$$

$$= \frac{\boxed{} \cdot 3}{6 \cdot \boxed{}}$$

$$= \frac{3}{\boxed{}}$$

22. Simplify: $\dfrac{18}{24}$

$$\frac{18}{24} = \frac{2 \cdot \boxed{} \cdot 3}{2 \cdot 2 \cdot 2 \cdot \boxed{}}$$

$$= \frac{\overset{1}{\cancel{2}} \cdot 3 \cdot \overset{1}{\cancel{3}}}{2 \cdot 2 \cdot 2 \cdot \underset{1}{\cancel{3}}}$$

$$= \frac{3}{\boxed{}}$$

GUIDED PRACTICE

Identify the numerator and denominator of each fraction.
See Example 1.

23. **a.** $\dfrac{4}{5}$ **b.** $\dfrac{7}{8}$

   c. $\dfrac{17}{10}$ **d.** $\dfrac{29}{21}$

24. Use the numbers 24 and 25 to write:

   a. a proper fraction   **b.** an improper fraction

Write a fraction to describe what part of the figure is shaded.
Write a fraction to describe what part of the figure is not shaded.
See Example 2.

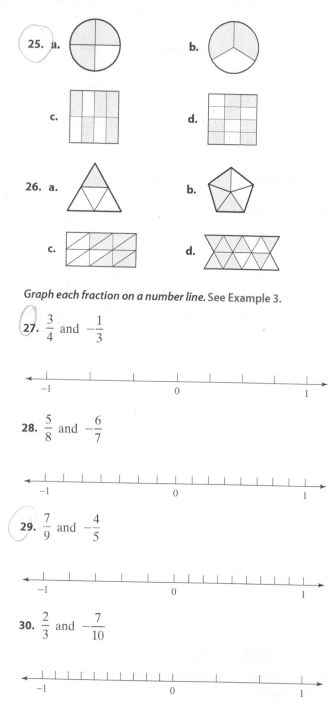

25. a. b.

c. d.

26. a. b.

c. d.

Graph each fraction on a number line. **See Example 3.**

27. $\frac{3}{4}$ and $-\frac{1}{3}$

28. $\frac{5}{8}$ and $-\frac{6}{7}$

29. $\frac{7}{9}$ and $-\frac{4}{5}$

30. $\frac{2}{3}$ and $-\frac{7}{10}$

Simplify, if possible. **See Example 3.**

31. a. $\frac{4}{1}$ **b.** $\frac{8}{8}$

c. $\frac{0}{12}$ **d.** $\frac{1}{0}$

32. a. $\frac{5}{0}$ **b.** $\frac{0}{50}$

c. $\frac{33}{33}$ **d.** $\frac{75}{1}$

Write each fraction as an equivalent fraction with the indicated denominator. **See Example 5.**

33. $\frac{7}{8}$, denominator 40   **34.** $\frac{3}{4}$, denominator 24

35. $\frac{4}{9}$, denominator 27   **36.** $\frac{5}{7}$, denominator 49

37. $\frac{5}{6}$, denominator 54   **38.** $\frac{2}{3}$, denominator 27

39. $\frac{2}{7}$, denominator 14   **40.** $\frac{3}{10}$, denominator 50

41. $\frac{1}{2}$, denominator 30   **42.** $\frac{1}{3}$, denominator 60

43. $\frac{11}{16}$, denominator 32   **44.** $\frac{9}{10}$, denominator 60

45. $\frac{5}{4}$, denominator 28   **46.** $\frac{9}{4}$, denominator 44

47. $\frac{16}{15}$, denominator 45   **48.** $\frac{13}{12}$, denominator 36

Write each whole number as an equivalent fraction with the indicated denominator. **See Example 6.**

49. 4, denominator 9   **50.** 4, denominator 3

51. 6, denominator 8   **52.** 3, denominator 6

53. 3, denominator 5   **54.** 7, denominator 4

55. 14, denominator 2   **56.** 10, denominator 9

Find the prime factorization of each number. **See Example 7.**

57. 75   **58.** 28

59. 81   **60.** 125

61. 117   **62.** 147

63. 220   **64.** 270

Are the following fractions in simplest form? **See Example 8.**

65. a. $\frac{12}{16}$ **b.** $\frac{3}{25}$

66. a. $\frac{9}{24}$ **b.** $\frac{7}{36}$

67. a. $\frac{35}{36}$ **b.** $\frac{18}{21}$

68. a. $\dfrac{22}{45}$ **b.** $\dfrac{21}{56}$

Simplify each fraction, if possible. See Example 9.

69. $\dfrac{6}{9}$ **70.** $\dfrac{15}{20}$

71. $\dfrac{16}{20}$ **72.** $\dfrac{25}{35}$

73. $\dfrac{5}{15}$ **74.** $\dfrac{6}{30}$

75. $\dfrac{2}{48}$ **76.** $\dfrac{2}{42}$

Simplify each fraction, if possible. See Example 10.

77. $\dfrac{36}{96}$ **78.** $\dfrac{48}{120}$

79. $\dfrac{16}{17}$ **80.** $\dfrac{14}{25}$

81. $\dfrac{55}{62}$ **82.** $\dfrac{41}{51}$

83. $\dfrac{50}{55}$ **84.** $\dfrac{22}{88}$

85. $\dfrac{60}{108}$ **86.** $\dfrac{75}{275}$

87. $\dfrac{180}{210}$ **88.** $\dfrac{90}{120}$

Simplify each fraction. See Example 11.

89. $\dfrac{15}{6}$ **90.** $\dfrac{24}{16}$

91. $\dfrac{216}{189}$ **92.** $\dfrac{208}{117}$

93. $-\dfrac{105}{90}$ **94.** $-\dfrac{126}{98}$

95. $-\dfrac{4}{68}$ **96.** $-\dfrac{3}{42}$

TRY IT YOURSELF

Tell whether each pair of fractions is equivalent by simplifying each fraction.

97. $\dfrac{2}{14}$ and $\dfrac{6}{36}$ **98.** $\dfrac{3}{12}$ and $\dfrac{4}{24}$

99. $\dfrac{22}{34}$ and $\dfrac{33}{51}$ **100.** $\dfrac{4}{30}$ and $\dfrac{12}{90}$

CONCEPT EXTENSIONS

101. a. Shade $\dfrac{1}{3}$ of the figure.

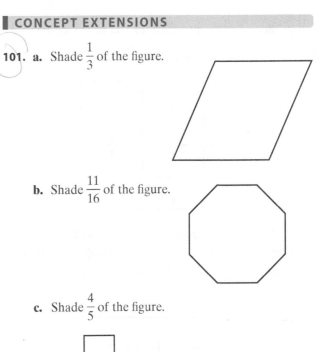

  b. Shade $\dfrac{11}{16}$ of the figure.

  c. Shade $\dfrac{4}{5}$ of the figure.

102. What part of the overall square region shown below has been shaded?

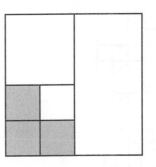

103. a. Shade $\dfrac{1}{6}$ of the figure. As a result of the shading, what fraction equivalent to $\dfrac{1}{6}$ is shown?

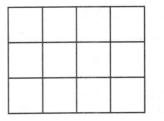

b. Shade $\frac{7}{10}$ of the figure. As a result of the shading, what fraction equivalent to $\frac{7}{10}$ is shown?

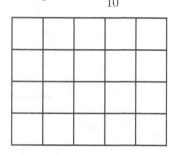

104. Shade the *same portion* of each of the figures below so that a fraction equivalent to $\frac{1}{4}$ is showing. Then, for each figure, give the equivalent fraction that is illustrated.

a.

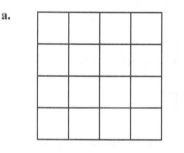

b.

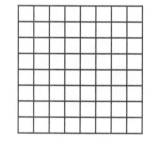

c.

APPLICATIONS

105. DENTISTRY Refer to the dental chart.

    a. How many teeth are shown on the chart?

    b. What fraction of this set of teeth have fillings?

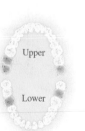

106. TIME CLOCKS For each clock, what fraction of the hour has passed? Write your answers in simplified form. (*Hint:* There are 60 minutes in an hour.)

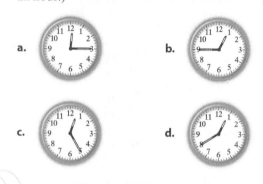

    a.   **b.**

    c.   **d.**

107. RULERS The illustration below shows a ruler.

    a. How many spaces are there between the numbers 0 and 1?

    b. To what fraction is the arrow pointing? Write your answer in simplified form.

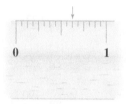

108. SINKHOLES The illustration below shows a side view of a drop in the sidewalk near a sinkhole. Describe the movement of the sidewalk using a signed fraction.

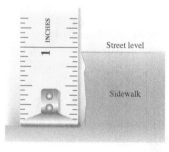

109. POLITICAL PARTIES The graph on the next page shows the number of Democrat and Republican governors of the 50 states, as of February 1, 2009.

    a. How many Democrat governors are there? How many Republican governors are there?

    b. What fraction of the governors are Democrats? Write your answer in simplified form.

c. What fraction of the governors are Republicans? Write your answer in simplified form.

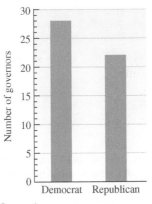

Source: thegreenpapers.com

110. GAS TANKS Write fractions to describe the amount of gas left in the tank and the amount of gas that has been used.

Use unleaded fuel

111. SELLING CONDOS The model below shows a new condominium development. The condos that have been sold are shaded.

a. How many units are there in the development?

b. What fraction of the units in the development have been sold? What fraction have not been sold? Write your answers in simplified form.

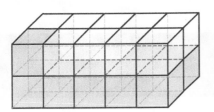

112. MUSIC The illustration shows a side view of the finger position needed to produce a length of string (from the bridge to the fingertip) that gives low C on a violin. To play other notes, fractions of that length are used. Locate these finger positions on the illustration.

a. $\frac{1}{2}$ of the length gives middle C.

b. $\frac{3}{4}$ of the length gives F above low C.

c. $\frac{2}{3}$ of the length gives G.

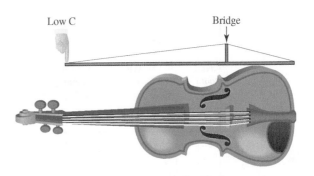

113. MEDICAL CENTERS Hospital designers have located a nurse's station at the center of a circular building. Show how to divide the surrounding office space (shaded in grey) so that each medical department has the fractional amount assigned to it. Label each department.

$\frac{2}{12}$: Radiology

$\frac{5}{12}$: Pediatrics

$\frac{1}{12}$: Laboratory

$\frac{3}{12}$: Orthopedics

$\frac{1}{12}$: Pharmacy

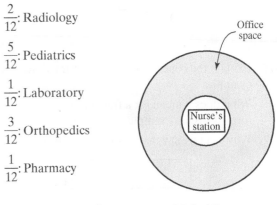

Medical Center

114. ARCHITECTURE The floor plan of a movie theater complex is shown on the next page. It has three Screen Rooms, a Lobby (that *includes* the Men's and Women's Restrooms), and an Entrance.

a. What fraction of the complex floor space is used for Screen Room 1?

b. What fraction of the complex floor space is used for the Lobby?

c. What fraction of the complex floor space is used for the Lobby and Entrance (combined)?

d. What fraction of the Lobby floor space is used for the Men's and Women's Restrooms (combined)?

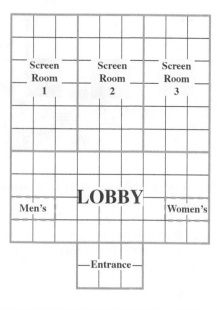

119. a. What type of problem is shown below? Explain the solution.

$$\frac{1}{2} = \frac{1}{2} \cdot \frac{4}{4} = \frac{4}{8}$$

b. What type of problem is shown below? Explain the solution.

$$\frac{15}{35} = \frac{3 \cdot \overset{1}{\cancel{5}}}{\cancel{5} \cdot 7} = \frac{3}{7}$$

120. Explain the difference in the two approaches used to simplify $\frac{20}{28}$. Are the results the same?

$$\frac{\overset{1}{\cancel{4}} \cdot 5}{\cancel{4} \cdot 7} \quad \text{and} \quad \frac{\overset{1}{\cancel{2}} \cdot \overset{1}{\cancel{2}} \cdot 5}{\cancel{2} \cdot \cancel{2} \cdot 7}$$

| WRITING

115. Explain the concept of equivalent fractions. Give an example.

116. What does it mean for a fraction to be in simplest form? Give an example.

117. Why can't we say that $\frac{2}{5}$ of the figure below is shaded?

118. Perhaps you have heard the following joke:

A pizza parlor waitress asks a customer if he wants the pizza cut into four pieces or six pieces or eight pieces. The customer then declares that he wants either four or six pieces of pizza "because I can't eat eight."

Explain what is wrong with the customer's thinking.

121. GDP The gross domestic product (GDP) is the official measure of the size of the U.S. economy. It represents the market value of all goods and services that have been bought during a given period of time. The GDP for the second quarter of 2008 is listed below. What is meant by the phrase *second quarter of 2008*?

Second quarter of 2008 $14,294,500,000,000

Source: *The World Almanac and Book of Facts,* 2009

122. Give some examples of how you use fractions in your everyday life.

Objectives

1 Multiply fractions.

2 Simplify answers when multiplying fractions.

3 Evaluate exponential expressions that have fractional bases.

4 Solve application problems by multiplying fractions.

5 Find the area of rectangles, squares, and triangles.

SECTION **2.2**

Multiplying Fractions

ARE YOU READY?

▼ *The following problems review some basic skills that are needed when multiplying fractions.*

1. Simplify

a. $\frac{18}{24}$ **b.** $\frac{5}{45}$

2. Prime factor 75.

3. Evaluate: **a.** 6^2 **b.** 4^3

4. Complete each rule for multiplying signed numbers.

a. The product of two numbers with like signs is _____.

b. The product of two numbers with unlike signs is _____.

In the next three sections, we discuss how to add, subtract, multiply, and divide fractions. We begin with the operation of multiplication.

1 Multiply fractions.

To develop a rule for multiplying fractions, let's consider a real-life application.

Suppose $\frac{3}{5}$ of the last page of a school newspaper is devoted to campus sports coverage. To show this, we can divide the page into fifths, and shade 3 of them red.

Sports coverage:
$\frac{3}{5}$ of the page

Furthermore, suppose that $\frac{1}{2}$ of the sports coverage is about women's teams. We can show that portion of the page by dividing the already colored region into two halves, and shading one of them in purple.

Women's teams coverage:
$\frac{1}{2}$ of $\frac{3}{5}$ of the page

To find the fraction represented by the purple shaded region, the page needs to be divided into equal-size parts. If we extend the dashed line downward, we see there are 10 equal-sized parts. The purple shaded parts are 3 out of 10, or $\frac{3}{10}$, of the page. Thus, $\frac{3}{10}$ of the last page of the school newspaper is devoted to women's sports.

Women's teams coverage:
$\frac{3}{10}$ of the page

In this example, we have found that

$$\frac{1}{2} \text{ of } \frac{3}{5} \text{ is } \frac{3}{10}$$

$$\frac{1}{2} \cdot \frac{3}{5} = \frac{3}{10}$$

Since the key word *of* indicates multiplication, and the key word *is* means equals, we can translate this statement to symbols.

Two observations can be made from this result.

- The numerator of the answer is the product of the numerators of the original fractions.

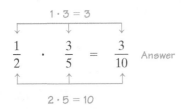

$1 \cdot 3 = 3$

$$\frac{1}{2} \cdot \frac{3}{5} = \frac{3}{10} \quad \text{Answer}$$

$2 \cdot 5 = 10$

- The denominator of the answer is the product of the denominators of the original fractions.

These observations illustrate the following rule for multiplying two fractions.

> **Multiplying Fractions**
>
> To multiply two fractions, multiply the numerators and multiply the denominators. Simplify the result, if possible.

> ***Success Tip***   In the newspaper example, we found a *part of a part* of a page. Multiplying proper fractions can be thought of in this way. When taking a *part of a part* of something, the result is always smaller than the original part that you began with.

Self Check 1

Multiply:

a. $\dfrac{1}{2} \cdot \dfrac{1}{8}$

b. $\dfrac{5}{9} \cdot \dfrac{2}{3}$

Now Try Problems 17 and 21

EXAMPLE 1

Multiply: **a.** $\dfrac{1}{6} \cdot \dfrac{1}{4}$ **b.** $\dfrac{7}{8} \cdot \dfrac{3}{5}$

Strategy We will multiply the numerators and denominators, and make sure that the result is in simplest form.

WHY This is the rule for multiplying two fractions.

Solution

a. $\dfrac{1}{6} \cdot \dfrac{1}{4} = \dfrac{1 \cdot 1}{6 \cdot 4}$ Multiply the numerators.
Multiply the denominators.

$= \dfrac{1}{24}$ Since 1 and 24 have no common factors other than 1, the result is in simplest form.

b. $\dfrac{7}{8} \cdot \dfrac{3}{5} = \dfrac{7 \cdot 3}{8 \cdot 5}$ Multiply the numerators.
Multiply the denominators.

$= \dfrac{21}{40}$ Since 21 and 40 have no common factors other than 1, the result is in simplest form.

The sign rules for multiplying integers also hold for multiplying fractions. When we multiply two fractions with *like* signs, the product is positive. When we multiply two fractions with *unlike* signs, the product is negative.

Self Check 2

Multiply: $\dfrac{5}{6}\left(-\dfrac{1}{3}\right)$

Now Try Problem 25

EXAMPLE 2

Multiply: $-\dfrac{3}{4}\left(\dfrac{1}{8}\right)$

Strategy We will use the rule for multiplying two fractions that have different (unlike) signs.

WHY One fraction is positive and one is negative.

Solution

$-\dfrac{3}{4}\left(\dfrac{1}{8}\right) = -\dfrac{3 \cdot 1}{4 \cdot 8}$ Multiply the numerators.
Multiply the denominators.
Since the fractions have unlike signs, make the answer negative.

$= -\dfrac{3}{32}$ Since 3 and 32 have no common factors other than 1, the result is in simplest form.

EXAMPLE 3   Multiply: $\dfrac{1}{2} \cdot 3$

Strategy We will begin by writing the integer 3 as a fraction.

WHY Then we can use the rule for multiplying two fractions to find the product.

Solution

$$\dfrac{1}{2} \cdot 3 = \dfrac{1}{2} \cdot \dfrac{3}{1} \qquad \text{Write 3 as a fraction: } 3 = \tfrac{3}{1}.$$

$$= \dfrac{1 \cdot 3}{2 \cdot 1} \qquad \begin{array}{l}\text{Multiply the numerators.}\\ \text{Multiply the denominators.}\end{array}$$

$$= \dfrac{3}{2} \qquad \begin{array}{l}\text{Since 3 and 2 have no common factors other than 1,}\\ \text{the result is in simplest form.}\end{array}$$

Self Check 3

Multiply: $\dfrac{1}{3} \cdot 7$

Now Try **Problem 29**

2 Simplify answers when multiplying fractions.

After multiplying two fractions, we need to simplify the result, if possible. To do that, we can use the procedure of removing pairs of common factors of the numerator and denominator.

EXAMPLE 4   Multiply and simplify: $\dfrac{5}{8} \cdot \dfrac{4}{5}$

Strategy We will multiply the numerators and denominators, and make sure that the result is in simplest form.

WHY This is the rule for multiplying two fractions.

Solution

$$\dfrac{5}{8} \cdot \dfrac{4}{5} = \dfrac{5 \cdot 4}{8 \cdot 5} \qquad \begin{array}{l}\text{Multiply the numerators.}\\ \text{Multiply the denominators.}\end{array}$$

$$= \dfrac{5 \cdot 2 \cdot 2}{2 \cdot 2 \cdot 2 \cdot 5} \qquad \begin{array}{l}\text{To prepare to simplify, write 4 and 8 in}\\ \text{prime-factored form.}\end{array}$$

$$= \dfrac{\overset{1}{\cancel{5}} \cdot \overset{1}{\cancel{2}} \cdot \overset{1}{\cancel{2}}}{\underset{1}{\cancel{2}} \cdot \underset{1}{\cancel{2}} \cdot 2 \cdot \underset{1}{\cancel{5}}} \qquad \begin{array}{l}\text{To simplify, remove the common factors of 2}\\ \text{and 5 from the numerator and denominator.}\end{array}$$

$$= \dfrac{1}{2} \qquad \begin{array}{l}\text{Multiply the remaining factors in the numerator: } 1 \cdot 1 \cdot 1 = 1.\\ \text{Multiple the remaining factors in the denominator: } 1 \cdot 1 \cdot 2 \cdot 1 = 2.\end{array}$$

Self Check 4

Multiply and simplify: $\dfrac{11}{25} \cdot \dfrac{10}{11}$

Now Try **Problem 33**

Success Tip If you recognized that 4 and 8 have a common factor of 4, you may remove that common factor from the numerator and denominator of the product without writing the prime factorizations. However, make sure that the numerator and denominator of the resulting fraction do not have any common factors. If they do, continue to simplify.

$$\dfrac{5}{8} \cdot \dfrac{4}{5} = \dfrac{5 \cdot 4}{8 \cdot 5} = \dfrac{\overset{1}{\cancel{5}} \cdot \overset{1}{\cancel{4}}}{2 \cdot \underset{1}{\cancel{4}} \cdot \underset{1}{\cancel{5}}} = \dfrac{1}{2} \qquad \begin{array}{l}\text{Factor 8 as } 2 \cdot 4, \text{ and then remove the}\\ \text{common factors of 4 and 5 in the numerator}\\ \text{and denominator.}\end{array}$$

The rule for multiplying two fractions can be extended to find the product of three or more fractions.

Self Check 5

Multiply and simplify:

$$\frac{2}{5}\left(-\frac{15}{22}\right)\left(-\frac{11}{26}\right)$$

Now Try Problem 37

EXAMPLE 5

Multiply and simplify: $\frac{2}{3}\left(-\frac{9}{14}\right)\left(-\frac{7}{10}\right)$

Strategy We will multiply the numerators and denominators, and make sure that the result is in simplest form.

WHY This is the rule for multiplying three (or more) fractions.

Solution A product is positive when there are an even number of negative factors. Since $\frac{2}{3}\left(-\frac{9}{14}\right)\left(-\frac{7}{10}\right)$ has *two* negative factors, the product is positive.

$$\frac{2}{3}\left(-\frac{9}{14}\right)\left(-\frac{7}{10}\right) = \frac{2}{3}\left(\frac{9}{14}\right)\left(\frac{7}{10}\right) \qquad \text{Since the answer is positive, drop both } - \text{ signs and continue.}$$

$$= \frac{2 \cdot 9 \cdot 7}{3 \cdot 14 \cdot 10} \qquad \text{Multiply the numerators. Multiply the denominators.}$$

$$= \frac{2 \cdot 3 \cdot 3 \cdot 7}{3 \cdot 2 \cdot 7 \cdot 2 \cdot 5} \qquad \text{To prepare to simplify, write 9, 14, and 10 in prime-factored form.}$$

$$= \frac{\overset{1}{2} \cdot \overset{1}{3} \cdot 3 \cdot \overset{1}{7}}{\underset{1}{3} \cdot 2 \cdot \underset{1}{7} \cdot 2 \cdot 5} \qquad \text{To simplify, remove the common factors of 2, 3, and 7 from the numerator and denominator.}$$

$$= \frac{3}{10} \qquad \text{Multiply the remaining factors in the numerator. Multiply the remaining factors in the denominator.}$$

Caution! In Example 5, it was very helpful to prime factor and simplify when we did (the third step of the solution). If, instead, you find the product of the numerators and the product of the denominators, the resulting fraction is difficult to simplify because the numerator, 126, and the denominator, 420, are large.

$$\frac{2}{3} \cdot \frac{9}{14} \cdot \frac{7}{10} \quad = \quad \frac{2 \cdot 9 \cdot 7}{3 \cdot 14 \cdot 10} \quad = \quad \frac{126}{420}$$

Factor and simplify at this stage, before multiplying in the numerator and denominator.

Don't multiply in the numerator and denominator and then try to simplify the result. You will get the same answer, but it takes much more work.

---

3 Evaluate exponential expressions that have fractional bases.

We have evaluated exponential expressions that have whole-number bases and integer bases. If the base of an exponential expression is a fraction, the exponent tells us how many times to write that fraction as a factor. For example,

$$\left(\frac{2}{3}\right)^2 = \frac{2}{3} \cdot \frac{2}{3} = \frac{2 \cdot 2}{3 \cdot 3} = \frac{4}{9} \qquad \text{Since the exponent is 2, write the base, } \frac{2}{3}, \text{ as a factor 2 times.}$$

EXAMPLE 6

Evaluate each expression: **a.** $\left(\frac{1}{4}\right)^3$ **b.** $\left(-\frac{2}{3}\right)^2$ **c.** $-\left(\frac{2}{3}\right)^2$

Strategy We will write each exponential expression as a product of repeated factors, and then perform the multiplication. This requires that we identify the base and the exponent.

WHY The exponent tells the number of times the base is to be written as a factor. ▼

Solution

Recall that exponents are used to represent repeated multiplication.

a. We read $\left(\frac{1}{4}\right)^3$ as "one-fourth raised to the third power," or as "one-fourth, cubed."

$$\left(\frac{1}{4}\right)^3 = \frac{1}{4} \cdot \frac{1}{4} \cdot \frac{1}{4}$$

Since the exponent is 3, write the base, $\frac{1}{4}$, as a factor 3 times.

$$= \frac{1 \cdot 1 \cdot 1}{4 \cdot 4 \cdot 4}$$

Multiply the numerators. Multiply the denominators.

$$= \frac{1}{64}$$

b. We read $\left(-\frac{2}{3}\right)^2$ as "negative two-thirds raised to the second power," or as "negative two-thirds, squared."

$$\left(-\frac{2}{3}\right)^2 = \left(-\frac{2}{3}\right)\left(-\frac{2}{3}\right)$$

Since the exponent is 2, write the base, $-\frac{2}{3}$, as a factor 2 times.

$$= \frac{2 \cdot 2}{3 \cdot 3}$$

The product of two fractions with like signs is positive: Drop the − signs. Multiply the numerators. Multiply the denominators.

$$= \frac{4}{9}$$

c. We read $-\left(\frac{2}{3}\right)^2$ as "the opposite of two-thirds squared." Recall that if the − symbol is not within the parantheses, it is not part of the base.

$$-\left(\frac{2}{3}\right)^2 = -\frac{2}{3} \cdot \frac{2}{3}$$

Since the exponent is 2, write the base, $\frac{2}{3}$, as a factor 2 times.

$$= -\frac{2 \cdot 2}{3 \cdot 3}$$

Multiply the numerators. Multiply the denominators.

$$= -\frac{4}{9}$$

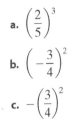

Self Check 6

Evaluate each expression:

a. $\left(\frac{2}{5}\right)^3$

b. $\left(-\frac{3}{4}\right)^2$

c. $-\left(\frac{3}{4}\right)^2$

Now Try **Problem 43**

4   Solve application problems by multiplying fractions.

The key word *of* often appears in application problems involving fractions. When a fraction is followed by the word *of*, such as $\frac{1}{2}$ *of* or $\frac{3}{4}$ *of*, it indicates that we are to find a part of some quantity using multiplication.

EXAMPLE 7   *How a Bill Becomes Law*   If the President vetoes (refuses to sign) a bill, it takes $\frac{2}{3}$ of those voting in the House of Representatives (and the Senate) to override the veto for it to become law. If all 435 members of the House cast a vote, how many of their votes does it take to override a presidential veto?

Solution

It is helpful to list what we know and what we are to find.

- It takes $\frac{2}{3}$ *of* those voting to override a veto.   · Given
- All 435 members of the House cast a vote.   Given
- How many votes does it take to override a Presidential veto?   Find

The key phrase $\frac{2}{3}$ *of* suggests that we are to find a part of the 435 possible votes using multiplication.
   We translate the words of the problem to numbers and symbols.

Self Check 7

HOW A BILL BECOMES LAW If only 96 Senators are present and cast a vote, how many of their votes does it takes to override a Presidential veto?

Now Try **Problem 95**

The number of votes needed in the House to override a veto	is equal to	$\frac{2}{3}$	of	the number of House members that vote.

The number of votes needed in the House to override a veto	$=$	$\frac{2}{3}$	$\cdot$	435

To find the product, we will express 435 as a fraction and then use the rule for multiplying two fractions.

$$\frac{2}{3} \cdot 435 = \frac{2}{3} \cdot \frac{435}{1}$$

Write 435 as a fraction: $435 = \frac{435}{1}$.

$$= \frac{2 \cdot 435}{3 \cdot 1}$$

Multiply the numerators.
Multiply the denominators.

$$= \frac{2 \cdot 3 \cdot 5 \cdot 29}{3 \cdot 1}$$

To prepare to simplify, write 435 in prime-factored form: $3 \cdot 5 \cdot 29$.

$$= \frac{2 \cdot \overset{1}{\cancel{3}} \cdot 5 \cdot 29}{\underset{1}{\cancel{3}} \cdot 1}$$

Remove the common factor of 3 from the numerator and denominator.

$$= \frac{290}{1}$$

Multiply the remaining factors in the numerator: $2 \cdot 1 \cdot 5 \cdot 29 = 290$.
Multiply the remaining factors in the denominator: $1 \cdot 1 = 1$.

$$= 290$$

Any whole number divided by 1 is equal to that number.

It would take 290 votes in the House to override a veto.

We can estimate to check the result. We will use 440 to approximate the number of House members voting. Since $\frac{1}{2}$ of 440 is 220, and since $\frac{2}{3}$ is a greater part than $\frac{1}{2}$, we would expect the number of votes needed to be *more than* 220. The result of 290 seems reasonable.

5 Find the area of rectangles, squares, and triangles.

The **area** of a plane (two-dimensional, flat) geometric figure is the amount of surface that it encloses. Area is measured in square units such as square feet, square yards, and square meters (written as ft^2, yd^2, and m^2, respectively). To find the **area of a square or the area of a rectangle,** we use the formulas listed below.

Figure	Name	Formula for Area
	Square	$A = s^2$, where s is the length of one side.
	Rectangle	$A = lw$, where l is the length and w is the width.

For example, to find the area of a square with sides $\frac{7}{8}$ inch long, we proceed as follows:

$A = s^2$ This is the formula for the area of a square.

$A = \left(\frac{7}{8}\right)^2$ Substitute $\frac{7}{8}$ for s, the length of one side.

$A = \frac{49}{64}$ Multiply: $\frac{7}{8} \cdot \frac{7}{8} = \frac{49}{64}$. The result does not simplify.

The area of the square is $\frac{49}{64}$ square inches, which can be written $\frac{49}{64}$ in.^{2}.

To find the area of a rectangle with length $\frac{15}{16}$ inch and width $\frac{1}{2}$ inch we proceed as follows:

$A = lw$ This is the formula for the area of a rectangle.

$A = \frac{15}{16} \cdot \frac{1}{2}$ Substitute $\frac{15}{16}$ for l, the length, and $\frac{1}{2}$ for w, the width.

$A = \frac{15}{32}$ Multiply the numerators: $15 \cdot 1 = 15$.

Multiply the denominators: $16 \cdot 2 = 32$. The result does not simplify.

The area of the rectangle is $\frac{15}{32}$ square inches, which can be written $\frac{15}{32}$ in.^{2}.

As the figures below show, a triangle has three sides. The length of the base of the triangle can be represented by the letter b and the height by the letter h. The height of a triangle is always perpendicular (makes a square corner) to the base. This is shown by using the symbol ⌐.

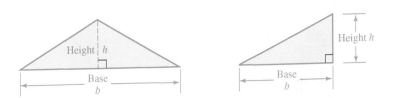

Recall that the area of a figure is the amount of surface that it encloses. The area of a triangle can be found by using the following formula.

Area of a Triangle

The area A of a triangle is one-half the product of its base b and its height h.

$$\text{Area} = \frac{1}{2}(\text{base})(\text{height}) \qquad \text{or} \qquad A = \frac{1}{2} \cdot b \cdot h$$

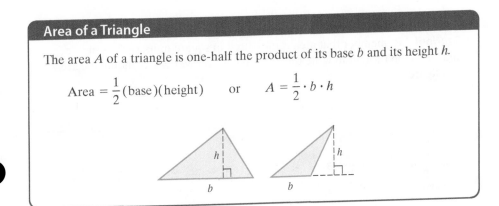

The segment perpendicular to the base and representing the height (shown on the previous page using a dashed line) is called an **altitude.**

> **The Language of Mathematics** The formula $A = \frac{1}{2} \cdot b \cdot h$ can be written more simply without the multiplication raised dots as $A = \frac{1}{2}bh$. The formula for the area of a triangle can also be written as $A = \frac{bh}{2}$.

Self Check 8

Find the area of the triangle shown below.

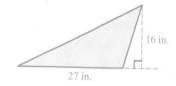

27 in.

Now Try Problems 53 and 107

EXAMPLE 8   *Geography*   Approximate the area of the state of Virginia (in square miles) using the triangle shown below.

Strategy We will find the product of $\frac{1}{2}$, 405, and 200.

WHY The formula for the area of a triangle is $A = \frac{1}{2}$ (base)(height).

Virginia

405 mi

Solution

$A = \dfrac{1}{2}bh$ This is the formula for the area of a triangle.

$= \dfrac{1}{2} \cdot 405 \cdot 200$ $\frac{1}{2}bh$ means $\frac{1}{2} \cdot b \cdot h$. Substitute 405 for b and 200 for h.

$= \dfrac{1}{2} \cdot \dfrac{405}{1} \cdot \dfrac{200}{1}$ Write 405 and 200 as fractions.

$= \dfrac{1 \cdot 405 \cdot 200}{2 \cdot 1 \cdot 1}$ Multiply the numerators.
Multiply the denominators.

$= \dfrac{1 \cdot 405 \cdot \overset{1}{\cancel{2}} \cdot 100}{\underset{1}{\cancel{2}} \cdot 1 \cdot 1}$ Factor 200 as $2 \cdot 100$. Then remove the common factor of 2 from the numerator and denominator.

$= 40{,}500$ In the numerator, multiply: $405 \cdot 100 = 40{,}500$.

The area of the state of Virginia is approximately 40,500 square miles. This can be written as 40,500 mi^2.

> **Caution!** Remember that area is measured in square units, such as in.^{2}, ft^2, and cm^2. Don't forget to write the units in your answer when finding the area of a figure.

ANSWERS TO SELF CHECKS

1. a. $\dfrac{1}{16}$ b. $\dfrac{10}{27}$ 2. $-\dfrac{5}{18}$ 3. $\dfrac{7}{3}$ 4. $\dfrac{2}{5}$ 5. $\dfrac{3}{26}$ 6. a. $\dfrac{8}{125}$ b. $\dfrac{9}{16}$ c. $-\dfrac{9}{16}$
7. 64 votes   8. 216 in.^{2}

SECTION 2.2   STUDY SET

VOCABULARY

Fill in the blanks.

1. When a fraction is followed by the word *of,* such as $\frac{1}{3}$ *of,* it indicates that we are to find a part of some quantity using _____.

2. The answer to a multiplication is called the _____.

3. To _____ a fraction, we remove common factors of the numerator and denominator.

4. In the expression $\left(\frac{1}{4}\right)^3$, the _____ is $\frac{1}{4}$ and the _____ is 3.

5. The _____ of a rectangle, square, or triangle is the amount of surface that it encloses.

6. The segment that represents the height of a triangle is called an _____. Label the *base* and the *height* of the triangle shown below.

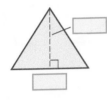

CONCEPTS

7. Fill in the blanks: To multiply two fractions, multiply the _____ and multiply the _____. Then _____, if possible.

8. Use the following rectangle to find $\frac{1}{3} \cdot \frac{1}{4}$.

   a. Draw three vertical lines that divide the given rectangle into four equal parts and lightly shade one part. What fractional part of the rectangle did you shade?

   b. To find $\frac{1}{3}$ of the shaded portion, draw two horizontal lines to divide the given rectangle into three equal parts and lightly shade one part. Into how many equal parts is the rectangle now divided? How many parts have been shaded twice?

   c. What is $\frac{1}{3} \cdot \frac{1}{4}$?

9. Determine whether each product is positive or negative. *You do not have to find the answer.*

   a. $-\frac{1}{8} \cdot \frac{3}{5}$

   b. $-\frac{7}{16}\left(-\frac{2}{21}\right)$

c. $-\frac{4}{5}\left(\frac{1}{3}\right)\left(-\frac{1}{8}\right)$

d. $-\frac{3}{4}\left(-\frac{8}{9}\right)\left(-\frac{1}{2}\right)$

10. Translate each phrase to symbols. *You do not have to find the answer.*

    a. $\frac{7}{10}$ of $\frac{4}{9}$

    b. $\frac{1}{5}$ of 40

11. Fill in the blanks:

    Area of a triangle $= \frac{1}{2}$(_____)(_____)   or

    $A =$ ____

12. Fill in the blank: Area is measured in _____ units, such as in.^{2} and ft^2.

NOTATION

13. Write each of the following integers as a fraction.

    a. 4

    b. –3

14. Fill in the blanks: $\left(\frac{1}{2}\right)^2$ represents the repeated multiplication ■ · ■.

Fill in the blanks to complete each step.

15. $$\frac{5}{8} \cdot \frac{7}{15} = \frac{5 \cdot \blacksquare}{8 \cdot \blacksquare}$$

    $$= \frac{5 \cdot 7}{\blacksquare \cdot 2 \cdot 2 \cdot \blacksquare \cdot 5}$$

    $$= \frac{\overset{1}{\cancel{5}} \cdot 7}{2 \cdot 2 \cdot 2 \cdot 3 \cdot \underset{1}{\cancel{5}}}$$

    $$= \frac{7}{\blacksquare}$$

16. $$\frac{7}{12} \cdot \frac{4}{21} = \frac{7 \cdot 4}{\blacksquare \cdot \blacksquare}$$

    $$= \frac{7 \cdot 4}{\blacksquare \cdot 4 \cdot 3 \cdot \blacksquare}$$

    $$= \frac{\overset{1}{\cancel{7}} \cdot \overset{1}{\cancel{4}}}{3 \cdot 4 \cdot 3 \cdot \underset{1}{\cancel{7}}}$$

    $$= \frac{\blacksquare}{9}$$

GUIDED PRACTICE

Multiply. Write the product in simplest form. See Example 1.

17. $\frac{1}{4} \cdot \frac{1}{2}$

18. $\frac{1}{3} \cdot \frac{1}{5}$

19. $\frac{1}{9} \cdot \frac{1}{5}$

20. $\frac{1}{2} \cdot \frac{1}{8}$

22. $\dfrac{3}{4} \cdot \dfrac{5}{7}$

23. $\dfrac{?}{11} \cdot \dfrac{3}{7}$

24. $\dfrac{11}{13} \cdot \dfrac{2}{3}$

Multiply. See Example 2.

25. $-\dfrac{4}{5} \cdot \dfrac{1}{3}$

26. $-\dfrac{7}{9} \cdot \dfrac{1}{4}$

27. $\dfrac{5}{6}\left(-\dfrac{7}{12}\right)$

28. $\dfrac{2}{15}\left(-\dfrac{4}{3}\right)$

Multiply. See Example 3.

29. $\dfrac{1}{8} \cdot 9$

30. $\dfrac{1}{6} \cdot 11$

31. $\dfrac{1}{2} \cdot 5$

32. $\dfrac{1}{2} \cdot 21$

Multiply. Write the product in simplest form. See Example 4.

33. $\dfrac{11}{10} \cdot \dfrac{5}{11}$

34. $\dfrac{5}{4} \cdot \dfrac{2}{5}$

35. $\dfrac{6}{49} \cdot \dfrac{7}{6}$

36. $\dfrac{13}{4} \cdot \dfrac{4}{39}$

Multiply. Write the product in simplest form. See Example 5.

37. $\dfrac{3}{4}\left(-\dfrac{8}{35}\right)\left(-\dfrac{7}{12}\right)$

38. $\dfrac{9}{10}\left(-\dfrac{4}{15}\right)\left(-\dfrac{5}{18}\right)$

39. $-\dfrac{5}{8}\left(\dfrac{16}{27}\right)\left(-\dfrac{9}{25}\right)$

40. $-\dfrac{15}{28}\left(\dfrac{7}{9}\right)\left(-\dfrac{18}{35}\right)$

Evaluate each expression. See Example 6.

41. a. $\left(\dfrac{3}{5}\right)^2$ **b.** $\left(-\dfrac{3}{5}\right)^2$

42. a. $\left(\dfrac{4}{9}\right)^2$ **b.** $\left(-\dfrac{4}{9}\right)^2$

43. a. $-\left(-\dfrac{1}{6}\right)^2$ **b.** $\left(-\dfrac{1}{6}\right)^3$

44. a. $-\left(-\dfrac{2}{5}\right)^2$ **b.** $\left(-\dfrac{2}{5}\right)^3$

Find each product. Write your answer in simplest form.
See Example 7.

45. $\dfrac{3}{4}$ of $\dfrac{5}{8}$

46. $\dfrac{4}{5}$ of $\dfrac{3}{7}$

47. $\dfrac{1}{6}$ of 54

48. $\dfrac{1}{9}$ of 36

Find the area of each rectangle or square. See Objective 5.

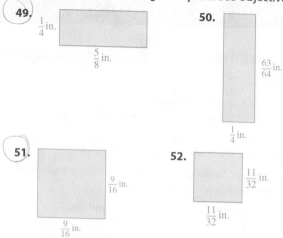

49. $\frac{1}{4}$ in., $\frac{5}{8}$ in.

50. $\frac{63}{64}$ in., $\frac{1}{4}$ in.

51. $\frac{9}{16}$ in., $\frac{9}{16}$ in.

52. $\frac{11}{32}$ in., $\frac{11}{32}$ in.

Find the area of each triangle. See Example 8.

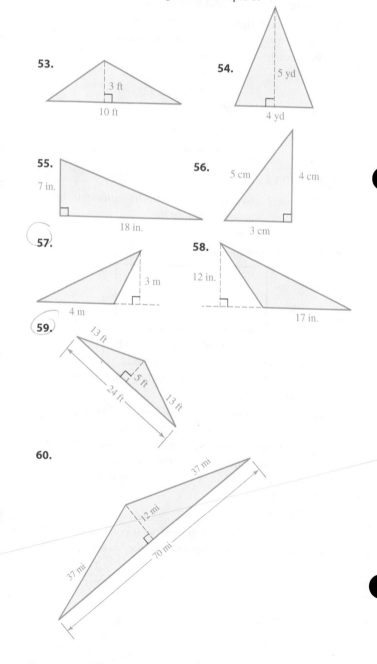

53. 3 ft, 10 ft

54. 5 yd, 4 yd

55. 7 in., 18 in.

56. 5 cm, 4 cm, 3 cm

57. 3 m, 4 m

58. 12 in., 17 in.

59. 13 ft, 5 ft, 24 ft, 13 ft

60. 37 mi, 12 mi, 37 mi, 70 mi

TRY IT YOURSELF

61. Complete the multiplication table of fractions.

·	$\frac{1}{2}$	$\frac{1}{3}$	$\frac{1}{4}$	$\frac{1}{5}$	$\frac{1}{6}$
$\frac{1}{2}$					
$\frac{1}{3}$					
$\frac{1}{4}$					
$\frac{1}{5}$					
$\frac{1}{6}$					

62. Complete the table by finding the original fraction, given its square.

Original fraction squared	Original fraction
$\frac{1}{9}$	
$\frac{1}{100}$	
$\frac{4}{25}$	
$\frac{16}{49}$	
$\frac{81}{36}$	
$\frac{9}{121}$	

Multiply. Write the product in simplest form.

63. $-\frac{15}{24} \cdot \frac{8}{25}$

64. $-\frac{20}{21} \cdot \frac{7}{16}$

65. $\frac{3}{8} \cdot \frac{7}{16}$

66. $\frac{5}{9} \cdot \frac{2}{7}$

67. $\left(\frac{2}{3}\right)\left(-\frac{1}{16}\right)\left(-\frac{4}{5}\right)$

68. $\left(\frac{3}{8}\right)\left(-\frac{2}{3}\right)\left(-\frac{12}{27}\right)$

69. $-\frac{5}{6} \cdot 18$

70. $6\left(-\frac{2}{3}\right)$

71. $\left(-\frac{3}{4}\right)^3$

72. $\left(-\frac{2}{5}\right)^3$

73. $\frac{3}{4} \cdot \frac{4}{3}$

74. $\frac{4}{5} \cdot \frac{5}{4}$

75. $\frac{5}{3}\left(-\frac{6}{15}\right)(-4)$

76. $\frac{5}{6}\left(-\frac{2}{3}\right)(-12)$

77. $-\frac{11}{12} \cdot \frac{18}{55} \cdot 5$

78. $-\frac{24}{5} \cdot \frac{7}{12} \cdot \frac{1}{14}$

79. $\left(-\frac{11}{21}\right)\left(-\frac{14}{33}\right)$

80. $\left(-\frac{16}{35}\right)\left(-\frac{25}{48}\right)$

81. $-\left(-\frac{5}{9}\right)^2$

82. $-\left(-\frac{5}{6}\right)^2$

83. $\frac{7}{10}\left(\frac{20}{21}\right)$

84. $\left(\frac{7}{6}\right)\frac{9}{49}$

85. $\frac{3}{4}\left(\frac{5}{7}\right)\left(\frac{2}{3}\right)\left(\frac{7}{3}\right)$

86. $-\frac{5}{4}\left(\frac{8}{15}\right)\left(\frac{2}{3}\right)\left(\frac{7}{2}\right)$

87. $-\frac{14}{15}\left(-\frac{11}{8}\right)$

88. $-\frac{5}{16}\left(-\frac{8}{3}\right)$

89. $\frac{3}{16} \cdot 4 \cdot \frac{2}{3}$

90. $5 \cdot \frac{7}{5} \cdot \frac{3}{14}$

CONCEPT EXTENSIONS

In problem 91 and 92, write a number sentence of the form
☐ · ☐ = ☐ *for each situation.*

91. a. The product of two negative fractions is $\frac{7}{32}$.

b. The product of two fractions is $-\frac{7}{32}$.

92. a. The product of an integer and a fraction is $\frac{1}{3}$.

b. The product of a proper fraction and an improper fraction is $\frac{1}{3}$.

93. a. Find two fractions whose product is greater than 1.

b. Find two fractions whose product is less than 1.

94. a. Divide the figure below into ten equal parts.

b. Now shade $\frac{2}{5}$ of the figure. How many of the equal parts did you shade?

c. Find $\frac{1}{2}$ of the parts that you shaded in part b. How many parts is that?

APPLICATIONS

95. SENATE RULES A *filibuster* is a method U.S. Senators sometimes use to block passage of a bill or appointment by talking endlessly. It takes $\frac{3}{5}$ of those voting in the Senate to break a filibuster. If all 100 Senators cast a vote, how many of their votes does it take to break a filibuster?

96. GENETICS Gregor Mendel (1822–1884), an Augustinian monk, is credited with developing a model that became the foundation of modern genetics. In his experiments, he crossed purple-flowered plants with white-flowered plants and found that $\frac{3}{4}$ of the offspring plants had purple flowers and $\frac{1}{4}$ of them had white flowers. Refer to the illustration on the next page, which shows a group of offspring plants. According to this concept, when the plants begin to flower, how many will have purple flowers?

97. BOUNCING BALLS A tennis ball is dropped from a height of 54 inches. Each time it hits the ground, it rebounds one-third of the previous height that it fell. Find the three missing rebound heights in the illustration.

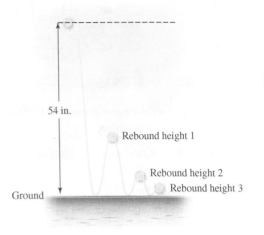

54 in.

Rebound height 1

Rebound height 2

Rebound height 3

Ground

98. ELECTIONS The final election returns for a city bond measure are shown below.

a. Find the total number of votes cast.

b. Find two-thirds of the total number of votes cast.

c. Did the bond measure pass?

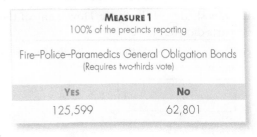

MEASURE 1
100% of the precincts reporting

Fire–Police–Paramedics General Obligation Bonds
(Requires two-thirds vote)

YES	No
125,599	62,801

99. COOKING Use the recipe below, along with the concept of multiplication of fractions, to find how much sugar and how much molasses are needed to make *one dozen* cookies. (*Hint:* this recipe is for *two dozen* cookies.)

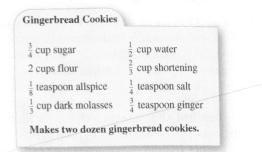

Gingerbread Cookies

$\frac{3}{4}$ cup sugar $\frac{1}{2}$ cup water

2 cups flour $\frac{2}{3}$ cup shortening

$\frac{1}{8}$ teaspoon allspice $\frac{1}{4}$ teaspoon salt

$\frac{1}{3}$ cup dark molasses $\frac{3}{4}$ teaspoon ginger

Makes two dozen gingerbread cookies.

100. THE EARTH'S SURFACE The surface of Earth covers an area of approximately 196,800,000 square miles. About $\frac{3}{4}$ of that area is covered by water. Find the number of square miles of the surface covered by water.

101. BOTANY In an experiment, monthly growth rates of three types of plants doubled when nitrogen was added to the soil. Complete the graph by drawing the improved growth rate bar next to each normal growth rate bar.

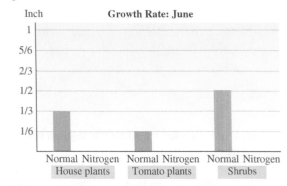

Inch   **Growth Rate: June**

1

5/6

2/3

1/2

1/3

1/6

Normal Nitrogen   Normal Nitrogen   Normal Nitrogen
House plants   Tomato plants   Shrubs

102. ICEBERGS About $\frac{9}{10}$ of the volume of an iceberg is below the water line.

a. What fraction of the volume of an iceberg is *above* the water line?

b. Suppose an iceberg has a total volume of 18,700 cubic meters. What is the volume of the part of the iceberg that is above the water line?

© Ralph A. Clevenger/Corbis

103. KITCHEN DESIGN Find the area of the *kitchen work triangle* formed by the paths between the refrigerator, the range, and the sink shown below.

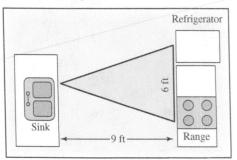

Refrigerator

6 ft

Sink

9 ft

Range

104. STARS AND STRIPES The illustration shows a folded U.S. flag. When it is placed on a table as part of an exhibit, how much area will it occupy?

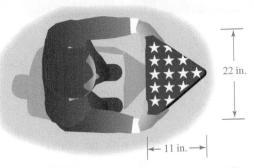

22 in.

11 in.

105. WINDSURFING Estimate the area of the sail on the windsurfing board.

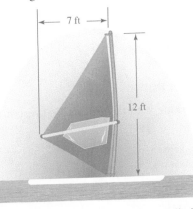

7 ft

12 ft

106. TILE DESIGN A design for bathroom tile is shown. Find the amount of area on a tile that is blue.

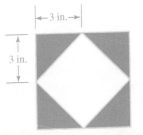

3 in.

3 in.

107. GEOGRAPHY Estimate the area of the state of New Hampshire, using the triangle in the illustration.

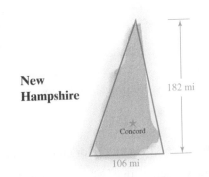

New Hampshire

182 mi

Concord

106 mi

108. STAMPS The best designs in a contest to create a wildlife stamp are shown. To save on paper costs, the postal service has decided to choose the stamp that has the smaller area. Which one did the postal service choose? (*Hint:* use the formula for the area of a rectangle.)

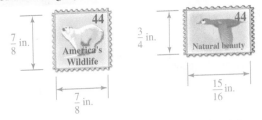

$\frac{7}{8}$ in.

44
America's Wildlife

$\frac{7}{8}$ in.

$\frac{3}{4}$ in.

44
Natural beauty

$\frac{15}{16}$ in.

109. VISES Each complete turn of the handle of the bench vise shown below tightens its jaws exactly $\frac{1}{16}$ of an inch. How much tighter will the jaws of the vice get if the handle is turned 12 complete times?

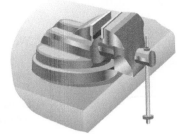

110. WOODWORKING Each time a board is passed through a power sander, the machine removes $\frac{1}{64}$ of an inch of thickness. If a rough pine board is passed through the sander 6 times, by how much will its thickness change?

WRITING

111. In a word problem, when a fraction is followed by the word *of*, multiplication is usually indicated. Give three real-life examples of this type of use of the word *of*.

112. Can you multiply the number 5 and another number and obtain an answer that is less than 5? Explain why or why not.

113. A MAJORITY The definition of the word *majority* is as follows: "a number greater than *one-half of* the total." Explain what it means when a teacher says, "A majority of the class voted to postpone the test until Monday." Give an example.

114. What does area measure? Give an example.

115. In the following solution, what step did the student forget to use that caused him to have to work with such large numbers?

Multiply. Simplify the product, if possible.

$$\frac{44}{63} \cdot \frac{27}{55} = \frac{44 \cdot 27}{63 \cdot 55}$$
$$= \frac{1,188}{3,465}$$

116. Is the product of two proper fractions always smaller than either of those fractions? Explain why or why not. Give an example.

Objectives

1 Find the reciprocal of a fraction.

2 Divide fractions.

3 Solve application problems by dividing fractions.

SECTION 2.3
Dividing Fractions

ARE YOU READY?

The following problems review some basic skills that are needed when dividing fractions.

1. Multiply: $\dfrac{14}{3} \cdot \dfrac{2}{21}$

2. Simplify: $\dfrac{2 \cdot 3 \cdot 3 \cdot 5}{2 \cdot 5 \cdot 5 \cdot 7}$

3. Find the opposite of each number:

    a. 16   **b.** -2

4. Complete each rule for dividing signed numbers.

    a. The quotient of two numbers with like signs is _____.

    b. The quotient of two numbers with unlike signs is _____.

We will now discuss how to divide fractions.

1 Find the reciprocal of a fraction.

Division with fractions involves working with *reciprocals*. To present the concept of reciprocal, we consider the problem $\frac{7}{8} \cdot \frac{8}{7}$.

$$\frac{7}{8} \cdot \frac{8}{7} = \frac{7 \cdot 8}{8 \cdot 7}$$ Multiply the numerators. Multiply the denominators.

$$= \frac{\overset{1}{7} \cdot \overset{1}{8}}{\underset{1}{8} \cdot \underset{1}{7}}$$ To simplify, remove the common factors of 7 and 8 from the numerator and denominator.

$$= \frac{1}{1}$$ Multiply the remaining factors in the numerator. Multiply the remaining factors in the denominator.

$$= 1$$ Any whole number divided by 1 is equal to that number.

The product of $\frac{7}{8}$ and $\frac{8}{7}$ is 1.

Whenever the product of two numbers is 1, we say that those numbers are *reciprocals*. Therefore, $\frac{7}{8}$ and $\frac{8}{7}$ are reciprocals. To find the reciprocal of a fraction, *we invert the numerator and the denominator.*

Reciprocals

Two numbers are called **reciprocals** if their product is 1.

Caution! Zero does not have a reciprocal, because the product of 0 and a number can never be 1.

Self Check 1

For each number, find its reciprocal and show that their product is 1.

a. $\dfrac{3}{5}$ **b.** $-\dfrac{5}{6}$ **c.** 8

Now Try Problem 13

EXAMPLE 1

For each number, find its reciprocal and show that their product is 1: **a.** $\dfrac{2}{3}$ **b.** $-\dfrac{3}{4}$ **c.** 5

Strategy To find each reciprocal, we will invert the numerator and denominator.

WHY This procedure will produce a new fraction that, when multiplied by the original fraction, gives a result of 1.

Solution

a. Fraction   Reciprocal

$$\frac{2}{3} \diagdown \frac{3}{2}$$
invert

The reciprocal of $\frac{2}{3}$ is $\frac{3}{2}$.

Check: $\dfrac{2}{3} \cdot \dfrac{3}{2} = \dfrac{\overset{1}{2} \cdot \overset{1}{3}}{\underset{1}{3} \cdot \underset{1}{2}} = 1$

b. Fraction   Reciprocal

$$-\frac{3}{4} \diagdown -\frac{4}{3}$$
invert

The reciprocal of $-\dfrac{3}{4}$ is $-\dfrac{4}{3}$.

Check: $-\dfrac{3}{4}\left(-\dfrac{4}{3}\right) = \dfrac{\overset{1}{3} \cdot \overset{1}{4}}{\underset{1}{4} \cdot \underset{1}{3}} = 1$ The product of two fractions with like signs is positive.

c. Since $5 = \dfrac{5}{1}$, the reciprocal of 5 is $\dfrac{1}{5}$.

Check: $5 \cdot \dfrac{1}{5} = \dfrac{5}{1} \cdot \dfrac{1}{5} = \dfrac{\overset{1}{5} \cdot 1}{1 \cdot \underset{1}{5}} = 1$

Caution!   Don't confuse the concepts of the *opposite* of a negative number and the *reciprocal* of a negative number. For example:

The reciprocal of $-\dfrac{9}{16}$ is $-\dfrac{16}{9}$.

The opposite of $-\dfrac{9}{16}$ is $\dfrac{9}{16}$.

---

2 Divide fractions.

To develop a rule for dividing fractions, let's consider a real-life application.

Suppose that the manager of a candy store buys large bars of chocolate and divides each one into four equal parts to sell. How many fourths can be obtained from 5 bars?

We are asking, "How many $\frac{1}{4}$'s are there in 5?" To answer the question, we need to use the operation of division. We can represent this division as $5 \div \frac{1}{4}$.

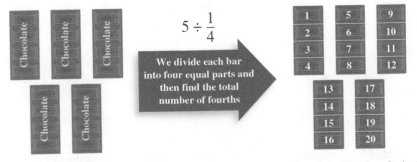

5 bars of chocolate

$5 \div \dfrac{1}{4}$

We divide each bar into four equal parts and then find the total number of fourths

Total number of fourths $= 5 \cdot 4 = 20$

There are 20 fourths in the 5 bars of chocolate. Two observations can be made from this result.

- This division problem involves a fraction: $5 \div \frac{1}{4}$.
- Although we were asked to find $5 \div \frac{1}{4}$, we solved the problem using *multiplication* instead of *division*: $5 \cdot 4 = 20$. That is, division by $\frac{1}{4}$ (a fraction) is the same as multiplication by 4 (its reciprocal).

$$5 \div \frac{1}{4} = 5 \cdot 4$$

These observations suggest the following rule for dividing two fractions.

Dividing Fractions

To divide two fractions, multiply the first fraction by the reciprocal of the second fraction. Simplify the result, if possible.

For example, to find $\frac{5}{7} \div \frac{3}{4}$, we multiply $\frac{5}{7}$ by the reciprocal of $\frac{3}{4}$.

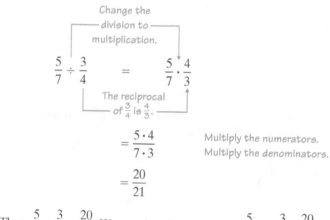

Change the division to multiplication.

$$\frac{5}{7} \div \frac{3}{4} = \frac{5}{7} \cdot \frac{4}{3}$$

The reciprocal of $\frac{3}{4}$ is $\frac{4}{3}$.

$$= \frac{5 \cdot 4}{7 \cdot 3} \qquad \text{Multiply the numerators.}$$
$$\text{Multiply the denominators.}$$

$$= \frac{20}{21}$$

Thus, $\frac{5}{7} \div \frac{3}{4} = \frac{20}{21}$. We say that the *quotient* of $\frac{5}{7}$ and $\frac{3}{4}$ is $\frac{20}{21}$.

Self Check 2

Divide: $\dfrac{2}{3} \div \dfrac{7}{8}$

Now Try **Problem 17**

EXAMPLE 2   Divide: $\dfrac{1}{3} \div \dfrac{4}{5}$

Strategy We will multiply the first fraction, $\frac{1}{3}$, by the reciprocal of the second fraction, $\frac{4}{5}$. Then, if possible, we will simplify the result.

WHY This is the rule for dividing two fractions.

Solution

$$\frac{1}{3} \div \frac{4}{5} = \frac{1}{3} \cdot \frac{5}{4} \qquad \text{Multiply } \tfrac{1}{3} \text{ by the reciprocal of } \tfrac{4}{5}, \text{ which is } \tfrac{5}{4}.$$

$$= \frac{1 \cdot 5}{3 \cdot 4} \qquad \text{Multiply the numerators.}$$
$$\text{Multiply the denominators.}$$

$$= \frac{5}{12}$$

Since 5 and 12 have no common factors other than 1, the result is in simplest form. ∎

EXAMPLE 3

Divide and simplify: $\dfrac{9}{16} \div \dfrac{3}{20}$

Strategy We will multiply the first fraction, $\frac{9}{16}$, by the reciprocal of the second fraction, $\frac{3}{20}$. Then, if possible, we will simplify the result.

WHY This is the rule for dividing two fractions.

Solution

$$\dfrac{9}{16} \div \dfrac{3}{20} = \dfrac{9}{16} \cdot \dfrac{20}{3}$$ Multiply $\frac{9}{16}$ by the reciprocal of $\frac{3}{20}$, which is $\frac{20}{3}$.

$$= \dfrac{9 \cdot 20}{16 \cdot 3}$$ Multiply the numerators.
Multiply the denominators.

$$= \dfrac{\overset{1}{\cancel{3}} \cdot 3 \cdot \overset{1}{\cancel{4}} \cdot 5}{\underset{1}{\cancel{4}} \cdot 4 \cdot \underset{1}{\cancel{3}}}$$ To simplify, factor 9 as $3 \cdot 3$, factor 20 as $4 \cdot 5$, and factor 16 as $4 \cdot 4$. Then remove out the common factors of 3 and 4 from the numerator and denominator.

$$= \dfrac{15}{4}$$ Multiply the remaining factors in the numerator: $1 \cdot 3 \cdot 1 \cdot 5 = 15$
Multiply the remaining factors in the denominator: $1 \cdot 4 \cdot 1 = 4$.

Self Check 3

Divide and simplify: $\dfrac{4}{5} \div \dfrac{8}{25}$

Now Try **Problem 21**

EXAMPLE 4

Divide and simplify: $120 \div \dfrac{10}{7}$

Strategy We will write 120 as a fraction and then multiply the first fraction by the reciprocal of the second fraction.

WHY This is the rule for dividing two fractions.

Solution

$$120 \div \dfrac{10}{7} = \dfrac{120}{1} \div \dfrac{10}{7}$$ Write 120 as a fraction: $120 = \frac{120}{1}$.

$$= \dfrac{120}{1} \cdot \dfrac{7}{10}$$ Multiply $\frac{120}{1}$ by the reciprocal of $\frac{10}{7}$, which is $\frac{7}{10}$.

$$= \dfrac{120 \cdot 7}{1 \cdot 10}$$ Multiply the numerators.
Multiply the denominators.

$$= \dfrac{\overset{1}{\cancel{10}} \cdot 12 \cdot 7}{1 \cdot \underset{1}{\cancel{10}}}$$ To simplify, factor 120 as $10 \cdot 12$, then remove the common factor of 10 from the numerator and denominator.

$$= \dfrac{84}{1}$$ Multiply the remaining factors in the numerator: $1 \cdot 12 \cdot 7 = 84$.
Multiply the remaining factors in the denominator: $1 \cdot 1 = 1$.

$$= 84$$ Any whole number divided by 1 is the same number.

Self Check 4

Divide and simplify:

$$80 \div \dfrac{20}{11}$$

Now Try **Problem 27**

Because of the relationship between multiplication and division, the sign rules for *dividing* fractions are the same as those for *multiplying* fractions.

EXAMPLE 5

Divide and simplify: $\dfrac{1}{6} \div \left(-\dfrac{1}{18} \right)$

Strategy We will multiply the first fraction, $\frac{1}{6}$, by the reciprocal of the second fraction, $-\frac{1}{18}$. To determine the sign of the result, we will use the rule for multiplying two fractions that have different (unlike) signs.

WHY One fraction is positive and one is negative.

Self Check 5

Divide and simplify:

$$\dfrac{2}{3} \div \left(-\dfrac{7}{6} \right)$$

Now Try **Problem 29**

Solution

$$\frac{1}{6} \div \left(-\frac{1}{18}\right) = \frac{1}{6}\left(-\frac{18}{1}\right) \qquad \text{Multiply } \tfrac{1}{6} \text{ by the reciprocal of } -\tfrac{1}{18}, \text{ which is } -\tfrac{18}{1}.$$

$$= -\frac{1 \cdot 18}{6 \cdot 1} \qquad \begin{array}{l}\text{Multiply the numerators.}\\ \text{Multiply the denominators.}\\ \text{Since the fractions have unlike signs,}\\ \text{make the answer negative.}\end{array}$$

$$= -\frac{1 \cdot 3 \cdot \overset{1}{\cancel{6}}}{\underset{1}{\cancel{6}} \cdot 1} \qquad \begin{array}{l}\text{To simplify, factor 18 as } 3 \cdot 6. \text{ Then remove the common}\\ \text{factor of 6 from the numerator and denominator.}\end{array}$$

$$= -\frac{3}{1} \qquad \begin{array}{l}\text{Multiply the remaining factors in the numerator.}\\ \text{Multiply the remaining factors in the denominator.}\end{array}$$

$$= -3$$

Self Check 6

Divide and simplify:

$$-\frac{35}{16} \div (-7)$$

Now Try **Problem 33**

EXAMPLE 6

Divide and simplify: $\quad -\dfrac{21}{36} \div (-3)$

Strategy We will multiply the first fraction, $-\frac{21}{36}$, by the reciprocal of -3. To determine the sign of the result, we will use the rule for multiplying two fractions that have the same (like) signs.

WHY Both fractions are negative.

Solution

$$-\frac{21}{36} \div (-3) = -\frac{21}{36}\left(-\frac{1}{3}\right) \qquad \text{Multiply } -\tfrac{21}{36} \text{ by the reciprocal of } -3, \text{ which is } -\tfrac{1}{3}.$$

$$= \frac{21}{36}\left(\frac{1}{3}\right) \qquad \begin{array}{l}\text{Since the product of two negative fractions is}\\ \text{positive, drop both } - \text{ signs and continue.}\end{array}$$

$$= \frac{21 \cdot 1}{36 \cdot 3} \qquad \begin{array}{l}\text{Multiply the numerators.}\\ \text{Multiply the denominators.}\end{array}$$

$$= \frac{\overset{1}{\cancel{3}} \cdot 7 \cdot 1}{36 \cdot \underset{1}{\cancel{3}}} \qquad \begin{array}{l}\text{To simplify, factor 21 as } 3 \cdot 7. \text{ Then remove the common}\\ \text{factor of 3 from the numerator and denominator.}\end{array}$$

$$= \frac{7}{36} \qquad \begin{array}{l}\text{Multiply the remaining factors in the numerator:}\\ 1 \cdot 7 \cdot 1 = 7.\\ \text{Multiply the remaining factors in the denominator:}\\ 36 \cdot 1 = 36.\end{array}$$

---

3 **Solve application problems by dividing fractions.**

Problems that involve forming equal-sized groups can be solved by division.

EXAMPLE 7 *Surfboard Designs* Most surfboards are made of a foam core covered with several layers of fiberglass to keep them water-tight. How many layers are needed to build up a finish $\frac{3}{8}$ of an inch thick if each layer of fiberglass has a thickness of $\frac{1}{16}$ of an inch?

Solution It is helpful to list what we know and what we are to find.

- The surfboard is to have a $\frac{3}{8}$-inch-thick fiberglass finish.   *Given*
- Each layer of fiberglass is $\frac{1}{16}$ of an inch thick.   *Given*
- How many layers of fiberglass need to be applied?   *Find*

Think of the $\frac{3}{8}$-inch-thick finish separated into an unknown number of equally thick layers of fiberglass. This indicates division.

We translate the words of the problem to numbers and symbols.

The number of layers of fiberglass that are needed	is equal to	the thickness of the finish	divided by	the thickness of 1 layer of fiberglass.
The number of layers of fiberglass that are needed	$=$	$\frac{3}{8}$	$\div$	$\frac{1}{16}$

To find the quotient, we will use the rule for dividing two fractions.

$$\frac{3}{8} \div \frac{1}{16} = \frac{3}{8} \cdot \frac{16}{1}$$ Multiply $\frac{3}{8}$ by the reciprocal of $\frac{1}{16}$, which is $\frac{16}{1}$.

$$= \frac{3 \cdot 16}{8 \cdot 1}$$ Multiply the numerators.
Multiply the denominators.

$$= \frac{3 \cdot 2 \cdot \overset{1}{8}}{\underset{1}{8} \cdot 1}$$ To simplify, factor 16 as $2 \cdot 8$. Then remove the common factor of 8 from the numerator and denominator.

$$= \frac{6}{1}$$ Multiply the remaining factors in the numerator.
Multiply the remaining factors in the denominator.

$$= 6$$ Any whole number divided by 1 is the same number.

The number of layers of fiberglass needed is 6.

If 6 layers of fiberglass, each $\frac{1}{16}$ of an inch thick, are used, the finished thickness will be $\frac{6}{16}$ of an inch. If we simplify $\frac{6}{16}$, we see that it is equivalent to the desired finish thickness:

$$\frac{6}{16} = \frac{\overset{1}{2} \cdot 3}{\underset{1}{2} \cdot 8} = \frac{3}{8}$$

The result checks.

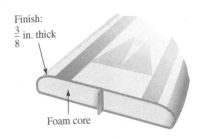

Finish:
$\frac{3}{8}$ in. thick

Foam core

ANSWERS TO SELF CHECKS

1. a. $\frac{5}{3}$ **b.** $-\frac{6}{5}$ **c.** $\frac{1}{8}$ **2.** $\frac{16}{21}$ **3.** $\frac{5}{2}$ **4.** 44 **5.** $-\frac{4}{7}$ **6.** $\frac{5}{16}$ **7.** 12

TION 2.3   STUDY SET

VOCABULARY

Fill in the blanks.

1. The _____ of $\frac{5}{12}$ is $\frac{12}{5}$.

2. To find the reciprocal of a fraction, _____ the numerator and denominator.

3. The answer to a division is called the _____.

4. To simplify $\frac{2 \cdot 2 \cdot 3}{2 \cdot 3 \cdot 5 \cdot 7}$, we _____ common factors of the numerator and denominator.

CONCEPTS

5. Fill in the blanks.

a. To divide two fractions, _____ the first fraction by the _____ of the second fraction.

b. 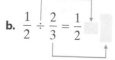 $\frac{1}{2} \div \frac{2}{3} = \frac{1}{2}$

6. a. What division problem is illustrated below?

b. What is the answer?

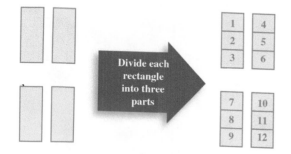

1	4
2	5
3	6

Divide each rectangle into three parts

7	10
8	11
9	12

7. Determine whether each quotient is positive or negative. *You do not have to find the answer.*

a. $-\frac{1}{4} \div \frac{3}{4}$ **b.** $-\frac{7}{8} \div \left(-\frac{21}{32}\right)$

8. Complete the table.

Number	Opposite	Reciprocal
$\frac{3}{10}$		
$-\frac{7}{11}$		
6		

9. a. Multiply $\frac{4}{5}$ and its reciprocal. What is the result?

b. Multiply $-\frac{3}{5}$ and its reciprocal. What is the result?

10. a. Find: $15 \div 3$

b. Rewrite $15 \div 3$ as multiplication by the reciprocal of 3, and find the result.

c. Complete this statement: Division by 3 is the same as multiplication by ☐.

NOTATION

Complete each step.

11. $\dfrac{4}{9} \div \dfrac{8}{27} = \dfrac{4}{9} \cdot \dfrac{\boxed{}}{8}$

$= \dfrac{4 \cdot \boxed{}}{9 \cdot \boxed{}}$

$= \dfrac{4 \cdot 3 \cdot \boxed{}}{9 \cdot \boxed{} \cdot \boxed{}}$

$= \dfrac{\overset{1}{\cancel{}} \cdot 3 \cdot \overset{1}{\cancel{9}}}{\underset{1}{\cancel{}} \cdot 2 \cdot \underset{1}{\cancel{4}}}$

$= \dfrac{\boxed{}}{2}$

12. $\dfrac{25}{31} \div 10 = \dfrac{25}{31} \div \dfrac{10}{\boxed{}}$

$= \dfrac{25}{31} \cdot \dfrac{1}{\boxed{}}$

$= \dfrac{25 \cdot \boxed{}}{31 \cdot \boxed{}}$

$= \dfrac{5 \cdot \boxed{} \cdot 1}{31 \cdot 2 \cdot 5}$

$= \dfrac{\overset{1}{\cancel{5}} \cdot 5 \cdot 1}{31 \cdot 2 \cdot \underset{1}{\cancel{}}}$

$= \dfrac{5}{\boxed{}}$

GUIDED PRACTICE

Find the reciprocal of each number. See Example 1.

13. a. $\frac{6}{7}$ **b.** $-\frac{15}{8}$ **c.** 10

14. a. $\frac{2}{9}$ **b.** $-\frac{9}{4}$ **c.** 7

15. a. $\frac{11}{8}$ **b.** $-\frac{1}{14}$ **c.** -63

16. a. $\frac{13}{2}$ **b.** $-\frac{1}{5}$ **c.** -21

Divide. Simplify each quotient, if possible. See Example 2.

17. $\frac{1}{8} \div \frac{2}{3}$ **18.** $\frac{1}{2} \div \frac{8}{9}$

19. $\frac{2}{23} \div \frac{1}{7}$ **20.** $\frac{4}{21} \div \frac{1}{5}$

Divide. Simplify each quotient, if possible. **See Example 3.**

21. $\dfrac{25}{32} \div \dfrac{5}{28}$ **22.** $\dfrac{4}{25} \div \dfrac{2}{35}$

23. $\dfrac{27}{32} \div \dfrac{9}{8}$ **24.** $\dfrac{16}{27} \div \dfrac{20}{21}$

Divide. Simplify each quotient, if possible. **See Example 4.**

25. $50 \div \dfrac{10}{9}$ **26.** $60 \div \dfrac{10}{3}$

27. $150 \div \dfrac{15}{32}$ **28.** $170 \div \dfrac{17}{6}$

Divide. Simplify each quotient, if possible. **See Example 5.**

29. $\dfrac{1}{8} \div \left(-\dfrac{1}{32}\right)$ **30.** $\dfrac{1}{9} \div \left(-\dfrac{1}{27}\right)$

31. $\dfrac{2}{5} \div \left(-\dfrac{4}{35}\right)$ **32.** $\dfrac{4}{9} \div \left(-\dfrac{16}{27}\right)$

Divide. Simplify each quotient, if possible. **See Example 6.**

33. $-\dfrac{28}{55} \div (-7)$ **34.** $-\dfrac{32}{45} \div (-8)$

35. $-\dfrac{33}{23} \div (-11)$ **36.** $-\dfrac{21}{31} \div (-7)$

TRY IT YOURSELF

Divide. Simplify each quotient, if possible.

37. $120 \div \dfrac{12}{5}$ **38.** $360 \div \dfrac{36}{5}$

39. $\dfrac{1}{2} \div \dfrac{3}{5}$ **40.** $\dfrac{1}{7} \div \dfrac{5}{6}$

41. $\left(-\dfrac{7}{4}\right) \div \left(-\dfrac{21}{8}\right)$ **42.** $\left(-\dfrac{15}{16}\right) \div \left(-\dfrac{5}{8}\right)$

43. $\dfrac{4}{5} \div \dfrac{4}{5}$ **44.** $\dfrac{2}{3} \div \dfrac{2}{3}$

45. Divide $-\dfrac{15}{32}$ by $\dfrac{3}{4}$ **46.** Divide $-\dfrac{7}{10}$ by $\dfrac{4}{5}$

47. $3 \div \dfrac{1}{12}$ **48.** $9 \div \dfrac{3}{4}$

49. $-\dfrac{4}{5} \div (-6)$ **50.** $-\dfrac{7}{8} \div (-14)$

51. $\dfrac{15}{16} \div 180$ **52.** $\dfrac{7}{8} \div 210$

53. $-\dfrac{9}{10} \div \dfrac{4}{15}$ **54.** $-\dfrac{3}{4} \div \dfrac{3}{2}$

55. $\dfrac{9}{10} \div \left(-\dfrac{3}{25}\right)$ **56.** $\dfrac{11}{16} \div \left(-\dfrac{9}{16}\right)$

57. $\dfrac{3}{16} \div \dfrac{1}{9}$ **58.** $\dfrac{5}{8} \div \dfrac{2}{9}$

59. $-\dfrac{1}{8} \div 8$ **60.** $-\dfrac{1}{15} \div 15$

The following problems involve multiplication and division. Perform each operation. Simplify the result, if possible.

61. $\dfrac{7}{6} \cdot \dfrac{9}{49}$ **62.** $\dfrac{7}{10} \cdot \dfrac{20}{21}$

63. $-\dfrac{4}{5} \div \left(-\dfrac{3}{2}\right)$ **64.** $-\dfrac{2}{3} \div \left(-\dfrac{3}{2}\right)$

65. $\dfrac{13}{16} \div 2$ **66.** $\dfrac{7}{8} \div 6$

67. $\left(-\dfrac{11}{21}\right)\left(-\dfrac{14}{33}\right)$ **68.** $\left(-\dfrac{16}{35}\right)\left(-\dfrac{25}{48}\right)$

69. $-\dfrac{15}{32} \div \dfrac{5}{64}$ **70.** $-\dfrac{28}{15} \div \dfrac{21}{10}$

71. $11 \cdot \dfrac{1}{6}$ **72.** $9 \cdot \dfrac{1}{8}$

73. $\dfrac{3}{4} \cdot \dfrac{5}{7}$ **74.** $\dfrac{2}{3} \cdot \dfrac{7}{9}$

75. $\dfrac{25}{7} \div \left(-\dfrac{30}{21}\right)$ **76.** $\dfrac{39}{25} \div \left(-\dfrac{13}{10}\right)$

CONCEPT EXTENSIONS

In problems 77 and 78, write a number sentence of the form ☐ ÷ ☐ = ☐ *for each situation.*

77. a. The quotient of two negative fractions is $\frac{1}{4}$.

   b. The quotient of two fractions is $-\frac{1}{4}$.

78. a. The quotient of an integer and a fraction is $\frac{5}{3}$.

   b. The quotient of a proper fraction and an improper fraction is $\frac{5}{3}$.

79. Graph the following numbers on the same number line.

   a. The reciprocal of $-\frac{8}{5}$

   b. The reciprocal of the opposite of $-\frac{9}{7}$

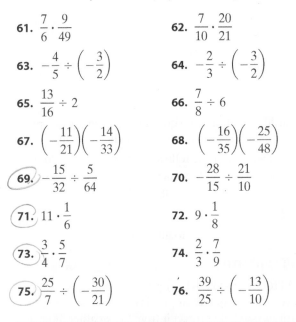

80. a. Given an example of a positive fraction whose reciprocal is less than that fraction.

   b. Give an example of a negative fraction whose reciprocal is greater than that fraction.

81. **a.** Divide each of the figures below into equal parts that have the shape ◇.

  b. What fraction division problem does this process illustrate?

  c. What is the answer to the division problem from part b?

82. Consider the following question: How many one pint ($\frac{1}{8}$-gallon) servings are there in $\frac{1}{2}$ gallon of milk?

  a. Which one of the following expressions could be used to answer this question?

  i. $\frac{1}{2} \cdot \frac{1}{8}$ **ii.** $\frac{1}{2} - \frac{1}{8}$

  iii. $\frac{1}{8} \div \frac{1}{2}$ **iv.** $\frac{1}{2} \div \frac{1}{8}$

  b. What is the answer to this problem?

▌APPLICATIONS

83. PATIO FURNITURE A production process applies several layers of a clear plastic coat to outdoor furniture to help protect it from the weather. If each protective coat is $\frac{3}{32}$-inch thick, how many applications will be needed to build up $\frac{3}{8}$ inch of clear finish?

84. MARATHONS Each lap around a stadium track is $\frac{1}{4}$ mile. How many laps would a runner have to complete to get a 26-mile workout?

85. COOKING A recipe calls for $\frac{3}{4}$ cup of flour, and the only measuring container you have holds $\frac{1}{8}$ cup. How many $\frac{1}{8}$ cups of flour would you need to add to follow the recipe?

86. LASERS A technician uses a laser to slice thin pieces of aluminum off the end of a rod that is $\frac{7}{8}$-inch long. How many $\frac{1}{64}$-inch-wide slices can be cut from this rod? (Assume that there is no waste in the process.)

87. UNDERGROUND CABLES Refer to the illustration and table.

  a. How many days will it take to install underground TV cable from the broadcasting station to the new homes using route 1?

  b. How long is route 2?

  c. How many days will it take to install the cable using route 2?

  d. Which route will require fewer days to install the cable?

Proposal	Amount of cable installed per day	Comments
Route 1	$\frac{2}{5}$ of a mile	Ground very rocky
Route 2	$\frac{3}{5}$ of a mile	Longer than Route 1

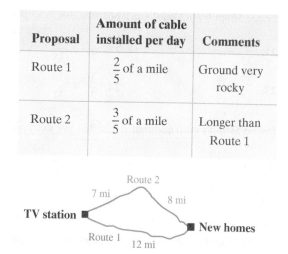

88. PRODUCTION PLANNING The materials used to make a pillow are shown. Examine the inventory list to decide how many pillows can be manufactured in one production run with the materials in stock.

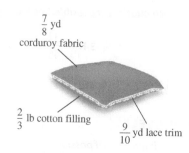

Factory Inventory List

Materials	Amount in stock
Lace trim	135 yd
Corduroy fabric	154 yd
Cotton filling	98 lb

89. NOTE CARDS Ninety 3 × 5 cards are stacked next to a ruler as shown.

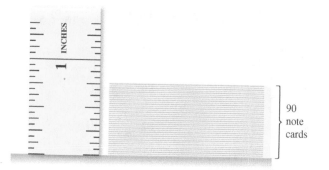

  a. Into how many parts is 1 inch divided on the ruler?

  b. How thick is the stack of cards?

  c. How thick is one 3 × 5 card?

90. COMPUTER PRINTERS The illustration shows how the letter E is formed by a dot matrix printer. What is the height of one dot?

$\frac{3}{32}$ in.

91. FORESTRY A set of forestry maps divides the 6,284 acres of an old-growth forest into $\frac{4}{5}$-acre sections. How many sections do the maps contain?

92. HARDWARE A hardware chain purchases large amounts of nails and packages them in $\frac{9}{16}$-pound bags for sale. How many of these bags of nails can be obtained from 2,871 pounds of nails?

WRITING

93. Explain how to divide two fractions.

94. Why do you need to know how to multiply fractions to be able to divide fractions?

95. Explain why 0 does not have a reciprocal.

96. What number is its own reciprocal? Explain why this is so.

97. Write an application problem that could be solved by finding $10 \div \frac{1}{5}$.

98. Explain why dividing a fraction by 2 is the same as finding $\frac{1}{2}$ of it. Give an example.

99. Explain why 6 divided by $\frac{1}{2}$ is larger than 6.

100. Is there a number whose opposite is the same as its reciprocal? Explain why or why not.

SECTION 2.4
Adding and Subtracting Fractions

Objectives

1 Add and subtract fractions that have the same denominator.

2 Add and subtract fractions that have different denominators.

3 Find the LCD using multiples.

4 Find the LCD using prime factorization.

5 Identify the greater of two fractions.

6 Solve application problems by adding and subtracting fractions.

ARE YOU READY?

The following problems review some basic skills that are needed when adding and subtracting fractions.

1. Evaluate: $-8 - (-4)$

2. Prime factor 280.

3. Fill in the blanks: 3, 6, ▨ , 12, ▨ , 18, 21, 24, ▨ , 30, . . .

4. Simplify: $\dfrac{35}{84}$

5. Which two fractions have the same denominator?

$$\frac{7}{24} \quad \frac{9}{16} \quad \frac{16}{15} \quad \frac{24}{49} \quad \frac{7}{16} \quad \frac{16}{9}$$

6. Multiply: $\dfrac{7}{10} \cdot \dfrac{3}{4}$

In mathematics and everyday life, we can only add (or subtract) objects that are similar. For example, we can add dollars to dollars, but we cannot add dollars to oranges. This concept is important when adding or subtracting fractions.

1 Add and subtract fractions that have the same denominator.

Consider the problem $\frac{3}{5} + \frac{1}{5}$. When we write it in words, it is apparent that we are adding similar objects.

three-**fifths** + one-**fifth**

└─ Similar objects ─┘

Because the denominators of $\frac{3}{5}$ and $\frac{1}{5}$ are the same, we say that they have a **common denominator.** Since the fractions have a common denominator, we can add them. The following figure explains the addition process.

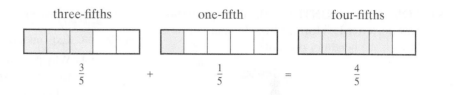

three-fifths	one-fifth	four-fifths

$$\frac{3}{5} \qquad + \qquad \frac{1}{5} \qquad = \qquad \frac{4}{5}$$

We can make some observations about the addition shown in the figure.

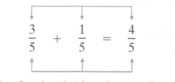

The sum of the numerators is the numerator of the answer.

$$\frac{3}{5} \quad + \quad \frac{1}{5} \quad = \quad \frac{4}{5}$$

The answer is a fraction that has the same denominator as the two fractions that were added.

These observations illustrate the following rule.

Adding and Subtracting Fractions That Have the Same Denominator

To add (or subtract) fractions that have the same denominator, add (or subtract) their numerators and write the sum (or difference) over the common denominator. Simplify the result, if possible.

Caution! We **do not** add fractions by adding the numerators and adding the denominators!

$$\frac{3}{5} + \frac{1}{5} = \frac{3+1}{5+5} = \frac{4}{10}$$

The same caution applies when subtracting fractions.

Self Check 1

Perform each operation and simplify the result, if possible.

a. Add: $\dfrac{5}{12} + \dfrac{1}{12}$

b. Subtract: $\dfrac{8}{9} - \dfrac{1}{9}$

Now Try **Problems 23 and 27**

EXAMPLE 1

Perform each operation and simplify the result, if possible.

a. Add: $\dfrac{1}{8} + \dfrac{5}{8}$ **b.** Subtract: $\dfrac{11}{15} - \dfrac{4}{15}$

Strategy We will use the rule for adding and subtracting fractions that have *the same* denominator.

WHY In part a, the fractions have the same denominator, 8. In part b, the fractions have the same denominator, 15.

Solution

a. $\dfrac{1}{8} + \dfrac{5}{8} = \dfrac{1+5}{8}$ *Add the numerators and write the sum over the common denominator 8.*

$= \dfrac{6}{8}$ *This fraction can be simplified.*

$= \dfrac{\overset{1}{\cancel{2}} \cdot 3}{\underset{1}{\cancel{2}} \cdot 4}$ *To simplify, factor 6 as 2 · 3 and 8 as 2 · 4. Then remove the common factor of 2 from the numerator and denominator.*

$= \dfrac{3}{4}$ *Multiply the remaining factors in the numerator: 1 · 3 = 3. Multiply the remaining factors in the denominator: 1 · 4 = 4.*

b. $\dfrac{11}{15} - \dfrac{4}{15} = \dfrac{11-4}{15}$ *Subtract the numerators and write the difference over the common denominator 15.*

$= \dfrac{7}{15}$

Since 7 and 15 have no common factors other than 1, the result is in simplest form. ■

To subtract two fractions, add the first to the opposite of the fraction to be subtracted.

EXAMPLE 2   Subtract: $-\dfrac{7}{3} - \left(-\dfrac{2}{3}\right)$

Strategy To find the difference, we will apply the rule for subtraction.

WHY It is easy to make an error when subtracting signed fractions. We will probably be more accurate if we write the subtraction as addition of the opposite.

Solution

We read $-\frac{7}{3} - \left(-\frac{2}{3}\right)$ as "negative seven-thirds *minus* negative two-thirds." Thus, the number to be subtracted is $-\frac{2}{3}$. Subtracting $-\frac{2}{3}$ is the same as adding its opposite, $\frac{2}{3}$.

$-\dfrac{7}{3} - \left(-\dfrac{2}{3}\right) = -\dfrac{7}{3} + \dfrac{2}{3}$ *Add the opposite of $-\frac{2}{3}$, which is $\frac{2}{3}$.*

$= \dfrac{-7}{3} + \dfrac{2}{3}$ *Write $-\frac{7}{3}$ as $\frac{-7}{3}$.*

$= \dfrac{-7+2}{3}$ *Add the numerators and write the sum over the common denominator 3.*

$= \dfrac{-5}{3}$ *Use the rule for adding two integers with different signs: $-7 + 2 = -5$.*

$= -\dfrac{5}{3}$ *Rewrite the result with the $-$ sign in front: $\frac{-5}{3} = -\frac{5}{3}$. This fraction is in simplest form.*

Note that the result is a negative improper fraction. In Section 2.5, we will see how an answer like this can be expressed in an alternate form as a **mixed number.** ■

Self Check 2

Subtract: $-\dfrac{9}{11} - \left(-\dfrac{3}{11}\right)$

***Now Try* Problem 31**

EXAMPLE 3   Perform the operations and simplify: $\dfrac{18}{25} - \dfrac{2}{25} - \dfrac{1}{25}$

Strategy We will use the rule for subtracting fractions that have *the same* denominator.

WHY All three fractions have the same denominator, 25.

Solution

$\dfrac{18}{25} - \dfrac{2}{25} - \dfrac{1}{25} = \dfrac{18-2-1}{25}$ *Subtract the numerators and write the difference over the common denominator 25.*

$= \dfrac{15}{25}$ *This fraction can be simplified.*

$= \dfrac{3 \cdot \overset{1}{\cancel{5}}}{\underset{1}{\cancel{5}} \cdot 5}$ *To simplify, factor 15 as $3 \cdot 5$ and 25 as $5 \cdot 5$. Then remove the common factor of 5 from the numerator and denominator.*

$= \dfrac{3}{5}$ *Multiply the remaining factors in the numerator: $3 \cdot 1 = 3$. Multiply the remaining factors in the denominator: $1 \cdot 5 = 5$.*

Self Check 3

Perform the operations and simplify:

$\dfrac{2}{9} + \dfrac{2}{9} + \dfrac{2}{9}$

***Now Try* Problem 35**

2 Add and subtract fractions that have different denominators.

Now we consider the problem $\frac{3}{5} + \frac{1}{3}$. Since the denominators are different, we cannot add these fractions in their present form.

three-**fifths**   +   one-**third**

└─Not similar objects─┘

To add (or subtract) fractions with different denominators, we express them as equivalent fractions that have a common denominator. The smallest common denominator, called the **least** or **lowest common denominator,** is usually the easiest common denominator to use.

Least Common Denominator

The **least common denominator (LCD)** for a set of fractions is the smallest number each denominator will divide exactly (divide with no remainder).

The denominators of $\frac{3}{5}$ and $\frac{1}{3}$ are 5 and 3. The numbers 5 and 3 divide many numbers exactly (30, 45, and 60, to name a few), but the smallest number that they divide exactly is 15. Thus, 15 is the LCD for $\frac{3}{5}$ and $\frac{1}{3}$.

To find $\frac{3}{5} + \frac{1}{3}$, we *build* equivalent fractions that have denominators of 15. Then we use the rule for adding fractions that have the same denominator.

$$\frac{3}{5} + \frac{1}{3} = \frac{3}{5} \cdot \frac{3}{3} + \frac{1}{3} \cdot \frac{5}{5}$$

We need to multiply this denominator by 5 to obtain 15. It follows that $\frac{5}{5}$ should be the form of 1 used to build $\frac{1}{3}$.

We need to multiply this denominator by 3 to obtain 15. It follows that $\frac{3}{3}$ should be the form of 1 that is used to build $\frac{3}{5}$.

$$= \frac{9}{15} + \frac{5}{15}$$

Multiply the numerators. Multiply the denominators. Note that the denominators are now the same.

$$= \frac{9 + 5}{15}$$

Add the numerators and write the sum over the common denominator 15.

$$= \frac{14}{15}$$

Since 14 and 15 have no common factors other than 1, this fraction is in simplest form.

The figure below shows $\frac{3}{5}$ and $\frac{1}{3}$ expressed as equivalent fractions with a denominator of 15. Once the denominators are the same, the fractions are similar objects and can be added easily.

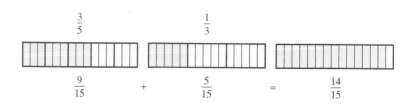

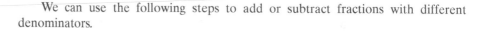

We can use the following steps to add or subtract fractions with different denominators.

Adding and Subtracting Fractions That Have Different Denominators

1. Find the LCD.
2. Rewrite each fraction as an equivalent fraction with the LCD as the denominator. To do so, build each fraction using a form of 1 that involves any factors needed to obtain the LCD.
3. Add or subtract the numerators and write the sum or difference over the LCD.
4. Simplify the result, if possible.

EXAMPLE 4   Add: $\dfrac{1}{7} + \dfrac{2}{3}$

Strategy We will express each fraction as an equivalent fraction that has the LCD as its denominator. Then we will use the rule for adding fractions that have the same denominator.

WHY To add (or subtract) fractions, the fractions must have *like* denominators.

Solution
Since the smallest number the denominators 7 and 3 divide exactly is 21, the LCD is 21.

$$\frac{1}{7} + \frac{2}{3} = \frac{1}{7} \cdot \frac{3}{3} + \frac{2}{3} \cdot \frac{7}{7}$$ To build $\frac{1}{7}$ and $\frac{2}{3}$ so that their denominators are 21, multiply each by a form of 1.

$$= \frac{3}{21} + \frac{14}{21}$$ Multiply the numerators. Multiply the denominators. The denominators are now the same.

$$= \frac{3 + 14}{21}$$ Add the numerators and write the sum over the common denominator 21.

$$= \frac{17}{21}$$ Since 17 and 21 have no common factors other than 1, this fraction is in simplest form.

Self Check 4

Add: $\dfrac{1}{2} + \dfrac{2}{5}$

Now Try **Problem 41**

EXAMPLE 5   Subtract: $\dfrac{5}{2} - \dfrac{7}{3}$

Strategy We will express each fraction as an equivalent fraction that has the LCD as its denominator. Then we will use the rule for subtracting fractions that have the same denominator.

WHY To add (or subtract) fractions, the fractions must have *like* denominators.

Solution
Since the smallest number the denominators 2 and 3 divide exactly is 6, the LCD is 6.

$$\frac{5}{2} - \frac{7}{3} = \frac{5}{2} \cdot \frac{3}{3} - \frac{7}{3} \cdot \frac{2}{2}$$ To build $\frac{5}{2}$ and $\frac{7}{3}$ so that their denominators are 6, multiply each by a form of 1.

$$= \frac{15}{6} - \frac{14}{6}$$ Multiply the numerators. Multiply the denominators. The denominators are now the same.

$$= \frac{15 - 14}{6}$$ Subtract the numerators and write the difference over the common denominator 6.

$$= \frac{1}{6}$$ This fraction is in simplest form.

Self Check 5

Subtract: $\dfrac{6}{7} - \dfrac{3}{5}$

Now Try **Problem 43**

Self Check 6

Subtract: $\dfrac{2}{3} - \dfrac{13}{6}$

Now Try **Problem 47**

EXAMPLE 6   Subtract: $\dfrac{2}{5} - \dfrac{11}{15}$

Strategy Since the smallest number the denominators 5 and 15 divide exactly is 15, the LCD is 15. We will only need to build an equivalent fraction for $\frac{2}{5}$.

WHY We do not have to build the fraction $\frac{11}{15}$ because it already has a denominator of 15.

Solution

$$\frac{2}{5} - \frac{11}{15} = \frac{2}{5}\cdot\frac{3}{3} - \frac{11}{15}$$ To build $\frac{2}{5}$ so that its denominator is 15, multiply it by a form of 1.

$$= \frac{6}{15} - \frac{11}{15}$$ Multiply the numerators. Multiply the denominators. The denominators are now the same.

$$= \frac{6 - 11}{15}$$ Subtract the numerators and write the difference over the common denominator 15.

$$= -\frac{5}{15}$$ If it is helpful, use the subtraction rule and add the opposite in the numerator: $6 + (-11) = -5$. Write the $-$ sign in front of the fraction.

$$= -\frac{\overset{1}{\cancel{5}}}{3\cdot\underset{1}{\cancel{5}}}$$ To simplify, factor 15 as $3\cdot 5$. Then remove the common factor of 5 from the numerator and denominator.

$$= -\frac{1}{3}$$ Multiply the remaining factors in the denominator: $3\cdot 1 = 3$.

Success Tip In Example 6, did you notice that the denominator 5 is a factor of the denominator 15, and that the LCD is 15. In general, when adding (or subtracting) two fractions with different denominators, *if the smaller denominator is a factor of the larger denominator, the larger denominator is the LCD.*

Caution! You might not have to build each fraction when adding or subtracting fractions with different denominators. For instance, the step in blue shown below is unnecessary when solving Example 6.

$$\frac{2}{5} - \frac{11}{15} = \frac{2}{5}\cdot\frac{3}{3} - \frac{11}{15}\cdot\cancel{\frac{1}{1}}$$

Self Check 7

Add: $-6 + \dfrac{3}{8}$

Now Try **Problem 51**

EXAMPLE 7   Add: $-5 + \dfrac{3}{4}$

Strategy We will write -5 as the fraction $\frac{-5}{1}$. Then we will follow the steps for adding fractions that have different denominators.

WHY The fractions $\frac{-5}{1}$ and $\frac{3}{4}$ have different denominators.

Solution

Since the smallest number the denominators 1 and 4 divide exactly is 4, the LCD is 4.

$$-5 + \frac{3}{4} = \frac{-5}{1} + \frac{3}{4}$$ Write -5 as $\frac{-5}{1}$.

$$= \frac{-5}{1}\cdot\frac{4}{4} + \frac{3}{4}$$ To build $\frac{-5}{1}$ so that its denominator is 4, multiply it by a form of 1.

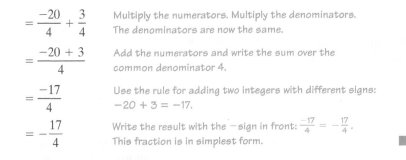

$= \dfrac{-20}{4} + \dfrac{3}{4}$ Multiply the numerators. Multiply the denominators.
The denominators are now the same.

$= \dfrac{-20 + 3}{4}$ Add the numerators and write the sum over the
common denominator 4.

$= \dfrac{-17}{4}$ Use the rule for adding two integers with different signs:
$-20 + 3 = -17$.

$= -\dfrac{17}{4}$ Write the result with the $-$ sign in front: $\frac{-17}{4} = -\frac{17}{4}$.
This fraction is in simplest form.

3 Find the LCD using multiples.

When we add or subtract fractions that have different denominators, the least common denominator is not always obvious. Two procedures we can use to determine the LCD for more difficult problems that involve larger denominators are called the **multiples method** and the **prime factorization method.**

As a child, you probably learned to count by 2's and 5's and 10's. Counting in that way is an example of an important concept in mathematics called *multiplies.* The **multiples** of a number are the products of that number and 1, 2, 3, 4, 5, and so on. For example, to find the multiples of 6, we proceed as follows:

$6 \cdot 1 = 6$ This is the first multiple of 6.
$6 \cdot 2 = 12$
$6 \cdot 3 = 18$
$6 \cdot 4 = 24$
$6 \cdot 5 = 30$
$6 \cdot 6 = 36$
$6 \cdot 7 = 42$
$6 \cdot 8 = 48$ This is the eighth multiple of 6.

The first eight multiples of 6 are 6, 12, 18, 24, 30, 36, 42, and 48.

To illustrate the multiples method for finding an LCD, let's find the least common denominator for $\dfrac{3}{8}$ and $\dfrac{1}{10}$. Note that the LCD *is not* 80. We have learned, however, that both 8 and 10 must divide the LCD exactly.

The Least Common Multiple (LCM)

The **least common multiple (LCM)** of two whole numbers is the smallest whole number that is divisible by both of those numbers.

Thus, the least common denominator of $\frac{3}{8}$ and $\frac{1}{10}$ is simply the *least common multiple* of 8 and 10.

We can find the LCM of 8 and 10 by listing multiples of the larger number, 10, until we find one that is divisible by the smaller number, 8.

Multiples of 10:   10,   20,   30,   **40**,   50,   60, . . .
                                            ↑
                        This is the first multiple of 10 that
                        is divisible by 8 (no remainder).

Since the LCM of 8 and 10 is 40, it follows that the LCD for $\frac{3}{8}$ and $\frac{1}{10}$ is 40.

4 Find the LCD using prime factorization.

We can also find the LCM of 8 and 10 using prime factorization. We begin by prime factoring 8 and 10.

$$8 = \boxed{2 \cdot 2 \cdot 2}$$
$$10 = 2 \cdot \boxed{5}$$

The LCM of 8 and 10 is a product of prime factors, where each factor is used the greatest number of times it appears in any one factorization.

- We will use the factor 2 three times, because 2 appears three times in the factorization of 8. Circle $2 \cdot 2 \cdot 2$, as shown.
- We will use the factor 5 once, because it appears one time in the factorization of 10. Circle 5 as shown.

Since there are no other prime factors in either prime factorization, we have

Use 2 three times.
Use 5 one time.

$$\text{LCM } (8, 10) = 2 \cdot 2 \cdot 2 \cdot 5 = 40$$

Finding the LCD

The least common denominator (LCD) of a set of fractions is the least common multiple (LCM) of the denominators of the fractions. Two ways to find the LCM of the denominators are as follows:

- Write the multiples of the largest denominator in increasing order, until one is found that is divisible (no remainder) by the other denominators.
- Prime factor each denominator. The LCM is a product of prime factors, where each factor is used the greatest number of times it appears in any one factorization.

Self Check 8

Add: $\dfrac{1}{8} + \dfrac{5}{6}$

Now Try **Problem 55**

EXAMPLE 8   Add: $\dfrac{7}{15} + \dfrac{3}{10}$

Strategy We begin by expressing each fraction as an equivalent fraction that has the LCD for its denominator. Then we use the rule for adding fractions that have the same denominator.

WHY To add (or subtract) fractions, the fractions must have *like* denominators.

Solution

To find the LCD using the multiples method, we find the LCM of 15 and 10 by listing the multiples of the larger number, 15, until we find one that is divisible by the smaller number, 10.

Multiples of 15:   15,   30,   45,   60,   75, . . .

This is the first multiple of 15 that
is divisible by 10 (no remainder).

$$15 \cdot 1 = 15$$
$$15 \cdot 2 = 30$$
$$15 \cdot 3 = 45$$
$$15 \cdot 4 = 65$$
$$15 \cdot 5 = 75$$

Since the LCM of 15 and 10 is 30, the LCD for $\dfrac{7}{15}$ and $\dfrac{3}{10}$ is 30.

To find the LCD using the prime factorization method, we find the prime factorization of both denominators and use each prime factor the *greatest* number of times it appears in any one factorization:

$$\left.\begin{array}{l} 15 = \text{③} \cdot \text{⑤} \\ 10 = \text{②} \cdot 5 \end{array}\right\} \text{LCD} = 2 \cdot 3 \cdot 5 = 30$$

2 appears once in the factorization of 10.
3 appears once in the factorization of 15.
5 appears once in the factorizations of 15 and 10.

As with the multiples method, we find that the LCD for $\dfrac{7}{15}$ and $\dfrac{3}{10}$ is 30.

$$\dfrac{7}{15} + \dfrac{3}{10} = \dfrac{7}{15} \cdot \dfrac{2}{2} + \dfrac{3}{10} \cdot \dfrac{3}{3}$$

To build $\frac{7}{15}$ and $\frac{3}{10}$ so that their denominators are 30, multiply each by a form of 1.

$$= \dfrac{14}{30} + \dfrac{9}{30}$$

Multiply the numerators. Multiply the denominators. The denominators are now the same.

$$= \dfrac{14 + 9}{30}$$

Add the numerators and write the sum over the common denominator 30.

$$= \dfrac{23}{30}$$

Since 23 and 30 have no common factors other than 1, this fraction is in simplest form.

EXAMPLE 9

Subtract and simplify: $\dfrac{13}{28} - \dfrac{1}{21}$

Strategy We begin by expressing each fraction as an equivalent fraction that has the LCD for its denominator. Then we use the rule for subtracting fractions with *like* denominators.

WHY To add (or subtract) fractions, the fractions must have like denominators.

Solution

To find the LCD using the multiples method, we find the LCM of 28 and 21 by listing the multiples of the larger number, 28, until we find one that is divisible by the smaller number, 21.

Multiples of 28:   28,   56,   **84**,   112,   140, . . .

$$\begin{array}{l} 28 \cdot 1 = 28 \\ 28 \cdot 2 = 56 \\ 28 \cdot 3 = 84 \\ 28 \cdot 4 = 112 \\ 28 \cdot 5 = 140 \end{array}$$

This is the first multiple of 28 that is divisible by 21 (no remainder).

Since the LCM of 28 and 21 is 84, the LCD for $\dfrac{13}{28}$ and $\dfrac{1}{21}$ is 84.

To find the LCD, using the prime factorization method, we use each prime factor the *greatest* number of times it appears in any one factorization:

$$\left.\begin{array}{l} 28 = \text{②} \cdot \text{②} \cdot \text{⑦} \\ 21 = \text{③} \cdot 7 \end{array}\right\} \text{LCD} = 2 \cdot 2 \cdot 3 \cdot 7 = 84$$

2 appears twice in the factorization of 28.
3 appears once in the factorization of 21.
7 appears once in the factorizations of 28 and 21.

The LCD for $\frac{13}{28}$ and $\frac{1}{21}$ is 84.

    We will compare the prime factorizations of 28, 21, and the prime factorization of the LCD, 84, to determine what forms of 1 to use to build equivalent fractions for $\frac{13}{28}$ and $\frac{1}{21}$ with a denominator of 84.

$$\text{LCD} = 2 \cdot 2 \cdot 3 \cdot 7 \qquad\qquad \text{LCD} = 2 \cdot 2 \cdot 3 \cdot 7$$

Cover the prime factorization of 28.
Since 3 is left uncovered,
use $\frac{3}{3}$ to build $\frac{13}{28}$.

Cover the prime factorization of 21.
Since $2 \cdot 2 = 4$ is left uncovered,
use $\frac{4}{4}$ to build $\frac{1}{21}$.

Self Check 9

Subtract and simplify:
$$\dfrac{21}{56} - \dfrac{9}{40}$$

Now Try **Problem 59**

$$\frac{13}{28} - \frac{1}{21} = \frac{13}{28} \cdot \frac{3}{3} - \frac{1}{21} \cdot \frac{4}{4}$$

To build $\frac{13}{28}$ and $\frac{1}{21}$ so that their denominators are 84, multiply each by a form of 1.

$$= \frac{39}{84} - \frac{4}{84}$$

Multiply the numerators. Multiply the denominators. The denominators are now the same.

$$= \frac{39 - 4}{84}$$

Subtract the numerators and write the difference over the common denominator.

$$= \frac{35}{84}$$

This fraction is not in simplest form.

$$= \frac{5 \cdot \overset{1}{7}}{2 \cdot 2 \cdot 3 \cdot \underset{1}{7}}$$

To simplify, factor 35 and 84. Then remove the common factor of 7 from the numerator and denominator.

$$= \frac{5}{12}$$

Multiply the remaining factors in the numerator: $5 \cdot 1 = 5$. Multiply the remaining factors in the denominator: $2 \cdot 2 \cdot 3 \cdot 1 = 12$.

(factor tree for 84: 84 → ②, 42 → ②, 21 → ③, ⑦)

5 Identify the greater of two fractions.

If two fractions have the same denominator, the fraction with the greater numerator is the greater fraction.

For example,

$$\frac{7}{8} > \frac{3}{8} \quad \text{because } 7 > 3 \qquad\qquad -\frac{1}{3} > -\frac{2}{3} \quad \text{because } -1 > -2$$

If the denominators of two fractions are different, we need to write the fractions with a common denominator (preferably the LCD) before we can make a comparison.

Self Check 10

Which fraction is larger:
$\frac{7}{12}$ or $\frac{3}{5}$?

Now Try Problem 63

EXAMPLE 10   Which fraction is larger: $\frac{5}{6}$ or $\frac{7}{8}$?

Strategy We will express each fraction as an equivalent fraction that has the LCD for its denominator. Then we will compare their numerators.

WHY We cannot compare the fractions as given. They are not similar objects.

five-**sixths**   seven-**eighths**

Solution

Since the smallest number the denominators will divide exactly is 24, the LCD for $\frac{5}{6}$ and $\frac{7}{8}$ is 24.

$$\frac{5}{6} = \frac{5}{6} \cdot \frac{4}{4} \qquad\qquad \frac{7}{8} = \frac{7}{8} \cdot \frac{3}{3}$$

To build $\frac{5}{6}$ and $\frac{7}{8}$ so that their denominators are 24, multiply each by a form of 1.

$$= \frac{20}{24} \qquad\qquad\qquad = \frac{21}{24}$$

Multiply the numerators.
Multiply the denominators.

Next, we compare the numerators. Since $21 > 20$, it follows that $\frac{21}{24}$ is greater than $\frac{20}{24}$. Thus, $\frac{7}{8} > \frac{5}{6}$.

6 Solve application problems by adding and subtracting fractions.

EXAMPLE 11   *Television Viewing Habits* Students on a college campus were asked to estimate to the nearest hour how much television they watched each day. The results are given in the **circle graph** below (also called a **pie chart**). For example, the chart tells us that $\frac{1}{4}$ of those responding watched 1 hour per day. What fraction of the student body watches from 0 to 2 hours daily?

Solution

It is helpful to list what we know and what we are to find.

- $\frac{1}{6}$ of the student body watches no TV daily.   *Given*
- $\frac{1}{4}$ of the student body watches 1 hour of TV daily.   *Given*
- $\frac{7}{15}$ of the student body watches 2 hours of TV daily.   *Given*
- What fraction of the student body watches 0 to 2 hours of TV daily? *Find*

We translate the words of the problem to numbers and symbols.

The fraction of the student body that watches from 0 to 2 hours of TV daily	is equal to	the fraction that watches no TV daily	plus	the fraction that watches 1 hour of TV daily	plus	the fraction that watches 2 hours of TV daily.

The fraction of the student body that watches from 0 to 2 hours of TV daily	=	$\frac{1}{6}$	+	$\frac{1}{4}$	+	$\frac{7}{15}$

We must find the sum of three fractions with different denominators. To find the LCD, we prime factor the denominators and use each prime factor the *greatest* number of times it appears in any one factorization:

$$\left.\begin{array}{l} 6 = 2 \cdot 3 \\ 4 = 2 \cdot 2 \\ 15 = 3 \cdot 5 \end{array}\right\} \text{LCD} = 2 \cdot 2 \cdot 3 \cdot 5 = 60$$

2 appears twice in the factorization of 4.
3 appears once in the factorization of 6 and 15.
5 appears once in the factorization of 15.

The LCD for $\frac{1}{6}$, $\frac{1}{4}$, and $\frac{7}{15}$ is 60.

$$\frac{1}{6} + \frac{1}{4} + \frac{7}{15} = \frac{1}{6} \cdot \frac{10}{10} + \frac{1}{4} \cdot \frac{15}{15} + \frac{7}{15} \cdot \frac{4}{4}$$

Build each fraction so that its denominator is 60.

$$= \frac{10}{60} + \frac{15}{60} + \frac{28}{60}$$

Multiply the numerators. Multiply the denominators. The denominators are now the same.

$$= \frac{10 + 15 + 28}{60}$$

Add the numerators and write the sum over the common denominator 60.

$$= \frac{53}{60}$$

This fraction is in simplest form.

$$\begin{array}{r} \overset{1}{10} \\ 15 \\ + 28 \\ \hline 53 \end{array}$$

Self Check 11

Refer to the circle graph for Example 11. Find the fraction of the student body that watches 2 or more hours of television daily.

Now Try **Problems 71 and 118**

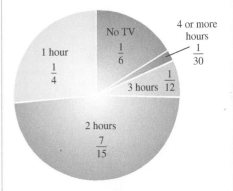

The fraction of the student body that watches 0 to 2 hours of TV daily is $\frac{53}{60}$.

We can check by estimation. The result, $\frac{53}{60}$, is approximately $\frac{50}{60}$, which simplifies to $\frac{5}{6}$. The red, yellow, and blue shaded areas appear to shade about $\frac{5}{6}$ of the pie chart. The result seems reasonable.

THINK IT THROUGH   *Budgets*

"Putting together a budget is crucial if you don't want to spend your way into serious problems. You're also developing a habit that can serve you well throughout your life."

Liz Pulliam Weston, MSN Money

The circle graph below shows a suggested budget for new college graduates as recommended by Springboard, a nonprofit consumer credit counseling service. What fraction of net take-home pay should be spent on housing?

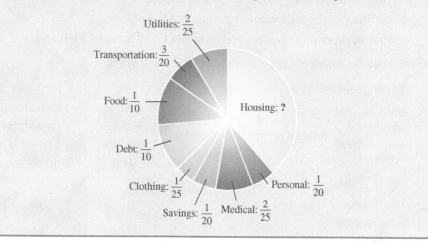

ANSWERS TO SELF CHECKS

1. a. $\frac{1}{2}$ **b.** $\frac{7}{9}$ · **2.** $-\frac{6}{11}$ **3.** $\frac{2}{3}$ **4.** $\frac{9}{10}$ **5.** $\frac{9}{35}$ **6.** $-\frac{3}{2}$ **7.** $-\frac{45}{8}$ **8.** $\frac{23}{24}$ **9.** $\frac{3}{20}$ **10.** $\frac{3}{5}$ **11.** $\frac{7}{12}$

SECTION 2.4   STUDY SET

▌VOCABULARY

Fill in the blanks.

1. Because the denominators of $\frac{3}{8}$ and $\frac{7}{8}$ are the same number, we say that they have a _____ denominator.

2. The _____ common denominator for a set of fractions is the smallest number each denominator will divide exactly (no remainder).

3. Consider the solution below. To _____ an equivalent fraction with a denominator of 18, we multiply $\frac{4}{9}$ by a 1 in the form of .

$$\frac{4}{9} = \frac{4}{9} \cdot \frac{2}{2}$$
$$= \frac{8}{18}$$

4. Consider the solution below. To _____ the fraction $\frac{15}{27}$, we factor 15 and 27, and then remove the common factor of 3 from the _____ and the _____.

$$\frac{15}{27} = \frac{\overset{1}{\cancel{3}} \cdot 5}{\underset{1}{\cancel{3}} \cdot 3 \cdot 3}$$

$$= \frac{5}{9}$$

5. The _____ of a number are the products of that number and 1, 2, 3, 4, 5, and so on.

6. One number is _____ by another if, when dividing them, we get a remainder of 0.

CONCEPTS

Fill in the blanks.

7. To add (or subtract) fractions that have the same denominator, add (or subtract) their _____ and write the sum (or difference) over the _____ denominator. _____ the result, if possible.

8. To add (or subtract) fractions that have different denominators, we express each fraction as an equivalent fraction that has the _____ for its denominator. Then we use the rule for adding (subtracting) fractions that have the _____ denominator.

9. When adding (or subtracting) two fractions with different denominators, if the smaller denominator is a factor of the larger denominator, the _____ denominator is the LCD.

10. Write the subtraction as addition of the opposite:

$$-\frac{1}{8} - \left(-\frac{5}{8}\right) = \boxed{} \boxed{} \boxed{}$$

11. Consider $\frac{3}{4}$. By what form of 1 should we multiply the numerator and denominator to express it as an equivalent fraction with a denominator of 36?

12. The *denominators* of two fractions are given. Find the least common denominator.

   a. 2 and 3   **b.** 3 and 5

   c. 4 and 8   **d.** 6 and 36

13. Find the first ten multiples of 9.

14. a. The first six multiples of 5 are 5, 10, 15, 20, 25, and 30. What is the first multiple of 5 that is divisible by 4?

   b. What is the LCM of 4 and 5?

15. Consider the following prime factorizations:

$$24 = 2 \cdot 2 \cdot 2 \cdot 3$$
$$90 = 2 \cdot 3 \cdot 3 \cdot 5$$

For any one factorization, what is the greatest number of times

   a. a 5 appears?

   b. a 3 appears?

   c. a 2 appears?

16. The *denominators* of two fractions have their prime-factored forms shown below. Fill in the blanks to find the LCD for the fractions.

$$\left. \begin{array}{l} 20 = 2 \cdot 2 \cdot 5 \\ 30 = 2 \cdot 3 \cdot 5 \end{array} \right\} LCD = \boxed{} \cdot \boxed{} \cdot \boxed{} \cdot \boxed{} = \boxed{}$$

17. The *denominators* of three fractions have their prime-factored forms shown below. Fill in the blanks to find the LCD for the fractions.

$$\left. \begin{array}{l} 20 = 2 \cdot 2 \cdot 5 \\ 30 = 2 \cdot 3 \cdot 5 \\ 90 = 2 \cdot 3 \cdot 3 \cdot 5 \end{array} \right\} LCD = \boxed{} \cdot \boxed{} \cdot \boxed{} \cdot \boxed{} \cdot \boxed{} = \boxed{}$$

18. Place a $>$ or $<$ symbol in the blank to make a true statement.

   a. $\frac{32}{35} \boxed{} \frac{31}{35}$

   b. $-\frac{13}{17} \boxed{} -\frac{11}{17}$

19. Use the three figures below to show how to find $\frac{3}{4} - \frac{1}{4}$.

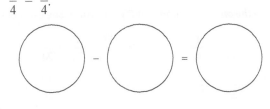

20. Use the three figures below to show how to find $\frac{1}{2} + \frac{3}{8}$.

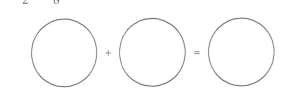

NOTATION

Fill in the blanks to complete each step.

21.
$$\frac{2}{5} + \frac{1}{7} = \frac{2}{5} \cdot \frac{}{} + \frac{1}{7} \cdot \frac{5}{5}$$

$$= \frac{\boxed{}}{35} + \frac{5}{\boxed{}}$$

$$= \frac{\boxed{} + \boxed{}}{35}$$

$$= \frac{\boxed{}}{35}$$

22. $\frac{7}{8} - \frac{2}{3} = \frac{7}{8} \cdot \frac{3}{3} - \frac{2}{3} \cdot \frac{\ }{\ }$

$\qquad = \frac{21}{\ } - \frac{16}{\ }$

$\qquad = \frac{21 - 16}{\ }$

$\qquad = \frac{\ }{24}$

GUIDED PRACTICE

Perform each operation and simplify, if possible. See Example 1.

23. $\frac{4}{9} + \frac{1}{9}$ **24.** $\frac{3}{7} + \frac{1}{7}$

25. $\frac{3}{8} + \frac{1}{8}$ **26.** $\frac{7}{12} + \frac{1}{12}$

27. $\frac{11}{15} - \frac{7}{15}$ **28.** $\frac{10}{21} - \frac{5}{21}$

29. $\frac{11}{20} - \frac{3}{20}$ **30.** $\frac{7}{18} - \frac{5}{18}$

Subtract and simplify, if possible. See Example 2.

31. $-\frac{11}{5} - \left(-\frac{8}{5}\right)$ **32.** $-\frac{15}{9} - \left(-\frac{11}{9}\right)$

33. $-\frac{7}{21} - \left(-\frac{2}{21}\right)$ **34.** $-\frac{21}{25} - \left(-\frac{9}{25}\right)$

Perform the operations and simplify, if possible. See Example 3.

35. $\frac{19}{40} - \frac{3}{40} - \frac{1}{40}$ **36.** $\frac{11}{24} - \frac{1}{24} - \frac{7}{24}$

37. $\frac{13}{33} + \frac{1}{33} + \frac{7}{33}$ **38.** $\frac{21}{50} + \frac{1}{50} + \frac{13}{50}$

Add and simplify, if possible. See Example 4.

39. $\frac{1}{3} + \frac{1}{7}$ **40.** $\frac{1}{4} + \frac{1}{5}$

41. $\frac{2}{5} + \frac{1}{2}$ **42.** $\frac{2}{7} + \frac{1}{2}$

Subtract and simplify, if possible. See Example 5.

43. $\frac{4}{5} - \frac{3}{4}$ **44.** $\frac{2}{3} - \frac{3}{5}$

45. $\frac{3}{4} - \frac{2}{7}$ **46.** $\frac{6}{7} - \frac{2}{3}$

Subtract and simplify, if possible. See Example 6.

47. $\frac{11}{12} - \frac{2}{3}$ **48.** $\frac{11}{18} - \frac{1}{6}$

49. $\frac{9}{14} - \frac{1}{7}$ **50.** $\frac{13}{15} - \frac{2}{3}$

Add and simplify, if possible. See Example 7.

51. $-2 + \frac{5}{9}$ **52.** $-3 + \frac{5}{8}$

53. $-3 + \frac{9}{4}$ **54.** $-1 + \frac{7}{10}$

Add and simplify, if possible. See Example 8.

55. $\frac{1}{6} + \frac{5}{8}$ **56.** $\frac{7}{12} + \frac{3}{8}$

57. $\frac{4}{9} + \frac{5}{12}$ **58.** $\frac{1}{9} + \frac{5}{6}$

Subtract and simplify, if possible. See Example 9.

59. $\frac{9}{10} - \frac{3}{14}$ **60.** $\frac{11}{12} - \frac{11}{30}$

61. $\frac{11}{12} - \frac{7}{15}$ **62.** $\frac{7}{15} - \frac{5}{12}$

Determine which fraction is larger. See Example 10.

63. $\frac{3}{8}$ or $\frac{5}{16}$ **64.** $\frac{5}{6}$ or $\frac{7}{12}$

65. $\frac{4}{5}$ or $\frac{2}{3}$ **66.** $\frac{7}{9}$ or $\frac{4}{5}$

67. $\frac{7}{9}$ or $\frac{11}{12}$ **68.** $\frac{3}{8}$ or $\frac{5}{12}$

69. $\frac{23}{20}$ or $\frac{7}{6}$ **70.** $\frac{19}{15}$ or $\frac{5}{4}$

Add and simplify, if possible. See Example 11.

71. $\frac{1}{6} + \frac{5}{18} + \frac{2}{9}$ **72.** $\frac{1}{10} + \frac{1}{8} + \frac{1}{5}$

73. $\frac{4}{15} + \frac{2}{3} + \frac{1}{6}$ **74.** $\frac{1}{2} + \frac{3}{5} + \frac{3}{20}$

TRY IT YOURSELF

Perform each operation.

75. $-\frac{1}{12} - \left(-\frac{5}{12}\right)$ **76.** $-\frac{1}{16} - \left(-\frac{15}{16}\right)$

77. $\frac{12}{25} - \frac{1}{25} - \frac{1}{25}$ **78.** $\frac{7}{9} + \frac{1}{9} + \frac{1}{9}$

79. $-\frac{7}{20} - \frac{1}{5}$ **80.** $-\frac{5}{8} - \frac{1}{3}$

81. $-\frac{7}{16} + \frac{1}{4}$ **82.** $-\frac{17}{20} + \frac{4}{5}$

83. $\frac{11}{12} - \frac{2}{3}$ **84.** $\frac{2}{3} - \frac{1}{6}$

85. $\dfrac{9}{20} - \dfrac{1}{30}$

86. $\dfrac{5}{6} - \dfrac{3}{10}$

87. $\dfrac{27}{50} + \dfrac{5}{16}$

88. $\dfrac{49}{50} - \dfrac{15}{16}$

89. $\dfrac{13}{20} - \dfrac{1}{5}$

90. $\dfrac{71}{100} - \dfrac{1}{10}$

91. $\dfrac{37}{103} - \dfrac{17}{103}$

92. $\dfrac{54}{53} - \dfrac{52}{53}$

93. $-\dfrac{3}{4} - 5$

94. $-2 - \dfrac{7}{8}$

95. $\dfrac{4}{27} + \dfrac{1}{6}$

96. $\dfrac{8}{9} - \dfrac{7}{12}$

97. $\dfrac{7}{30} - \dfrac{19}{75}$

98. $\dfrac{73}{75} - \dfrac{31}{30}$

99. Find the difference of $\dfrac{11}{60}$ and $\dfrac{2}{45}$.

100. Find the sum of $\dfrac{9}{48}$ and $\dfrac{7}{40}$.

101. Subtract $\dfrac{5}{12}$ from $\dfrac{2}{15}$.

102. What is the sum of $\dfrac{11}{24}$ and $\dfrac{7}{36}$ increased by $\dfrac{5}{48}$?

LOOK ALIKES . . .

103. **a.** $\dfrac{4}{9} + \dfrac{3}{7}$ **b.** $\dfrac{4}{9} - \dfrac{3}{7}$ **c.** $\dfrac{4}{9} \cdot \dfrac{3}{7}$ **d.** $\dfrac{4}{9} \div \dfrac{3}{7}$

104. **a.** $\dfrac{3}{5} + \dfrac{5}{12}$ **b.** $\dfrac{3}{5} - \dfrac{5}{12}$

   c. $\dfrac{3}{5} \cdot \dfrac{5}{12}$ **d.** $\dfrac{3}{5} \div \dfrac{5}{12}$

CONCEPT EXTENSIONS

Find the perimeter of each figure.

105.

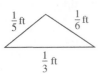

$\frac{1}{5}$ ft $\frac{1}{6}$ ft

$\frac{1}{3}$ ft

106.

$\frac{1}{3}$ in.

$\frac{1}{8}$ in.

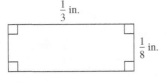

107. **a.** Find two fractions whose sum is 1.

   b. Find two fractions whose difference is 1.

   c. Find two fractions whose product is 1.

   d. Find two fractions whose quotient is 1.

108. **a.** What number, when added to $\dfrac{3}{5}$, produces a result of 1?

   b. What number, when subtracted from $\dfrac{3}{5}$, produces a result of 1?

   c. What number, when multiplied by $\dfrac{3}{5}$, produces a result of 1?

   d. What number, when divided by $\dfrac{3}{5}$, produces a result of 1?

APPLICATIONS

109. BOTANY To determine the effects of smog on tree development, a scientist cut down a pine tree and measured the width of the growth rings for the last two years.

   a. What was the growth over this two-year period?

   b. What is the difference in the widths of the two rings?

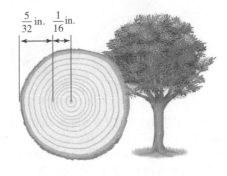

$\frac{5}{32}$ in. $\frac{1}{16}$ in.

110. GARAGE DOOR OPENERS What is the difference in strength between a $\frac{1}{3}$-hp and a $\frac{1}{2}$-hp garage door opener?

111. MAGAZINE COVERS The page design for the magazine cover shown below includes a blank strip at the top, called a *header*, and a blank strip at the bottom of the page, called a *footer*. How much page length is lost because of the header and footer?

112. DELIVERY TRUCKS A truck can safely carry a one-ton load. Should it be used to deliver one-half ton of sand, one-third ton of gravel, and one-fifth ton of cement in one trip to a job site?

113. DINNERS A family bought two large pizzas for dinner. Some pieces of each pizza were not eaten, as shown.

   a. What fraction of the first pizza was not eaten?

   b. What fraction of the second pizza was not eaten?

   c. What fraction of a pizza was left?

   d. Could the family have been fed with just one pizza?

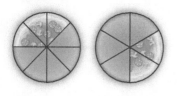

114. GASOLINE BARRELS Three identical-sized barrels are shown below. If their contents of the two of the barrels are poured into the empty third barrel, what fraction of the third barrel will be filled?

115. WEIGHTS AND MEASURES A consumer protection agency determines the accuracy of butcher shop scales by placing a known three-quarter-pound weight on the scale and then comparing that to the scale's readout. According to the illustration, by how much is this scale off? Does it result in undercharging or overcharging customers on their meat purchases?

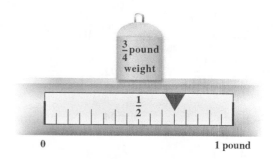

116. FIGURE DRAWING As an aid in drawing the human body, artists divide the body into three parts. Each part is then expressed as a fraction of the total body height. For example, the torso is $\frac{4}{15}$ of the body height. What fraction of body height is the head?

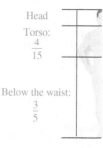

117. Suppose you work as a school guidance counselor at a community college and your department has conducted a survey of the full-time students to learn more about their study habits. As part of a *Power Point* presentation of the survey results to the school board, you show the following circle graph. At that time, you are asked, "What fraction of the full-time students study 2 hours or more daily?" What would you answer?

from Campus to Careers
School Guidance Counselor

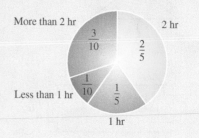

118. HEALTH STATISTICS The circle graph below shows the leading causes of death in the United States for 2006. For example, $\frac{13}{50}$ of all of the deaths that year were caused by heart disease. What fraction of all the deaths were caused by heart disease, cancer, or stroke, combined?

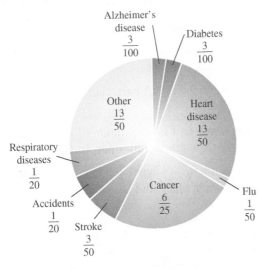

Source: National Center for Health Statistics

119. MUSICAL NOTES The notes used in music have fractional values. Their names and the symbols used to represent them are shown in illustration (a). In common time, the values of the notes in each measure must add to 1. Is the measure in illustration (b) complete?

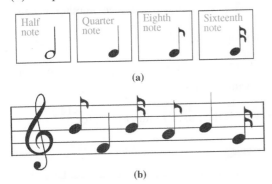

120. TOOLS A mechanic likes to hang his wrenches above his tool bench in order of narrowest to widest. What is the proper order of the wrenches in the illustration?

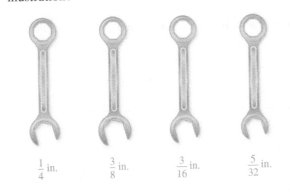

121. TIRE TREAD A mechanic measured the tire tread depth on each of the tires on a car and recorded them on the form shown below. (The letters LF stand for *left front*, RR stands for *right rear*, and so on.)

a. Which tire has the most tread?

b. Which tire has the least tread?

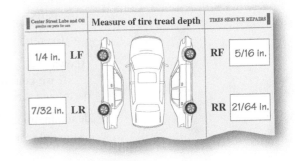

122. HIKING The illustration below shows the length of each part of a three-part hike. Rank the lengths of the parts from longest to shortest.

WRITING

123. Explain why we cannot add or subtract the fractions $\frac{2}{9}$ and $\frac{2}{5}$ as they are written.

124. To multiply fractions, must they have the same denominators? Explain why or why not. Give an example.

125. What are equivalent fractions? Give an example.

126. Explain the error in the following addition.

$$\frac{4}{3} + \frac{3}{2} = \frac{4+3}{3+2} = \frac{7}{5}$$

SECTION 2.5

Applications Introduction: Improper Fractions and Mixed Numbers

To graph a **proper fraction** such as $\frac{1}{3}$ on a number line, we think of the distance between 0 and 1 as one whole. The denominator of $\frac{1}{3}$ indicates that we should divide that distance into 3 equal parts. The numerator indicates that we should consider 1 of those parts.

To graph $\frac{1}{3}$, we start at 0 and move to the right 1 part. There, we draw a heavy dot (shown in red below) and label the fraction.

If we continue to divide each whole unit on the number line into three equal parts, and keep counting them, we can graph **improper fractions** that have a denominator of 3. For example, to graph $\frac{11}{3}$, we begin at 0 and move 11 equal parts to the right, draw a heavy dot (as shown in blue), and label the fraction.

The point on the number line that represents $\frac{11}{3}$ can be described in another way. Beginning at 0, we can move to the right 3 whole units plus two equal parts $\left(\frac{2}{3}\right)$ to locate it. It follows that $\frac{11}{3} = 3\frac{2}{3}$. We call $3\frac{2}{3}$ a **mixed number** because it is the sum of a whole number and a proper fraction: $3 + \frac{2}{3}$.

1. **a.** Graph $\frac{1}{5}$ and $\frac{14}{5}$ on a number line. Label the complete list of improper fractions as shown in the example above.

   b. From your number line, what is the mixed number form for $\frac{14}{5}$?

   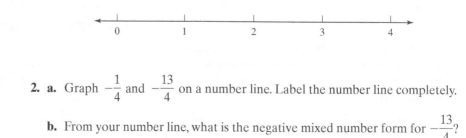

2. **a.** Graph $-\frac{1}{4}$ and $-\frac{13}{4}$ on a number line. Label the number line completely.

   b. From your number line, what is the negative mixed number form for $-\frac{13}{4}$?

SECTION 2.5
Multiplying and Dividing Mixed Numbers

Objectives

1 Identify the whole-number and fractional parts of a mixed number.

2 Write mixed numbers as improper fractions.

3 Write improper fractions as mixed numbers.

4 Graph fractions and mixed numbers on a number line.

5 Multiply and divide mixed numbers.

6 Solve application problems by multiplying and dividing mixed numbers.

ARE YOU READY?

The following problems review some basic skills that are needed when multiplying and dividing mixed numbers.

1. Divide: $5\overline{)11}$

2. Evaluate: $4 \cdot 7 + 2$

3. Graph $-3, 2, -1,$ and 4 on a number line.

4. Multiply: $\dfrac{26}{5} \cdot \dfrac{15}{13}$

5. Divide: $-\dfrac{27}{8} \div \left(-\dfrac{9}{4}\right)$

6. What is the formula for the area of a triangle?

In the next two sections, we show how to add, subtract, multiply, and divide *mixed numbers*. These numbers are widely used in daily life.

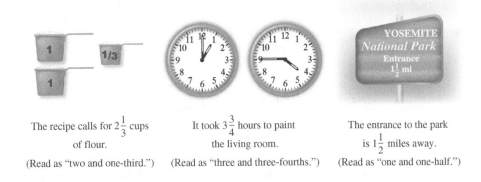

The recipe calls for $2\frac{1}{3}$ cups of flour.

(Read as "two and one-third.")

It took $3\frac{3}{4}$ hours to paint the living room.

(Read as "three and three-fourths.")

The entrance to the park is $1\frac{1}{2}$ miles away.

(Read as "one and one-half.")

1 Identify the whole-number and fractional parts of a mixed number.

A **mixed number** is the *sum* of a whole number and a proper fraction. For example, $3\frac{3}{4}$ is a mixed number.

$$3\frac{3}{4} \qquad = \qquad 3 \qquad + \qquad \frac{3}{4}$$

Mixed number   Whole-number part   Fractional part

Mixed numbers can be represented by shaded regions. In the illustration below, each rectangular region outlined in black represents one whole. To represent $3\frac{3}{4}$, we shade 3 *whole* rectangular regions and 3 out of 4 *parts* of another.

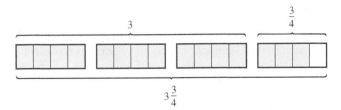

Caution!   Note that $3\frac{3}{4}$ means $3 + \frac{3}{4}$, even though the $+$ symbol is not written. Do not confuse $3\frac{3}{4}$ with $3 \cdot \frac{3}{4}$ or $3\left(\frac{3}{4}\right)$, which indicate the multiplication of 3 by $\frac{3}{4}$.

Self Check 1

In the illustration below, each oval region represents one whole. Write an improper fraction and a mixed number to represent the shaded portion.

Now Try **Problem 19**

EXAMPLE 1   In the illustration below, each disk represents one whole. Write an improper fraction and a mixed number to represent the shaded portion.

Strategy We will determine the number of equal parts into which a disk is divided. Then we will determine how many of those *parts* are shaded and how many of the *whole* disks are shaded.

WHY To write an improper fraction, we need to find its numerator and its denominator. To write a mixed number, we need to find its whole number part and its fractional part.

Solution

Since each disk is divided into 5 equal parts, the denominator of the improper fraction is 5. Since a total of 11 of those parts are shaded, the numerator is 11, and we say that

$\dfrac{11}{5}$ is shaded.   Write: $\dfrac{\text{total number of parts shaded}}{\text{number of equal parts in one disk}}$

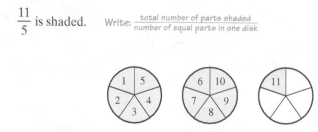

Since 2 whole disks are shaded, the whole number part of the mixed number is 2. Since 1 out of 5 of the parts of the last disk is shaded, the fractional part of the mixed number is $\frac{1}{5}$, and we say that

$2\dfrac{1}{5}$ is shaded.

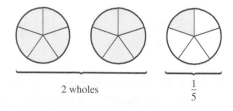

2 wholes $\dfrac{1}{5}$

In this section, we will work with negative as well as positive mixed numbers. For example, the negative mixed number $-3\frac{3}{4}$ could be used to represent $3\frac{3}{4}$ feet below sea level. Think of $-3\frac{3}{4}$ as $-3 - \frac{3}{4}$ or as $-3 + \left(-\frac{3}{4}\right)$.

2 Write mixed numbers as improper fractions.

In Example 1, we saw that the shaded portion of the illustration can be represented by the mixed number $2\frac{1}{5}$ and by the improper fraction $\frac{11}{5}$. To develop a procedure to write any mixed number as an improper fraction, consider the following steps that show how to do this for $2\frac{1}{5}$. The objective is to find how many *fifths* that the mixed number $2\frac{1}{5}$ represents.

$$2\frac{1}{5} = 2 + \frac{1}{5} \qquad \text{Write the mixed number } 2\frac{1}{5} \text{ as a sum.}$$

$$= \frac{2}{1} + \frac{1}{5} \qquad \text{Write 2 as a fraction: } 2 = \frac{2}{1}.$$

$$= \frac{2}{1} \cdot \frac{5}{5} + \frac{1}{5} \qquad \text{To build } \frac{2}{1} \text{ so that its denominator is 5, multiply it by a form of 1.}$$

$$= \frac{10}{5} + \frac{1}{5} \qquad \begin{array}{l}\text{Multiply the numerators.}\\ \text{Multiply the denominators.}\end{array}$$

$$= \frac{11}{5} \qquad \begin{array}{l}\text{Add the numerators and write the sum over}\\ \text{the common denominator 5.}\end{array}$$

Thus, $2\frac{1}{5} = \frac{11}{5}$.

We can obtain the same result with far less work. To change $2\frac{1}{5}$ to an improper fraction, we simply multiply 5 by 2 and add 1 to get the numerator, and keep the denominator of 5.

$$2\frac{1}{5} = \frac{5 \cdot 2 + 1}{5} = \frac{10 + 1}{5} = \frac{11}{5}$$

This example illustrates the following procedure.

Writing a Mixed Number as an Improper Fraction

To write a mixed number as an improper fraction:

1. Multiply the denominator of the fraction by the whole-number part.
2. Add the numerator of the fraction to the result from Step 1.
3. Write the sum from Step 2 over the original denominator.

EXAMPLE 2   Write the mixed number $7\frac{5}{6}$ as an improper fraction.

Strategy   We will use the 3-step procedure to find the improper fraction.

WHY   It's faster than writing $7\frac{5}{6}$ as $7 + \frac{5}{6}$, building to get an LCD, and adding.

Solution
To find the numerator of the improper fraction, multiply 6 by 7, and add 5 to that result. The denominator of the improper fraction is the same as the denominator of the fractional part of the mixed number.

Step 2: add

$$7\frac{5}{6} = \frac{6 \cdot 7 + 5}{6} = \frac{42 + 5}{6} = \frac{47}{6} \qquad \begin{array}{l}\text{By the order of operations rule,}\\ \text{multiply first, and then add in}\\ \text{the numerator.}\end{array}$$

Step 1: multiply   Step 3: Use the same denominator

Self Check 2

Write the mixed number $3\frac{3}{8}$ as an improper fraction.

Now Try **Problems 23 and 27**

To write a *negative mixed number* in fractional form, ignore the $-$ sign and use the method shown in Example 2 on the positive mixed number. Once that procedure is completed, write a $-$ sign in front of the result. For example,

$$-6\frac{1}{4} = -\frac{25}{4} \qquad\qquad -1\frac{9}{10} = -\frac{19}{10} \qquad\qquad -12\frac{3}{8} = -\frac{99}{8}$$

3 Write improper fractions as mixed numbers.

To write an improper fraction as a mixed number, we must find two things: the *whole-number part* and the *fractional part* of the mixed number. To develop a procedure to do this, let's consider the improper fraction $\frac{7}{3}$. To find the number of groups of 3 in 7, we can divide 7 by 3. This will find the whole-number part of the mixed number. The remainder is the numerator of the fractional part of the mixed number.

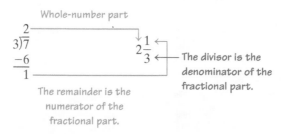

This example suggests the following procedure.

Writing an Improper Fraction as a Mixed Number

To write an improper fraction as a mixed number:

1. Divide the numerator by the denominator to obtain the whole-number part.

2. The remainder over the divisor is the fractional part.

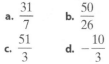

Write each improper fraction as a mixed number or a whole number:

a. $\dfrac{31}{7}$ **b.** $\dfrac{50}{26}$

c. $\dfrac{51}{3}$ **d.** $-\dfrac{10}{3}$

Now Try Problems 31, 35, 39, and 43

EXAMPLE 3   Write each improper fraction as a mixed number or a whole number: **a.** $\dfrac{29}{6}$ **b.** $\dfrac{40}{16}$ **c.** $\dfrac{84}{3}$ **d.** $-\dfrac{9}{5}$

Strategy We will divide the numerator by the denominator and write the remainder over the divisor.

WHY A fraction bar indicates division.

Solution

a. To write $\frac{29}{6}$ as a mixed number, divide 29 by 6:

$$\begin{array}{r} 4 \leftarrow \text{The whole-number part is 4.} \\ 6\overline{)29} \\ -24 \\ \hline 5 \leftarrow \text{Write the remainder 5 over the} \\ \text{divisor 6 to get the fractional part.} \end{array}$$

Thus, $\dfrac{29}{6} = 4\dfrac{5}{6}$.

b. To write $\frac{40}{16}$ as a mixed number, divide 40 by 16:

$$\begin{array}{r} 2 \\ 16\overline{)40} \\ -32 \\ \hline 8 \end{array}$$

Thus, $\dfrac{40}{16} = 2\dfrac{8}{16} = 2\dfrac{1}{2}$.

Simplify the fractional part: $\frac{8}{16} = \frac{\overset{1}{\cancel{8}}}{2 \cdot \cancel{8}} = \frac{1}{2}$.

c. For $\dfrac{84}{3}$, divide 84 by 3:

$$\begin{array}{r} 28 \\ 3\overline{)84} \\ -6 \\ \hline 24 \\ -24 \\ \hline 0 \leftarrow \end{array}$$

Thus, $\dfrac{84}{3} = 28$.

Since the remainder is 0, the improper fraction represents a whole number.

d. To write $-\frac{9}{5}$ as a mixed number, ignore the $-$ sign, and use the method for the positive improper fraction $\frac{9}{5}$. Once that procedure is completed, write a $-$ sign in front of the result.

$$\begin{array}{r} 1 \\ 5\overline{)9} \\ \underline{-5} \\ 4 \end{array}$$ Thus, $-\frac{9}{5} = -1\frac{4}{5}$.

4   Graph fractions and mixed numbers on a number line.

Fractions and mixed numbers can be graphed on a number line.

EXAMPLE 4   Graph $-2\frac{3}{4}, -1\frac{1}{2}, -\frac{1}{8}$, and $\frac{13}{5}$ on a number line.

Strategy   We will locate the position of each fraction and mixed number on the number line and draw a bold dot.

WHY   To *graph a number* means to make a drawing that represents the number.

Solution

- Since $-2\frac{3}{4} < -2$, the graph of $-2\frac{3}{4}$ is to the left of -2 on the number line.
- The number $-1\frac{1}{2}$ is between -1 and -2.
- The number $-\frac{1}{8}$ is less than 0.
- Expressed as a mixed number, $\frac{13}{5} = 2\frac{3}{5}$.

Self Check 4

Graph $-1\frac{7}{8}, -\frac{2}{3}, \frac{3}{5}$, and $\frac{9}{4}$ on a number line.

Now Try   **Problem 47**

5   Multiply and divide mixed numbers.

We will use the same procedures for multiplying and dividing mixed numbers as those that were used in Sections 2.2 and 2.3 to multiply and divide fractions. However, we must write the mixed numbers as improper fractions before we actually multiply or divide.

Multiplying and Dividing Mixed Numbers

To multiply or divide mixed numbers, first change the mixed numbers to improper fractions. Then perform the multiplication or division of the fractions. Write the result as a mixed number or a whole number in simplest form.

The sign rules for multiplying and dividing integers also hold for multiplying and dividing mixed numbers.

EXAMPLE 5   Multiply and simplify, if possible.

a. $1\frac{3}{4} \cdot 2\frac{1}{3}$ **b.** $5\frac{1}{5} \cdot \left(1\frac{2}{13}\right)$ **c.** $-4\frac{1}{9}(3)$

Strategy   We will write the mixed numbers and whole numbers as improper fractions.

Self Check 5

Multiply and simplify, if possible.

a. $3\frac{1}{3} \cdot 2\frac{1}{3}$ b. $9\frac{3}{5} \cdot \left(3\frac{3}{4}\right)$

c. $-4\frac{5}{6}(2)$

Now Try **Problems 51, 55, and 57**

WHY Then we can use the rule for multiplying two fractions from Section 2.2.

Solution

a. $1\frac{3}{4} \cdot 2\frac{1}{3} = \frac{7}{4} \cdot \frac{7}{3}$ Write $1\frac{3}{4}$ and $2\frac{1}{3}$ as improper fractions.

$= \frac{7 \cdot 7}{4 \cdot 3}$ Use the rule for multiplying two fractions. Multiply the numerators and the denominators.

$= \frac{49}{12}$ Since there are no common factors to remove, perform the multiplication in the numerator and in the denominator. The result is an improper fraction.

$$\begin{array}{r} 4 \\ 12\overline{)49} \\ -48 \\ \hline 1 \end{array}$$

$= 4\frac{1}{12}$ Write the improper fraction $\frac{49}{12}$ as a mixed number.

b. $5\frac{1}{5}\left(1\frac{2}{13}\right) = \frac{26}{5} \cdot \frac{15}{13}$ Write $5\frac{1}{5}$ and $1\frac{2}{13}$ as improper fractions.

$= \frac{26 \cdot 15}{5 \cdot 13}$ Multiply the numerators. Multiply the denominators.

$= \frac{2 \cdot 13 \cdot 3 \cdot 5}{5 \cdot 13}$ To prepare to simplify, factor 26 as $2 \cdot 13$ and 15 as $3 \cdot 5$.

$= \frac{2 \cdot \overset{1}{\cancel{13}} \cdot 3 \cdot \overset{1}{\cancel{5}}}{\underset{1}{\cancel{5}} \cdot \underset{1}{\cancel{13}}}$ Remove the common factors of 13 and 5 from the numerator and denominator.

$= \frac{6}{1}$ Multiply the remaining factors in the numerator: $2 \cdot 1 \cdot 3 \cdot 1 = 6$.
Multiply the remaining factors in the denominator: $1 \cdot 1 = 1$.

$= 6$ Any whole number divided by 1 remains the same.

c. $-4\frac{1}{9} \cdot 3 = -\frac{37}{9} \cdot \frac{3}{1}$ Write $-4\frac{1}{9}$ as an improper fraction and write 3 as a fraction.

$= -\frac{37 \cdot 3}{9 \cdot 1}$ Multiply the numerators and multiply the denominators. Since the fractions have unlike signs, make the answer negative.

$= -\frac{37 \cdot \overset{1}{\cancel{3}}}{\underset{1}{\cancel{3}} \cdot 3 \cdot 1}$ To simplify, factor 9 as $3 \cdot 3$, and then remove the common factor of 3 from the numerator and denominator.

$= -\frac{37}{3}$ Multiply the remaining factors in the numerator and in the denominator. The result is an improper fraction.

$$\begin{array}{r} 12 \\ 3\overline{)37} \\ -3 \\ \hline 7 \\ -6 \\ \hline 1 \end{array}$$

$= -12\frac{1}{3}$ Write the negative improper fraction $-\frac{37}{3}$ as a negative mixed number.

Success Tip   We can use rounding to check the results when multiplying mixed numbers. If the fractional part of the mixed number is $\frac{1}{2}$ *or greater*, round up by adding 1 to the whole-number part and dropping the fraction. If the fractional part of the mixed number is less than $\frac{1}{2}$, round down by dropping the fraction and using only the whole-number part. To check the answer $4\frac{1}{12}$ from Example 5, part a, we proceed as follows:

$$1\frac{3}{4} \cdot 2\frac{1}{3} \approx 2 \cdot 2 = 4$$ Since $\frac{3}{4}$ is greater than $\frac{1}{2}$, round $1\frac{3}{4}$ up to 2.
Since $\frac{1}{3}$ is less than $\frac{1}{2}$, round $2\frac{1}{3}$ down to 2.

Since $4\frac{1}{12}$ is close to 4, it is a reasonable answer.

EXAMPLE 6 Divide and simplify, if possible:

a. $-3\frac{3}{8} \div \left(-2\frac{1}{4}\right)$ **b.** $1\frac{11}{16} \div \frac{3}{4}$

Strategy We will write the mixed numbers as improper fractions.

WHY Then we can use the rule for dividing two fractions from Section 2.3.

Solution

a. $-3\frac{3}{8} \div \left(-2\frac{1}{4}\right) = -\frac{27}{8} \div \left(-\frac{9}{4}\right)$ Write $-3\frac{3}{8}$ and $-2\frac{1}{4}$ as improper fractions.

$= -\frac{27}{8}\left(-\frac{4}{9}\right)$ Use the rule for dividing two fractions.: Multiply $-\frac{27}{8}$ by the reciprocal of $-\frac{9}{4}$, which is $-\frac{4}{9}$.

$= \frac{27}{8}\left(\frac{4}{9}\right)$ Since the product of two negative fractions is positive, drop both $-$ signs and continue.

$= \frac{27 \cdot 4}{8 \cdot 9}$ Multiply the numerators. Multiply the denominators.

$= \frac{3 \cdot \overset{1}{\cancel{9}} \cdot \overset{1}{\cancel{4}}}{2 \cdot \underset{1}{\cancel{4}} \cdot \underset{1}{\cancel{9}}}$ To simplify, factor 27 as $3 \cdot 9$ and 8 as $2 \cdot 4$. Then remove the common factors of 9 and 4 from the numerator and denominator.

$= \frac{3}{2}$ Multiply the remaining factors in the numerator: $3 \cdot 1 \cdot 1 = 3$. Multiply the remaining factors in the denominator: $2 \cdot 1 \cdot 1 = 2$.

$= 1\frac{1}{2}$ Write the improper fraction $\frac{3}{2}$ as a mixed number by dividing 3 by 2.

b. $1\frac{11}{16} \div \frac{3}{4} = \frac{27}{16} \div \frac{3}{4}$ Write $1\frac{11}{16}$ as an improper fraction.

$= \frac{27}{16} \cdot \frac{4}{3}$ Multiply $\frac{27}{16}$ by the reciprocal of $\frac{3}{4}$, which is $\frac{4}{3}$.

$= \frac{27 \cdot 4}{16 \cdot 3}$ Multiply the numerators. Multiply the denominators.

$= \frac{\overset{1}{\cancel{3}} \cdot 9 \cdot \overset{1}{\cancel{4}}}{\underset{1}{\cancel{4}} \cdot 4 \cdot \underset{1}{\cancel{3}}}$ To simplify, factor 27 as $3 \cdot 9$ and 16 as $4 \cdot 4$. Then remove the common factors of 3 and 4 from the numerator and denominator.

$= \frac{9}{4}$ Multiply the remaining factors in the numerator and in the denominator. The result is an improper fraction.

$= 2\frac{1}{4}$ Write the improper fraction $\frac{9}{4}$ as a mixed number by dividing 9 by 4.

Self Check 6
Divide and simplify, if possible:

a. $-3\frac{4}{15} \div \left(-2\frac{1}{10}\right)$

b. $5\frac{3}{5} \div \frac{7}{8}$

Now Try **Problems 59 and 65**

6 **Solve application problems by multiplying and dividing mixed numbers.**

EXAMPLE 7 *Toys* The dimensions of the rectangular-shaped screen of an Etch-a-Sketch are shown in the illustration on the next page. Find the area of the screen.

BUMPER STICKERS A rectangular-shaped bumper sticker is $8\frac{1}{4}$ inches long by $3\frac{1}{4}$ inches wide. Find its area.

Now Try Problem 103

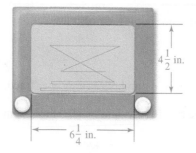

$4\frac{1}{2}$ in.

$6\frac{1}{4}$ in.

Strategy To find the area, we will multiply $6\frac{1}{4}$ by $4\frac{1}{2}$.

WHY The formula for the area of a rectangle is Area = length · width.

Solution

$$A = lw \qquad \text{This is the formula for the area of a rectangle.}$$

$$= 6\frac{1}{4} \cdot 4\frac{1}{2} \qquad \text{Substitute } 6\frac{1}{4} \text{ for } l \text{ and } 4\frac{1}{2} \text{ for } w.$$

$$= \frac{25}{4} \cdot \frac{9}{2} \qquad \text{Write } 6\frac{1}{4} \text{ and } 4\frac{1}{2} \text{ as improper fractions.}$$

$$= \frac{25 \cdot 9}{4 \cdot 2} \qquad \begin{array}{l}\text{Multiply the numerators.}\\ \text{Multiply the denominators.}\end{array}$$

$$= \frac{225}{8} \qquad \begin{array}{l}\text{Since there are no common factors to remove,}\\ \text{perform the multiplication in the numerator and in}\\ \text{the denominator. The result is an improper fraction.}\end{array}$$

$$= 28\frac{1}{8} \qquad \text{Write the improper fraction } \frac{225}{8} \text{ as a mixed number.}$$

$$\begin{array}{r}28\\ 8\overline{)225}\\ -16\\ \hline 65\\ -64\\ \hline 1\end{array}$$

The area of the screen of an Etch-a-Sketch is $28\frac{1}{8}$ in.^{2}.

TV INTERVIEWS An $18\frac{3}{4}$-minute taped interview with an actor was played in equally long segments over 5 consecutive nights on a celebrity news program. How long was each interview segment?

Now Try Problem 111

EXAMPLE 8   *Government Grants*   If $\$12\frac{1}{2}$ million is to be split equally among five cities to fund recreation programs, how much will each city receive?

Solution It is helpful to list what we know and what we are to find.

- There is $\$12\frac{1}{2}$ million in grant money.   *Given*
- 5 cities will split the money equally.   *Given*
- How much grant money will each city receive?   *Find*

The key phrase *split equally* suggests division.
  We translate the words of the problem to numbers and symbols.

The amount of money that each city will receive (in millions of dollars)	is equal to	the total amount of grant money (in millions of dollars)	divided by	the number of cities receiving money.
The amount of money that each city will receive (in millions of dollars)	=	$12\frac{1}{2}$	÷	5

To find the quotient, we will express $12\frac{1}{2}$ and 5 as fractions and then use the rule for dividing two fractions.

$$12\frac{1}{2} \div 5 = \frac{25}{2} \div \frac{5}{1} \qquad \text{Write } 12\frac{1}{2} \text{ as an improper fraction, and write 5 as a fraction.}$$

$$= \frac{25}{2} \cdot \frac{1}{5} \qquad \text{Multiply by the reciprocal of } \frac{5}{1}, \text{ which is } \frac{1}{5}.$$

$$= \frac{25 \cdot 1}{2 \cdot 5} \qquad \begin{array}{l}\text{Multiply the numerators.}\\ \text{Multiply the denominators.}\end{array}$$

$$= \frac{\overset{1}{\cancel{5}} \cdot 5 \cdot 1}{2 \cdot \underset{1}{\cancel{5}}} \qquad \begin{array}{l}\text{To simplify, factor 25 as } 5 \cdot 5. \text{ Then remove the common}\\ \text{factor of 5 from the numerator and denominator.}\end{array}$$

$$= \frac{5}{2} \qquad \begin{array}{l}\text{Multiply the remaining factors in the numerator.}\\ \text{Multiply the remaining factors in the denominator.}\end{array}$$

$$= 2\frac{1}{2} \qquad \begin{array}{l}\text{Write the improper fraction } \frac{5}{2} \text{ as a mixed number}\\ \text{by dividing 5 by 2. The units are in millions of dollars.}\end{array}$$

Each city will receive $\$2\frac{1}{2}$ million in grant money.

We can estimate to check the result. If there was \$10 million in grant money, each city would receive $\frac{\$10 \text{ million}}{5}$, or \$2 million. Since there is actually $\$12\frac{1}{2}$ million in grant money, the answer that each city would receive $\$2\frac{1}{2}$ million seems reasonable.

ANSWERS TO SELF CHECKS

$-1\frac{7}{8} \quad -\frac{2}{3} \quad \frac{3}{5} \quad \frac{9}{4}=2\frac{1}{4}$.

1. $\frac{9}{2}$, $4\frac{1}{2}$ **2.** $\frac{27}{8}$ **3. a.** $4\frac{3}{7}$ **b.** $1\frac{12}{13}$ **c.** 17 **d.** $-3\frac{1}{3}$ **4.** (number line: $-3 \quad -2 \quad -1 \quad 0 \quad 1 \quad 2 \quad 3$)
5. a. $7\frac{7}{9}$ **b.** 36 **c.** $-9\frac{2}{3}$ **6. a.** $1\frac{5}{9}$ **b.** $6\frac{2}{5}$ **7.** $26\frac{13}{16}$ in.^{2} **8.** $3\frac{3}{4}$ min

---

SECTION 2.5   STUDY SET

VOCABULARY

Fill in the blanks.

1. A _____ number, such as $8\frac{4}{5}$, is the sum of a whole number and a proper fraction.

2. In the mixed number $8\frac{4}{5}$, the _____-number part is 8 and the _____ part is $\frac{4}{5}$.

3. The numerator of an _____ fraction is greater than or equal to its denominator.

4. To _____ a number means to locate its position on the number line and highlight it using a dot.

CONCEPTS

5. What signed mixed number could be used to describe each situation?

  a. A temperature of five and one-third degrees above zero

  b. The depth of a sprinkler pipe that is six and seven-eighths inches below the sidewalk

6. What signed mixed number could be used to describe each situation?

  a. A rain total two and three-tenths of an inch lower than the average

  b. Three and one-half minutes after the liftoff of a rocket

Fill in the blanks.

7. To write a mixed number as an improper fraction:

  1. _____ the denominator of the fraction by the whole-number part.

  2. _____ the numerator of the fraction to the result from Step 1.

  3. Write the sum from Step 2 over the original _____.

8. To write an improper fraction as a mixed number:

1. _____ the numerator by the denominator to obtain the whole-number part.

2. The _____ over the divisor is the fractional part.

9. What fractions have been graphed on the number line?

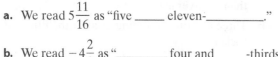

10. What mixed numbers have been graphed on the number line?

11. Fill in the blank: To multiply or divide mixed numbers, first change the mixed numbers to _____ fractions. Then perform the multiplication or division of the fractions as usual.

12. Simplify the fractional part of each mixed number.

a. $11\dfrac{2}{4}$

b. $1\dfrac{3}{9}$

c. $7\dfrac{15}{27}$

13. Use *estimation* to determine whether the following answer seems reasonable:

$$4\dfrac{1}{5} \cdot 2\dfrac{5}{7} = 7\dfrac{2}{35}$$

14. What is the formula for the

a. area of a rectangle?

b. area of a triangle?

▌NOTATION

15. Fill in the blanks.

a. We read $5\dfrac{11}{16}$ as "five _____ eleven-_____."

b. We read $-4\dfrac{2}{3}$ as "_____ four and _____-thirds."

16. Determine the sign of the result. *You do not have to find the answer.*

a. $1\dfrac{1}{9}\left(-7\dfrac{3}{14}\right)$

b. $-3\dfrac{4}{15} \div \left(-1\dfrac{5}{6}\right)$

Fill in the blanks to complete each solution.

17. Multiply: $5\dfrac{1}{4} \cdot 1\dfrac{1}{7}$

$$5\dfrac{1}{4} \cdot 1\dfrac{1}{7} = \dfrac{21}{\boxed{}} \cdot \dfrac{\boxed{}}{7}$$

$$= \dfrac{21 \cdot \boxed{}}{\boxed{} \cdot 7}$$

$$= \dfrac{3 \cdot \overset{1}{\cancel{7}} \cdot 2 \cdot \overset{1}{\cancel{}}}{\underset{1}{\cancel{}} \cdot \underset{1}{\cancel{7}}}$$

$$= \dfrac{\boxed{}}{1}$$

$$= \boxed{}$$

18. Divide: $-5\dfrac{5}{6} \div 2\dfrac{1}{12}$

$$-5\dfrac{5}{6} \div 2\dfrac{1}{12} = -\dfrac{\boxed{}}{6} \div \dfrac{25}{\boxed{}}$$

$$= -\dfrac{\boxed{}}{6} \cdot \dfrac{12}{\boxed{}}$$

$$= -\dfrac{35 \cdot 12}{6 \cdot \boxed{}}$$

$$= -\dfrac{\overset{1}{\cancel{5}} \cdot \boxed{} \cdot 2 \cdot \overset{1}{\cancel{6}}}{\underset{1}{\cancel{6}} \cdot \underset{1}{\cancel{5}} \cdot \boxed{}}$$

$$= -\dfrac{\boxed{}}{5}$$

$$= -2\dfrac{\boxed{}}{5}$$

▌GUIDED PRACTICE

Each region outlined in black represents one whole. Write an improper fraction and a mixed number to represent the shaded portion. **See Example 1.**

19.

20.

21.

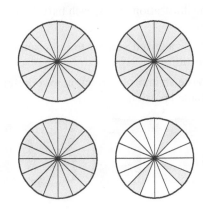

22.

Write each mixed number as an improper fraction.
See Example 2.

23. $6\frac{1}{2}$

24. $8\frac{2}{3}$

25. $20\frac{4}{5}$

26. $15\frac{3}{8}$

27. $-7\frac{5}{9}$

28. $-7\frac{1}{12}$

29. $-8\frac{2}{3}$

30. $-9\frac{3}{4}$

Write each improper fraction as a mixed number or a whole
number. Simplify the result, if possible. See Example 3.

31. $\frac{13}{4}$

32. $\frac{41}{6}$

33. $\frac{28}{5}$

34. $\frac{28}{3}$

35. $\frac{42}{9}$

36. $\frac{62}{8}$

37. $\frac{84}{8}$

38. $\frac{93}{9}$

39. $\frac{52}{13}$

40. $\frac{80}{16}$

41. $\frac{34}{17}$

42. $\frac{38}{19}$

43. $-\frac{58}{7}$

44. $-\frac{33}{7}$

45. $-\frac{20}{6}$

46. $-\frac{28}{8}$

Graph the given numbers on a number line. See Example 4.

47. $-2\frac{8}{9}, 1\frac{2}{3}, \frac{16}{5}, -\frac{1}{2}$

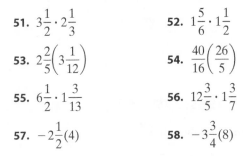

48. $-\frac{3}{4}, -3\frac{1}{4}, \frac{5}{2}, 4\frac{3}{4}$

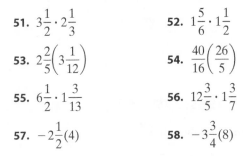

49. $3\frac{1}{7}, -\frac{98}{99}, -\frac{10}{3}, \frac{3}{2}$

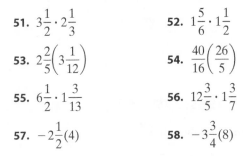

50. $-2\frac{1}{5}, \frac{4}{5}, -\frac{11}{3}, \frac{17}{4}$

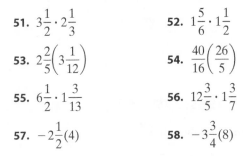

Multiply and simplify, if possible. See Example 5.

51. $3\frac{1}{2} \cdot 2\frac{1}{3}$

52. $1\frac{5}{6} \cdot 1\frac{1}{2}$

53. $2\frac{2}{5}\left(3\frac{1}{12}\right)$

54. $\frac{40}{16}\left(\frac{26}{5}\right)$

55. $6\frac{1}{2} \cdot 1\frac{3}{13}$

56. $12\frac{3}{5} \cdot 1\frac{3}{7}$

57. $-2\frac{1}{2}(4)$

58. $-3\frac{3}{4}(8)$

Divide and simplify, if possible. See Example 6.

59. $-1\frac{13}{15} \div \left(-4\frac{1}{5}\right)$

60. $-2\frac{5}{6} \div \left(-8\frac{1}{2}\right)$

61. $15\frac{1}{3} \div 2\frac{2}{9}$

62. $6\frac{1}{4} \div 3\frac{3}{4}$

63. $1\frac{3}{4} \div \frac{3}{4}$

64. $5\frac{3}{5} \div \frac{9}{10}$

65. $1\frac{7}{24} \div \frac{7}{8}$

66. $4\frac{1}{2} \div \frac{3}{17}$

TRY IT YOURSELF

Perform each operation and simplify, if possible.

67. $-6 \cdot 2\frac{7}{24}$

68. $-7 \cdot 1\frac{3}{28}$

69. $-6\frac{3}{5} \div 7\frac{1}{3}$

70. $-4\frac{1}{4} \div 4\frac{1}{2}$

71. $\left(1\frac{2}{3}\right)^2$

72. $\left(3\frac{1}{2}\right)^2$

73. $8 \div 3\frac{1}{5}$

74. $15 \div 3\frac{1}{3}$

75. $-20\frac{1}{4} \div \left(-1\frac{11}{16}\right)$

76. $-2\frac{7}{10} \div \left(-1\frac{1}{14}\right)$

77. $3\frac{1}{16} \cdot 4\frac{4}{7}$

78. $5\frac{3}{5} \cdot 1\frac{11}{14}$

79. Find the quotient of $-4\frac{1}{2}$ and $2\frac{1}{4}$.

80. Find the quotient of 25 and $-10\frac{5}{7}$.

81. $2\frac{1}{2}\left(-3\frac{1}{3}\right)$

82. $\left(-3\frac{1}{4}\right)\left(1\frac{1}{5}\right)$

83. $2\frac{5}{8} \cdot \frac{5}{27}$

84. $3\frac{1}{9} \cdot \frac{3}{32}$

85. $6\frac{1}{4} \div 20$

86. $4\frac{2}{5} \div 11$

87. Find the product of $1\frac{2}{3}$, 6, and $-\frac{1}{8}$.

88. Find the product of $-\frac{5}{6}$, -8, and $-2\frac{1}{10}$.

89. $\left(-1\frac{1}{3}\right)^3$

90. $\left(-1\frac{1}{5}\right)^3$

CONCEPT EXTENSIONS

91. **a.** Draw an illustration of $3\frac{4}{3}$.

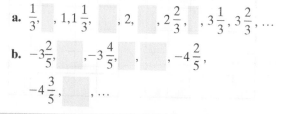

b. Explain why $3\frac{4}{3}$ is not a mixed number. Write it as a mixed number.

92. Write $7 + \frac{53}{49}$ as a mixed number.

93. Draw a number line.

a. On the number line, label where positive proper fractions are graphed.

b. On the number line, label where negative mixed numbers are graphed.

94. Fill in the blanks to complete the pattern.

a. $\frac{1}{3}$, ___, $1, 1\frac{1}{3}$, ___, 2, ___, $2\frac{2}{3}$, ___, $3\frac{1}{3}$, $3\frac{2}{3}$, ...

b. $-3\frac{2}{5}$, ___, $-3\frac{4}{5}$, ___, ___, $-4\frac{2}{5}$, $-4\frac{3}{5}$, ___, ...

APPLICATIONS

95. In the illustration below, each barrel represents one whole.

a. Write a mixed number to represent the shaded portion.

b. Write an improper fraction to represent the shaded portion.

96. Draw $\frac{17}{8}$ pizzas.

97. DIVING Fill in the blank with a mixed number to describe the dive shown below: forward ___ somersaults

98. PRODUCT LABELING Several mixed numbers appear on the label shown below. Write each mixed number as an improper fraction.

99. READING METERS

   a. Use a mixed number to describe the value to which the arrow is currently pointing.

   b. If the arrow moves twelve tick marks to the left, to what value will it be pointing?

100. READING METERS

   a. Use a mixed number to describe the value to which the arrow is currently pointing.

   b. If the arrow moves up six tick marks, to what value will it be pointing?

101. ONLINE SHOPPING A mother is ordering a pair of jeans for her daughter from the screen shown below. If the daughter's height is $60\frac{3}{4}$ in. and her waist is $24\frac{1}{2}$ in., on what size and what cut (regular or slim) should the mother point and click?

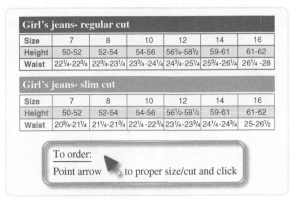

Girl's jeans- regular cut

Size	7	8	10	12	14	16
Height	50-52	52-54	54-56	56¼-58½	59-61	61-62
Waist	22¼-22¾	22¾-23¼	23¾-24¼	24¾-25¼	25¾-26¼	26¼-28

Girl's jeans- slim cut

Size	7	8	10	12	14	16
Height	50-52	52-54	54-56	56½-58½	59-61	61-62
Waist	20¾-21¼	21¼-21¾	22¼-22¾	23¼-23¾	24¼-24¾	25-26½

To order:
Point arrow ▶ to proper size/cut and click

102. SEWING Use the following table to determine the number of yards of fabric needed . . .

   a. to make a size 16 top if the fabric to be used is 60 inches wide.

   b. to make size 18 pants if the fabric to be used is 45 inches wide.

8767 Pattern
stitch'n save

Front

SIZES		8	10	12	14	16	18	20	
Top									
45"		2¼	2⅜	2⅜	2⅜	2½	2⅝	2¾	**Yds**
60"		2	2	2⅛	2⅛	2⅛	2⅛	2⅛	
Pants									
45"		2⅝	2⅝	2⅝	2⅝	2⅝	2⅝	2⅝	**Yds**
60"		1¾	2	2¼	2¼	2¼	2¼	2½	

103. LICENSE PLATES Find the area of the license plate shown below.

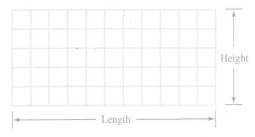

104. GRAPH PAPER Mathematicians use specially marked paper, called graph paper, when drawing figures. It is made up of squares that are $\frac{1}{4}$-inch long by $\frac{1}{4}$-inch high.

   a. Find the length of the piece of graph paper shown below.

   b. Find its height.

   c. What is the area of the piece of graph paper?

Height

Length

105. EMERGENCY EXITS The following sign marks the emergency exit on a school bus. Find the area of the sign.

106. CLOTHING DESIGN Find the number of square yards of material needed to make the triangular-shaped shawl shown in the illustration.

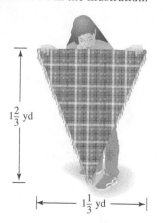

$1\frac{2}{3}$ yd

$\leftarrow 1\frac{1}{3}$ yd $\rightarrow$

107. CALORIES A company advertises that its mints contain only $3\frac{1}{5}$ calories a piece. What is the calorie intake if you eat an entire package of 20 mints?

108. CEMENT MIXERS A cement mixer can carry $9\frac{1}{2}$ cubic yards of concrete. If it makes 8 trips to a job site, how much concrete will be delivered to the site?

109. SHOPPING In the illustration, what is the cost of buying the fruit in the scale? Give your answer in cents and in dollars.

Oranges
84 cents a pound

110. PICTURE FRAMES How many inches of molding is needed to make the square picture frame below?

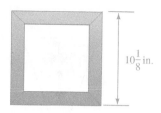

$10\frac{1}{8}$ in.

111. BREAKFAST CEREAL A box of cereal contains about $13\frac{3}{4}$ cups. Refer to the nutrition label shown in the next column and determine the recommended size of one serving.

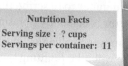

Nutrition Facts
Serving size : ? cups
Servings per container: 11

112. BREAKFAST CEREAL A box of cereal contains about $14\frac{1}{4}$ cups. Refer to the nutrition label shown below. Determine how many servings there are for children under 4 in one box.

Nutrition Facts
Serving size
Children under 4: $\frac{3}{4}$ cup

Servings per Container
Children Under 4: ?

113. CATERING How many people can be served $\frac{1}{3}$-pound hamburgers if a caterer purchases 200 pounds of ground beef?

114. SUBDIVISIONS A developer donated to the county 100 of the 1,000 acres of land she owned. She divided the remaining acreage into $1\frac{1}{3}$-acre lots. How many lots were created?

115. HORSE RACING The race tracks on which thoroughbred horses run are marked off in $\frac{1}{8}$-mile-long segments called *furlongs*. How many furlongs are there in a $1\frac{1}{16}$-mile race?

116. FIRE ESCAPES Part of the fire escape stairway for one story of an office building is shown below. Each riser is $7\frac{1}{2}$ inches high and each story of the building is 105 inches high.

 a. How many stairs are there in one story of the fire escape stairway?

 b. If the building has 43 stories, how many stairs are there in the entire fire escape stairway?

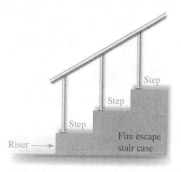

Step

Step

Step

Riser ⟶   Fire escape
                 stair case

▌WRITING

117. Explain the difference between $2\frac{3}{4}$ and $2\left(\frac{3}{4}\right)$.

118. Give three examples of how you use mixed numbers in daily life.

Applications Introduction: Estimation with Mixed Numbers

When adding, subtracting, multiplying, or dividing mixed numbers, and we don't need exact results, we can use **estimation.** There are several ways to estimate, but the objective is the same: Simplify the numbers in the problem so that the calculations can be made easily and quickly.

We have learned that every mixed number has a **whole-number part** and a **fractional part.** One method of estimation with mixed numbers is to consider the relative size of the fractional part. If the fractional part of the mixed number is greater than or equal to $\frac{1}{2}$, drop the fractional part and add 1 to its whole-number part. If the fractional part of the mixed number is less than $\frac{1}{2}$, simply drop its fractional part. An estimation of the sum of $83\frac{1}{4}$ and $52\frac{4}{5}$ using this method is shown below.

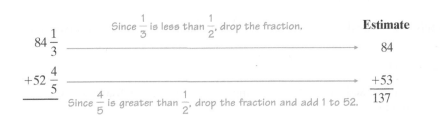

$$
\begin{array}{ll}
84\frac{1}{3} & \text{Since } \frac{1}{3} \text{ is less than } \frac{1}{2}, \text{ drop the fraction.} \\
+52\frac{4}{5} & \text{Since } \frac{4}{5} \text{ is greater than } \frac{1}{2}, \text{ drop the fraction and add 1 to 52.}
\end{array}
\qquad
\begin{array}{l}
\textbf{Estimate} \\
84 \\
+53 \\
\hline
137
\end{array}
$$

Use the estimation method shown above for the following problems.

1. LUGGAGE On many flights, airlines do not accept luggage whose total dimensions (length + width + height) exceed 62 inches. Estimate the total dimensions of the piece of luggage shown below.

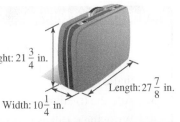

Height: $21\frac{3}{4}$ in.

Length: $27\frac{7}{8}$ in.

Width: $10\frac{1}{4}$ in.

2. FREEWAY SIGNS Estimate the distance between the Downtown San Diego off ramp and the Sea World off ramp on the 5 Freeway.

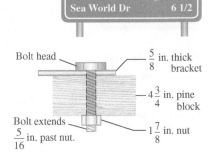

3. HARDWARE Estimate the length of a bolt needed to secure the bracket to the stock.

Bolt head

$\frac{5}{8}$ in. thick bracket

$4\frac{3}{4}$ in. pine block

Bolt extends $\frac{5}{16}$ in. past nut.

$1\frac{7}{8}$ in. nut

4. COOKING Estimate the amount of butter that is left in a $85\frac{1}{4}$-pound tub of butter if $8\frac{2}{3}$ pounds are used to make a wedding cake.

Objectives

1 Add mixed numbers.

2 Add mixed numbers in vertical form.

3 Subtract mixed numbers.

4 Solve application problems by adding and subtracting mixed numbers.

SECTION 2.6

Adding and Subtracting Mixed Numbers

ARE YOU READY?

The following problems review some basic skills that are needed when adding and subtracting mixed numbers.

1. Write $3\frac{5}{12}$ as an improper fraction.

2. Write $\frac{19}{16}$ as a mixed number.

3. Add: $\frac{3}{7} + \frac{2}{9}$

4. Add (Do not simplify the result):
$\frac{3}{24} + \frac{24}{24}$

5. Add: $75 + 43 + 54$

6. Subtract: $418 - 53$

In this section, we discuss several methods for adding and subtracting mixed numbers.

1 Add mixed numbers.

We can add mixed numbers by writing them as improper fractions. To do so, we follow these steps.

Adding Mixed Numbers: Method 1

1. Write each mixed number as an improper fraction.

2. Write each improper fraction as an equivalent fraction with a denominator that is the LCD.

3. Add the fractions.

4. Write the result as a mixed number, if desired.

Method 1 works well when the whole-number parts of the mixed numbers are small.

Self Check 1

Add: $3\frac{2}{3} + 1\frac{1}{5}$

Now Try **Problem 13**

EXAMPLE 1   Add: $4\frac{1}{6} + 2\frac{3}{4}$

Strategy We will write each mixed number as an improper fraction, and then use the rule for adding two fractions that have different denominators.

WHY We cannot add the mixed numbers as they are; their fractional parts are not similar objects.

$$4\frac{1}{6} + 2\frac{3}{4}$$

Four and one-sixth ⟶   ⟵ Two and three-fourths

Solution

$$4\frac{1}{6} + 2\frac{3}{4} = \frac{25}{6} + \frac{11}{4}$$ Write $4\frac{1}{6}$ and $2\frac{3}{4}$ as improper fractions.

By inspection, we see that the lowest common denominator is 12.

$$= \frac{25 \cdot 2}{6 \cdot 2} + \frac{11 \cdot 3}{4 \cdot 3}$$ To build $\frac{25}{6}$ and $\frac{11}{4}$ so that their denominators are 12, multiply each by a form of 1.

$$= \frac{50}{12} + \frac{33}{12}$$ Multiply the numerators.
Multiply the denominators.

$$= \frac{83}{12}$$ Add the numerators and write the sum over the common denominator 12. The result is an improper fraction.

$$= 6\frac{11}{12}$$ Write the improper fraction $\frac{83}{12}$ as a mixed number.

$$\begin{array}{r} 6 \\ 12\overline{)83} \\ -72 \\ \hline 11 \end{array}$$

Success Tip   We can use rounding to check the results when adding (or subtracting) mixed numbers. To check the answer $6\frac{11}{12}$ from Example 1, we proceed as follows:

$$4\frac{1}{6} + 2\frac{3}{4} \approx 4 + 3 = 7$$ Since $\frac{1}{6}$ is less than $\frac{1}{2}$, round $4\frac{1}{6}$ down to 4.
Since $\frac{3}{4}$ is greater than $\frac{1}{2}$, round $2\frac{3}{4}$ up to 3.

Since $6\frac{11}{12}$ is close to 7, it is a reasonable answer.

EXAMPLE 2   Add: $-3\frac{1}{8} + 1\frac{1}{2}$

Strategy   We will write each mixed number as an improper fraction, and then use the rule for adding two fractions that have different denominators.

WHY   We cannot add the mixed numbers as they are; their fractional parts are not similar objects.

$$-3\frac{1}{8} + 1\frac{1}{2}$$

Negative three and one-eighth ⎯⎯⎯⎯⎯↑   ↑⎯⎯⎯ One and one-half

Solution

$$-3\frac{1}{8} + 1\frac{1}{2} = -\frac{25}{8} + \frac{3}{2}$$ Write $-3\frac{1}{8}$ and $1\frac{1}{2}$ as improper fractions.

Since the smallest number the denominators 8 and 2 divide exactly is 8, the LCD is 8. We will only need to build an equivalent fraction for $\frac{3}{2}$.

$$= -\frac{25}{8} + \frac{3}{2} \cdot \frac{4}{4}$$ To build $\frac{3}{2}$ so that its denominator is 8, multiply it by a form of 1.

$$= -\frac{25}{8} + \frac{12}{8}$$ Multiply the numerators.
Multiply the denominators.

$$= \frac{-25 + 12}{8}$$ Add the numerators and write the sum over the common denominator 8.

$$= \frac{-13}{8}$$ Use the rule for adding integers that have different signs: $-25 + 12 = -13$.

$$= -1\frac{5}{8}$$ Write $\frac{-13}{8}$ as a negative mixed number by dividing 13 by 8.

Self Check 2
Add: $-4\frac{1}{12} + 2\frac{1}{4}$

Now Try **Problem 17**

We can also add mixed numbers by adding their whole-number parts and their fractional parts. To do so, we follow these steps.

Adding Mixed Numbers: Method 2

1. Write each mixed number as the sum of a whole number and a fraction.
2. Use the commutative property of addition to write the whole numbers together and the fractions together.
3. Add the whole numbers and the fractions separately.
4. Write the result as a mixed number, if necessary.

Method 2 works well when the whole number parts of the mixed numbers are large.

Self Check 3

Add: $275\frac{1}{6} + 81\frac{3}{5}$

Now Try **Problem 21**

EXAMPLE 3   Add: $168\frac{3}{7} + 85\frac{2}{9}$

Strategy We will write each mixed number as the sum of a whole number and a fraction. Then we will add the whole numbers and the fractions separately.

WHY If we change each mixed number to an improper fraction, build equivalent fractions, and add, the resulting numerators will be very large and difficult to work with.

Solution
We will write the solution in *horizontal* form.

$$168\frac{3}{7} + 85\frac{2}{9} = 168 + \frac{3}{7} + 85 + \frac{2}{9}$$

Write each mixed number as the sum of a whole number and a fraction.

$$= \text{_____} + \text{\_\_\_\_}$$

Use the commutative property of addition to change the order of the addition so that the whole numbers are together and the fractions are together.

$$= 253 + \frac{3}{7} + \frac{2}{9}$$

Add the whole numbers.

$$\begin{array}{r} \overset{1\,1}{168} \\ +\ 85 \\ \hline 253 \end{array}$$

$$= 253 + \frac{3}{7} \cdot \frac{9}{9} + \frac{2}{9} \cdot \frac{7}{7}$$

Prepare to add the fractions. To build $\frac{3}{7}$ and $\frac{2}{9}$ so that their denominators are 63, multiply each by a form of 1.

$$= 253 + \frac{27}{63} + \frac{14}{63}$$

Multiply the numerators.
Multiply the denominators.

$$= 253 + \frac{41}{63}$$

Add the numerators and write the sum over the common denominator 63.

$$\begin{array}{r} \overset{1}{27} \\ +\ 14 \\ \hline 41 \end{array}$$

$$= 253\frac{41}{63}$$

Write the sum as a mixed number.

Caution! If we use method 1 to add the mixed numbers in Example 3, the numbers we encounter are very large. As expected, the result is the same: $253\frac{41}{63}$.

$$168\frac{3}{7} + 85\frac{2}{9} = \frac{1{,}179}{7} + \frac{767}{9}$$ Write $168\frac{3}{7}$ and $85\frac{2}{9}$ as improper fractions.

$$= \frac{1{,}179}{7} \cdot \frac{9}{9} + \frac{767}{9} \cdot \frac{7}{7}$$ The LCD is 63.

$$= \frac{10{,}611}{63} + \frac{5{,}369}{63}$$ Note how large the numerators are.

$$= \frac{15{,}980}{63}$$ Add the numerators and write the sum over the common denominator 63.

$$= 253\frac{41}{63}$$ To write the improper fraction as a mixed number, divide 15,980 by 63.

Generally speaking, the larger the whole-number parts of the mixed numbers, the more difficult it becomes to add those mixed numbers using method 1.

2 Add mixed numbers in vertical form.

We can add mixed numbers quickly when they are written in **vertical form** by working in columns. The strategy is the same as in Example 2: Add whole numbers to whole numbers and fractions to fractions.

EXAMPLE 4 Add: $25\frac{3}{4} + 31\frac{1}{5}$

Strategy We will perform the addition in *vertical form* with the fractions in a column and the whole numbers lined up in columns. Then we will add the fractional parts and the whole-number parts separately.

WHY It is often easier to add the fractional parts and the whole-number parts of mixed numbers vertically—especially if the whole-number parts contain two or more digits, such as 25 and 31.

Solution

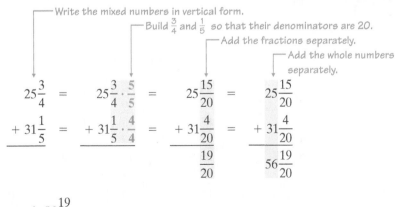

The sum is $56\frac{19}{20}$.

Self Check 4

Add: $71\frac{5}{8} + 23\frac{1}{3}$

Now Try **Problem 25**

Self Check 5

Add and simplify, if possible:

$68\frac{1}{6} + 37\frac{5}{18} + 52\frac{1}{9}$

Now Try **Problem 29**

EXAMPLE 5   Add and simplify, if possible: $75\frac{1}{12} + 43\frac{1}{4} + 54\frac{1}{6}$

Strategy We will write the problem in *vertical form*. We will make sure that the fractional part of the answer is in simplest form.

WHY When adding, subtracting, multiplying, or dividing fractions or mixed numbers, the answer should always be written in simplest form.

Solution

The LCD for $\frac{1}{12}, \frac{1}{4}$, and $\frac{1}{6}$ is 12.

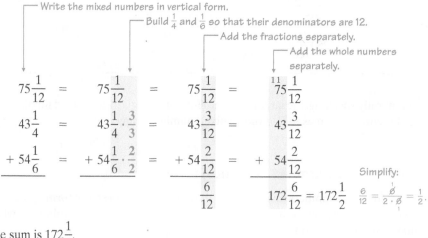

The sum is $172\frac{1}{2}$.

When we add mixed numbers, sometimes the sum of the fractions is an improper fraction.

Self Check 6

Add: $76\frac{11}{12} + 49\frac{5}{8}$

Now Try **Problem 33**

EXAMPLE 6   Add: $45\frac{2}{3} + 96\frac{4}{5}$

Strategy We will write the problem in *vertical form*. We will make sure that the fractional part of the answer is in simplest form.

WHY When adding, subtracting, multiplying, or dividing fractions or mixed numbers, the answer should always be written in simplest form.

Solution

The LCD for $\frac{2}{3}$ and $\frac{4}{5}$ is 15.

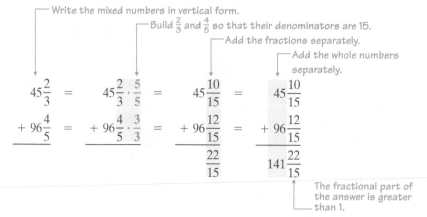

Since we don't want an improper fraction in the answer, we write $\frac{22}{15}$ as a mixed number. Then we *carry* 1 from the fraction column to the whole-number column.

$$141\frac{22}{15} = 141 + \frac{22}{15} \qquad \text{Write the mixed number as the sum of a whole number and a fraction.}$$

$$= 141 + 1\frac{7}{15} \qquad \text{To write the improper fraction as a mixed number divide 22 by 15.}$$

$$= 142\frac{7}{15} \qquad \text{Carry the 1 and add it to 141 to get 142.}$$

$$\begin{array}{r} 1 \\ 15\overline{)22} \\ -15 \\ \hline 7 \end{array}$$

3 Subtract mixed numbers.

Subtracting mixed numbers is similar to adding mixed numbers.

EXAMPLE 7

Subtract and simplify, if possible: $\quad 16\frac{7}{10} - 9\frac{8}{15}$

Strategy We will perform the subtraction in *vertical form* with the fractions in a column and the whole numbers lined up in columns. Then we will subtract the fractional parts and the whole-number parts separately.

WHY It is often easier to subtract the fractional parts and the whole-number parts of mixed numbers vertically.

Solution

The LCD for $\dfrac{7}{10}$ and $\dfrac{8}{15}$ is 30.

Write the mixed numbers in vertical form.
Build $\frac{7}{10}$ and $\frac{8}{15}$ so that their denominators are 30.
Subtract the fractions separately.
Subtract the whole numbers separately.

$$
\begin{array}{rcccccl}
16\dfrac{7}{10} & = & 16\dfrac{7}{10}\cdot\dfrac{3}{3} & = & 16\dfrac{21}{30} & = & 16\dfrac{21}{30} \\[2mm]
-\;9\dfrac{8}{15} & = & -\;9\dfrac{8}{15}\cdot\dfrac{2}{2} & = & -\;9\dfrac{16}{30} & = & -\;9\dfrac{16}{30} \\
\hline
 & & & & \dfrac{5}{30} & & 7\dfrac{5}{30} = 7\dfrac{1}{6}
\end{array}
$$

Simplify: $\dfrac{5}{30} = \dfrac{\cancel{5}}{\cancel{5}\cdot 6} = \dfrac{1}{6}$.

The difference is $7\dfrac{1}{6}$.

Subtraction of mixed numbers (like subtraction of whole numbers) sometimes involves borrowing. When the fraction we are subtracting is greater than the fraction we are subtracting it from, it is necessary to borrow.

EXAMPLE 8

Subtract: $\quad 34\frac{1}{8} - 11\frac{2}{3}$

Strategy We will perform the subtraction in *vertical form* with the fractions in a column and the whole numbers lined up in columns. Then we will subtract the fractional parts and the whole-number parts separately.

WHY It is often easier to subtract the fractional parts and the whole-number parts of mixed numbers vertically.

Self Check 7

Subtract and simplify, if possible:

$$12\frac{9}{20} - 8\frac{1}{30}$$

Now Try **Problem 37**

Self Check 8

Subtract: $\quad 258\frac{3}{4} - 175\frac{15}{16}$

Now Try **Problem 41**

Solution

The LCD for $\frac{1}{8}$ and $\frac{2}{3}$ is 24.

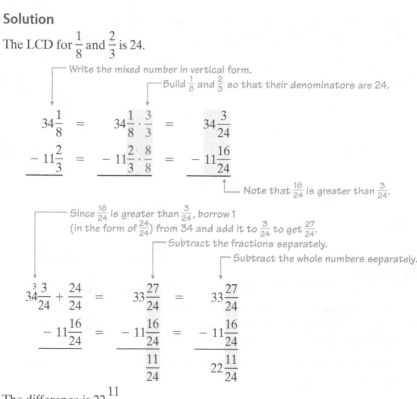

Write the mixed number in vertical form.

Build $\frac{1}{8}$ and $\frac{2}{3}$ so that their denominators are 24.

$$34\frac{1}{8} \quad = \quad 34\frac{1}{8} \cdot \frac{3}{3} \quad = \quad 34\frac{3}{24}$$

$$-11\frac{2}{3} \quad = \quad -11\frac{2}{3} \cdot \frac{8}{8} \quad = \quad -11\frac{16}{24}$$

Note that $\frac{16}{24}$ is greater than $\frac{3}{24}$.

Since $\frac{16}{24}$ is greater than $\frac{3}{24}$, borrow 1 (in the form of $\frac{24}{24}$) from 34 and add it to $\frac{3}{24}$ to get $\frac{27}{24}$.

Subtract the fractions separately.

Subtract the whole numbers separately.

$$34\overset{3}{\frac{3}{24}} + \frac{24}{24} \quad = \quad 33\frac{27}{24} \quad = \quad 33\frac{27}{24}$$

$$-11\frac{16}{24} \quad = \quad -11\frac{16}{24} \quad = \quad -11\frac{16}{24}$$

$$\frac{11}{24} \qquad\qquad 22\frac{11}{24}$$

The difference is $22\frac{11}{24}$.

Success Tip   We can use rounding to check the results when subtracting mixed numbers. To check the answer $22\frac{11}{24}$ from Example 8, we proceed as follows:

$$34\frac{1}{8} - 11\frac{2}{3} \approx 34 - 12 = 22$$

Since $\frac{1}{8}$ is less than $\frac{1}{2}$, round $34\frac{1}{8}$ down to 34.

Since $\frac{2}{3}$ is greater than $\frac{1}{2}$, round $11\frac{2}{3}$ up to 12.

Since $22\frac{11}{24}$ is close to 22, it is a reasonable answer.

EXAMPLE 9

Subtract: $419 - 53\frac{11}{16}$

Strategy We will write the numbers in vertical form and borrow 1 $\left(\text{in the form of } \frac{16}{16}\right)$ from 419.

WHY In the fraction column, we need to have a fraction from which to subtract $\frac{11}{16}$.

Solution

Write the mixed number in vertical form.

Borrow 1 (in the form of $\frac{16}{16}$) from 419.
Then subtract the fractions separately.

Subtract the whole numbers separately.
This also requires borrowing.

$$419 \quad = \quad 418\frac{16}{16} \quad = \quad \overset{311}{4\cancel{1}8}\frac{16}{16}$$

$$-53\frac{11}{16} \quad = \quad -53\frac{11}{16} \quad = \quad -53\frac{11}{16}$$

$$\frac{5}{16} \qquad\qquad 365\frac{5}{16}$$

The difference is $365\frac{5}{16}$.

4 Solve application problems by adding and subtracting mixed numbers.

EXAMPLE 10 *Horse Racing* In order to become the *Triple Crown Champion,* a thoroughbred horse must win three races: the Kentucky Derby ($1\frac{1}{4}$ miles long), the Preakness Stakes ($1\frac{3}{16}$ miles long), and the Belmont Stakes ($1\frac{1}{2}$ miles long). What is the combined length of the three races of the Triple Crown?

Solution It is helpful to list what we know and what we are to find.

- The Kentucky Derby is $1\frac{1}{4}$ miles long.
- The Preakness Stakes is $1\frac{3}{16}$ miles long.
- The Belmont Stakes is $1\frac{1}{2}$ miles long.
- What is the combined length of the three races?

Affirmed, in 1978, was the last of only 11 horses in history to win the Triple Crown.

The key phrase *combined length* indicates addition.
We translate the words of the problem to numbers and symbols.

The combined length of the three races	is equal to	the length of the Kentucky Derby	plus	the length of the Preakness Stakes	plus	the length of the Belmont Stakes.

$$\text{The combined length of the three races} \quad = \quad 1\frac{1}{4} \quad + \quad 1\frac{3}{16} \quad + \quad 1\frac{1}{2}$$

To find the sum, we will write the mixed numbers in vertical form. To add in the fraction column, the LCD for $\frac{1}{4}, \frac{3}{16},$ and $\frac{1}{2}$ is 16.

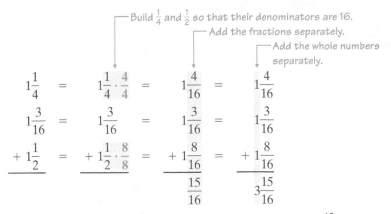

Build $\frac{1}{4}$ and $\frac{1}{2}$ so that their denominators are 16.
Add the fractions separately.
Add the whole numbers separately.

$$1\frac{1}{4} \;=\; 1\frac{1}{4}\cdot\frac{4}{4} \;=\; 1\frac{4}{16} \;=\; 1\frac{4}{16}$$
$$1\frac{3}{16} \;=\; 1\frac{3}{16} \;=\; 1\frac{3}{16} \;=\; 1\frac{3}{16}$$
$$+\,1\frac{1}{2} \;=\; +\,1\frac{1}{2}\cdot\frac{8}{8} \;=\; +\,1\frac{8}{16} \;=\; +\,1\frac{8}{16}$$
$$\frac{15}{16} \qquad 3\frac{15}{16}$$

The combined length of the three races of the Triple Crown is $3\frac{15}{16}$ miles.

We can estimate to check the result. If we round $1\frac{1}{4}$ down to 1, round $1\frac{3}{16}$ down to 1, and round $1\frac{1}{2}$ up to 2, the approximate combined length of the three races is $1 + 1 + 2 = 4$ miles. Since $3\frac{15}{16}$ is close to 4, the result seems reasonable.

Self Check 10

SALADS A three-bean salad calls for one can of green beans ($14\frac{1}{2}$ ounces), one can of garbanzo beans ($10\frac{3}{4}$ ounces), and one can of kidney beans ($15\frac{7}{8}$ ounces). How many ounces of beans are called for in the recipe?

***Now Try* Problem 93**

THINK IT THROUGH

"Americans are not getting the sleep they need which may affect their ability to perform well during the workday."

National Sleep Foundation Report, 2008

The 1,000 people who took part in the 2008 *Sleep in America* poll were asked when they typically wake up, when they go to bed, and how long they sleep on both workdays and non-workdays. The results are shown on the right. Write the average hours slept on a workday and on a non-workday as mixed numbers. How much longer does the average person sleep on a non-workday?

Typical Workday and Non-workday Sleep Schedules

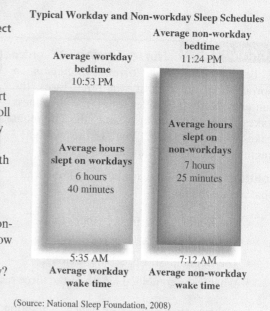

Average workday bedtime
10:53 PM

Average non-workday bedtime
11:24 PM

Average hours slept on workdays
6 hours 40 minutes

Average hours slept on non-workdays
7 hours 25 minutes

5:35 AM
Average workday wake time

7:12 AM
Average non-workday wake time

(Source: National Sleep Foundation, 2008)

Self Check 11

TRUCKING The mixing barrel of a cement truck holds 9 cubic yards of concrete. How much concrete is left in the barrel if $6\frac{3}{4}$ cubic yards have already been unloaded?

Now Try **Problem 95**

EXAMPLE 11   *Baking*   How much butter is left in a 10-pound tub if $2\frac{2}{3}$ pounds are used for a wedding cake?

Solution   It is helpful to list what we know and what we are to find.

- The tub contained 10 pounds of butter.   *Given*
- $2\frac{2}{3}$ pounds of butter are used for a cake.   *Given*
- How much butter is left in the tub?   *Find*

The key phrase *how much butter is left* indicates subtraction. We translate the words of the problem to numbers and symbols.

The amount of butter left in the tub	is equal to	the amount of butter in one tub	minus	the amount of butter used for the cake.
The amount of butter left in the tub	=	10	−	$2\frac{2}{3}$

To find the difference, we will write the numbers in vertical form and borrow 1 (in the form of $\frac{3}{3}$) from 10.

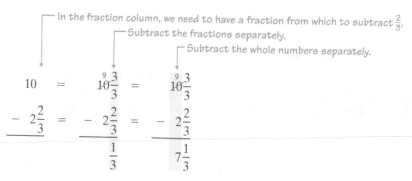

In the fraction column, we need to have a fraction from which to subtract $\frac{2}{3}$.
Subtract the fractions separately.
Subtract the whole numbers separately.

$$10 = 10\overset{9}{}\frac{3}{3} = \overset{9}{10}\frac{3}{3}$$
$$-2\frac{2}{3} = -2\frac{2}{3} = -2\frac{2}{3}$$
$$\frac{1}{3} \qquad 7\frac{1}{3}$$

There are $7\frac{1}{3}$ pounds of butter left in the tub.

We can check using addition. If $2\frac{2}{3}$ pounds of butter were used and $7\frac{1}{3}$ pounds of butter are left in the tub, then the tub originally contained $2\frac{2}{3} + 7\frac{1}{3} = 9\frac{3}{3} = 10$ pounds of butter. The result checks.

ANSWER TO SELF CHECKS

1. $4\frac{13}{15}$ **2.** $-1\frac{5}{6}$ **3.** $356\frac{23}{30}$ **4.** $94\frac{23}{24}$ **5.** $157\frac{5}{9}$ **6.** $126\frac{13}{24}$ **7.** $4\frac{5}{12}$ **8.** $82\frac{13}{16}$

9. $2{,}170\frac{1}{32}$ **10.** $41\frac{1}{8}$ oz   **11.** $2\frac{1}{4}$ yd^3

SECTION 2.6   STUDY SET

VOCABULARY

Fill in the blanks.

1. A _____ number, such as $1\frac{7}{8}$, contains a whole-number part and a fractional part.

2. We can add (or subtract) mixed numbers quickly when they are written in _____ form by working in columns.

3. To add (or subtract) mixed numbers written in vertical form, we add (or subtract) the _____ separately and the _____ numbers separately.

4. Fractions such as $\frac{11}{8}$, that are greater than or equal to 1, are called _____ fractions.

5. Consider the following problem:

$$36\frac{5}{7}$$
$$+\ 42\frac{4}{7}$$
$$\overline{78\frac{9}{7}} = 78 + 1\frac{2}{7} = 79\frac{2}{7}$$

   Since we don't want an improper fraction in the answer, we write $\frac{9}{7}$ as $1\frac{2}{7}$, _____ the 1, and add it to 78 to get 79.

6. Consider the following problem:

$$86\frac{1}{3} = \quad 86\frac{1}{3} + \frac{3}{3}$$
$$-\ 24\frac{2}{3} = \ -24\frac{2}{3}$$

   To subtract in the fraction column, we _____ 1 from 86 in the form of $\frac{3}{3}$.

CONCEPTS

7. **a.** For $76\frac{3}{4}$, list the whole-number part and the fractional part.

   b. Write $76\frac{3}{4}$ as a sum.

8. Use the commutative property of addition to rewrite the following expression with the whole numbers together and the fractions together. *You do not have to find the answer.*

$$14 + \frac{5}{8} + 53 + \frac{1}{6}$$

9. The *denominators* of two fractions are given. Find the least common denominator.

   a. 3 and 4   **b.** 5 and 6

   c. 6 and 9   **d.** 8 and 12

10. Simplify.

   a. $9\frac{17}{16}$ **b.** $1{,}288\frac{7}{3}$

   c. $16\frac{12}{8}$ **d.** $45\frac{24}{20}$

NOTATION

Fill in the blanks to complete each solution.

11. $$6\frac{3}{5} = \quad 6\frac{3}{5}\cdot\frac{7}{7} = \quad 6\frac{}{35}$$
$$+\ 3\frac{2}{7} = \ +3\frac{2}{7}\cdot\frac{}{} = \ +3\frac{10}{}$$
$$\overline{9\frac{}{}}$$

12. $$67\frac{3}{8} = \quad 67\frac{3}{8}\cdot\frac{}{} = \quad 67\frac{9}{24} = \quad 67\overset{6}{\frac{9}{24}} + \frac{}{} = \quad 66\frac{}{24}$$
$$-\ 23\frac{2}{3} = \ -23\frac{2}{3}\cdot\frac{8}{8} = \ -23\frac{}{24} = \ -23\frac{16}{24} = \ -23\frac{16}{24}$$
$$\overline{\frac{}{24}}$$

GUIDED PRACTICE

Add. See Example 1.

13. $1\frac{1}{4} + 2\frac{1}{3}$ 14. $2\frac{2}{5} + 3\frac{1}{4}$

15. $2\frac{1}{3} + 4\frac{2}{5}$ **16.** $4\frac{1}{3} + 1\frac{1}{7}$

Add. See Example 2.

17. $-4\frac{1}{8} + 1\frac{3}{4}$ **18.** $-3\frac{11}{15} + 2\frac{1}{5}$

19. $-6\frac{5}{6} + 3\frac{2}{3}$ **20.** $-6\frac{3}{14} + 1\frac{2}{7}$

Add. See Example 3.

21. $334\frac{1}{7} + 42\frac{2}{3}$ **22.** $259\frac{3}{8} + 40\frac{1}{3}$

23. $667\frac{1}{5} + 47\frac{3}{4}$ **24.** $568\frac{1}{6} + 52\frac{3}{4}$

Add. See Example 4.

25. $41\frac{2}{9} + 18\frac{2}{5}$ **26.** $60\frac{3}{11} + 24\frac{2}{3}$

27. $89\frac{6}{11} + 43\frac{1}{3}$ **28.** $77\frac{5}{8} + 55\frac{1}{7}$

Add and simplify, if possible. See Example 5.

29. $14\frac{1}{4} + 29\frac{1}{20} + 78\frac{3}{5}$ **30.** $11\frac{1}{12} + 59\frac{1}{4} + 82\frac{1}{6}$

31. $106\frac{5}{18} + 22\frac{1}{2} + 19\frac{1}{9}$ **32.** $75\frac{2}{5} + 43\frac{7}{30} + 54\frac{1}{3}$

Add and simplify, if possible. See Example 6.

33. $39\frac{5}{8} + 62\frac{11}{12}$ **34.** $53\frac{5}{6} + 47\frac{3}{8}$

35. $82\frac{8}{9} + 46\frac{11}{15}$ **36.** $44\frac{2}{9} + 76\frac{20}{21}$

Subtract and simplify, if possible. See Example 7.

37. $19\frac{11}{12} - 9\frac{2}{3}$ **38.** $32\frac{2}{3} - 7\frac{1}{6}$

39. $21\frac{5}{6} - 8\frac{3}{10}$ **40.** $41\frac{2}{5} - 6\frac{3}{20}$

Subtract. See Example 8.

41. $47\frac{1}{11} - 15\frac{2}{3}$ **42.** $58\frac{4}{11} - 15\frac{1}{2}$

43. $84\frac{5}{8} - 12\frac{6}{7}$ **44.** $95\frac{4}{7} - 23\frac{5}{6}$

Subtract. See Example 9.

45. $674 - 94\frac{11}{15}$ **46.** $437 - 63\frac{6}{23}$

47. $112 - 49\frac{9}{32}$ **48.** $221 - 88\frac{35}{64}$

TRY IT YOURSELF

Add or subtract and simplify, if possible.

49. $140\frac{5}{6} - 129\frac{4}{5}$ **50.** $291\frac{1}{4} - 289\frac{1}{12}$

51. $4\frac{1}{6} + 1\frac{1}{5}$ **52.** $2\frac{2}{5} + 3\frac{1}{4}$

53. $5\frac{1}{2} + 3\frac{4}{5}$ **54.** $6\frac{1}{2} + 2\frac{2}{3}$

55. $2 + 1\frac{7}{8}$ **56.** $3\frac{3}{4} + 5$

57. $8\frac{7}{9} - 3\frac{1}{9}$ **58.** $9\frac{9}{10} - 6\frac{3}{10}$

59. $140\frac{3}{16} - 129\frac{3}{4}$ **60.** $442\frac{1}{8} - 429\frac{2}{3}$

61. $380\frac{1}{6} + 17\frac{1}{4}$ **62.** $103\frac{1}{2} + 210\frac{2}{5}$

63. $-2\frac{5}{6} + 1\frac{3}{8}$ **64.** $-4\frac{5}{9} + 2\frac{1}{6}$

65. $3\frac{1}{4} + 4\frac{1}{4}$ **66.** $2\frac{1}{8} + 3\frac{3}{8}$

67. $-3\frac{3}{4} + \left(-1\frac{1}{2}\right)$ **68.** $-3\frac{2}{3} + \left(-1\frac{4}{5}\right)$

69. $7 - \frac{2}{3}$ **70.** $6 - \frac{1}{8}$

71. $12\frac{1}{2} + 5\frac{3}{4} + 35\frac{1}{6}$ **72.** $31\frac{1}{3} + 20\frac{2}{5} + 10\frac{1}{15}$

73. $16\frac{1}{4} - 13\frac{3}{4}$ **74.** $40\frac{1}{7} - 19\frac{6}{7}$

75. $-4\frac{5}{8} - 1\frac{1}{4}$ **76.** $-2\frac{1}{16} - 3\frac{7}{8}$

77. $6\frac{5}{8} - 3$ **78.** $10\frac{1}{2} - 6$

79. $\frac{7}{3} + 2$ **80.** $\frac{9}{7} + 3$

81. $58\frac{7}{8} + 340\frac{1}{2} + 61\frac{3}{4}$ **82.** $191\frac{1}{2} + 233\frac{1}{16} + 16\frac{5}{8}$

83. $9 - 8\frac{3}{4}$ **84.** $11 - 10\frac{4}{5}$

LOOK ALIKES . . .

85. **a.** $4\frac{1}{8} + 1\frac{5}{6}$ **b.** $4\frac{1}{8} - 1\frac{5}{6}$

     c. $4\frac{1}{8} \cdot 1\frac{5}{6}$ **d.** $4\frac{1}{8} \div 1\frac{5}{6}$

86. **a.** $3\frac{1}{12} + 2\frac{2}{5}$ **b.** $3\frac{1}{12} - 2\frac{2}{5}$

     c. $3\frac{1}{12}\left(2\frac{2}{5}\right)$ **d.** $3\frac{1}{12} \div 2\frac{2}{5}$

CONCEPT EXTENSIONS

87. The perimeter of the triangle shown below is $17\frac{1}{8}$ in. What is the length of the third side?

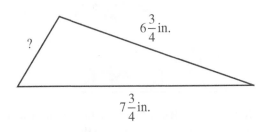

88. Subtract. Express the result using circular figures like those given.

89. Add. Express the result using square figures like those given.

90. Which two numbers below are equal?

$$23\frac{4}{5}, \quad 20\frac{17}{5}, \quad 22\frac{8}{5}, \quad 21\frac{14}{5}, \quad 19\frac{20}{5}$$

APPLICATIONS

91. AIR TRAVEL A businesswoman's flight left Los Angeles, and in $3\frac{3}{4}$ hours she landed in Minneapolis. She then boarded a commuter plane in Minneapolis and arrived at her final destination in $1\frac{1}{2}$ hours. Find the total time she spent on the flights.

92. SHIPPING A passenger ship and a cargo ship left San Diego harbor at midnight. During the first hour, the passenger ship traveled south at $16\frac{1}{2}$ miles per hour, while the cargo ship traveled north at a rate of $5\frac{1}{5}$ miles per hour. How far apart were they at 1:00 A.M.?

93. TRAIL MIX How many cups of trail mix will the recipe shown below make?

> **Trail Mix**
>
> *A healthy snack–great for camping trips*
>
> $2\frac{3}{4}$ cups peanuts $\frac{1}{3}$ cup coconut
>
> $\frac{1}{2}$ cup sunflower seeds $2\frac{2}{3}$ cups oat flakes
>
> $\frac{2}{3}$ cup raisins $\frac{1}{4}$ cup pretzels

94. HARDWARE Refer to the illustration below. How long should the threaded part of the bolt be?

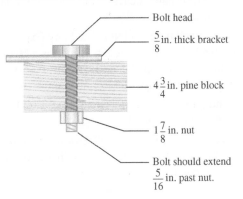

Bolt head

$\frac{5}{8}$ in. thick bracket

$4\frac{3}{4}$ in. pine block

$1\frac{7}{8}$ in. nut

Bolt should extend $\frac{5}{16}$ in. past nut.

95. OCTUPLETS On January 26, 2009, at Kaiser Permanente Bellflower Medical Center in California, Nadya Suleman gave birth to eight babies. (The United States' first live octuplets were born in Houston in 1998 to Nkem Chukwu and Iyke Louis Udobi). Find the combined birthweights of the babies from the information shown below. (Source: The Nadya Suleman family website)

No. 1: Noah, male, $2\frac{11}{16}$ pounds

No. 2: Maliah, female, $2\frac{3}{4}$ pounds

No. 3: Isaiah, male, $3\frac{1}{4}$ pounds

No. 4: Nariah, female, $2\frac{1}{2}$ pounds

No. 5: Makai, male, $1\frac{1}{2}$ pounds

No. 6: Josiah, male, $2\frac{3}{4}$ pounds

No. 7: Jeremiah, male, $1\frac{15}{16}$ pounds

No. 8: Jonah, male, $2\frac{11}{16}$ pounds

96. SEPTUPLETS On November 19, 1997, at Iowa Methodist Medical Center, Bobbie McCaughey gave birth to seven babies. Find the combined birthweights of the babies from the following information. (Source: *Los Angeles Times*, Nov. 20, 1997)

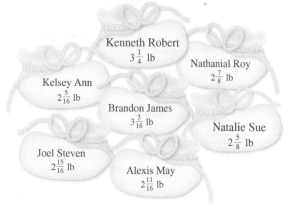

Kenneth Robert $3\frac{1}{4}$ lb

Nathanial Roy $2\frac{7}{8}$ lb

Kelsey Ann $2\frac{5}{16}$ lb

Brandon James $3\frac{3}{16}$ lb

Natalie Sue $2\frac{5}{8}$ lb

Joel Steven $2\frac{15}{16}$ lb

Alexis May $2\frac{11}{16}$ lb

97. HISTORICAL DOCUMENTS The Declaration of Independence on display at the National Archives in Washington, D.C., is $24\frac{1}{2}$ inches wide by $29\frac{3}{4}$ inches high. How many inches of molding would be needed to frame it?

98. STAMP COLLECTING The Pony Express Stamp, shown below, was issued in 1940. It is a favorite of collectors all over the world. A Postal Service document describes its size in an unusual way:

"The dimensions of the stamp are $\frac{84}{100}$ by $1\frac{44}{100}$ inches, arranged horizontally."

To display the stamp, a collector wants to frame it with gold braid. How many inches of braid are needed?

Smithsonian National Postal Museum

99. FREEWAY SIGNS A freeway exit sign is shown. How far apart are the Citrus Ave. and Grand Ave. exits?

Citrus Ave. $\frac{3}{4}$ mi
Grand Ave. $3\frac{1}{2}$ mi

100. BASKETBALL See the graph below. What is the difference in height between the tallest and the shortest of the starting players?

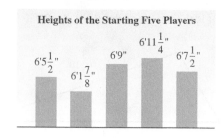

Heights of the Starting Five Players

$6'5\frac{1}{2}"$ $6'1\frac{7}{8}"$ $6'9"$ $6'11\frac{1}{4}"$ $6'7\frac{1}{2}"$

101. HOSE REPAIRS To repair a bad connector, a gardener removes $1\frac{1}{2}$ feet from the end of a 50-foot hose. How long is the hose after the repair?

102. HAIRCUTS A mother makes her child get a haircut when his hair measures 3 inches in length. His barber uses clippers with attachment #2 that leaves $\frac{3}{8}$-inch of hair. How many inches does the child's hair grow between haircuts?

103. SERVICE STATIONS Use the service station sign below to answer the following questions.

a. What is the difference in price between the least and most expensive types of gasoline at the self-service pump?

b. For each type of gasoline, how much more is the cost per gallon for full service compared to self service?

	Self Serve	Full Serve
PREMIUM UNLEADED	$269\frac{9}{10}$	$289\frac{9}{10}$
UNLEADED	$259\frac{9}{10}$	$279\frac{9}{10}$
PREMIUM PLUS	$279\frac{9}{10}$	$299\frac{9}{10}$

cents per gallon

104. WATER SLIDES An amusement park added a new section to a water slide to create a slide $311\frac{5}{12}$ feet long. How long was the slide before the addition?

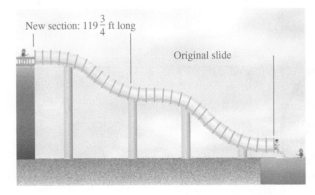

New section: $119\frac{3}{4}$ ft long

Original slide

105. JEWELRY A jeweler cut a 7-inch-long silver wire into three pieces. To do this, he aligned a 6-inch-long ruler directly below the wire and made the proper cuts. Find the length of piece 2 of the wire.

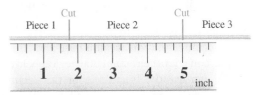

Cut   Cut

Piece 1   Piece 2   Piece 3

1   2   3   4   5

inch

106. SEWING To make some draperies, an interior decorator needs $12\frac{1}{4}$ yards of material for the den and $8\frac{1}{2}$ yards for the living room. If the material comes only in 21-yard bolts, how much will be left over after completing both sets of draperies?

WRITING

107. Of the methods studied to add mixed numbers, which do you like better, and why?

108. LEAP YEAR It actually takes Earth $365\frac{1}{4}$ days, give or take a few minutes, to make one revolution around the sun. Explain why every four years we add a day to the calendar to account for this fact.

109. Explain the process of simplifying $12\frac{7}{5}$.

110. Consider the following problem:

$$\begin{array}{r} 108\frac{1}{3} \\ -\ 99\frac{2}{3} \end{array}$$

   a. Explain why borrowing is necessary.

   b. Explain how the borrowing is done.

SECTION **2.7**

An Introduction to Decimals

ARE YOU READY?

The following problems review some basic skills that are needed when working with decimals.

1. Consider: 256,791

   a. What digit is in the hundreds column?

   b. What digit is in the ten thousands column?

   c. What digit is in the tens column?

2. Write each fraction in words:

   a. $\dfrac{7}{10}$

   b. $\dfrac{41}{100}$

   c. $\dfrac{213}{1,000}$

3. What fraction of the figure is shaded?

4. What fraction of the figure is shaded?

Objectives

1. Identify the place value of a digit in a decimal number.

2. Write decimals in expanded form.

3. Read decimals and write them in standard form.

4. Compare decimals using inequality symbols.

5. Graph decimals on a number line.

6. Round decimals.

7. Read tables and graphs involving decimals.

The place value system for whole numbers can be extended to create the **decimal numeration system.** Numbers written using **decimal notation** are often simply called **decimals.** They are used in measurement, because it is easy to put them in order and compare them. And as you probably know, our money system is based on decimals.

The decimal 1,537.6 on the odometer represents the distance, in miles, that the car has traveled.

The decimal 82.94 repesents the amount of the check, in dollars.

---

1 **Identify the place value of a digit in a decimal number.**

Like fraction notation, decimal notation is used to represent part of a whole. However, when writing a number in decimal notation, we don't use a fraction bar, nor is a denominator shown. For example, consider the rectangular region below that has 1 of 10 equal parts colored red. We can use the fraction $\frac{1}{10}$ or the decimal 0.1 to describe the amount of the figure that is shaded. Both are read as "one-tenth," and we can write:

$$\frac{1}{10} = 0.1$$

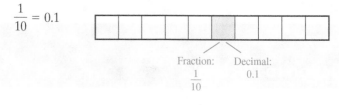

Fraction: Decimal:
$\frac{1}{10}$ 0.1

The square region on the right has 1 of 100 equal parts colored red. We can use the fraction $\frac{1}{100}$ or the decimal 0.01 to describe the amount of the figure that is shaded. Both are read as "one one-hundredth," and we can write:

$$\frac{1}{100} = 0.01$$

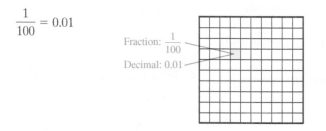

Fraction: $\frac{1}{100}$

Decimal: 0.01

Decimals are written by entering the digits 0, 1, 2, 3, 4, 5, 6, 7, 8, and 9 into place-value columns that are separated by a **decimal point.** The following **place-value chart** shows the names of the place-value columns. Those to the left of the decimal point form the **whole-number part** of the decimal number, and they have the familiar names ones, tens, hundreds, and so on. The columns to the right of the decimal point form the **fractional part.** Their place value names are similar to those in the whole-number part, but they end in "*ths.*" Notice that there is no one*ths* place in the chart.

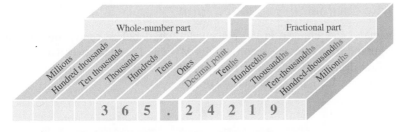

The decimal 365.24219, entered in the place-value chart above, represents the number of days it takes Earth to make one full orbit around the sun. We say that the decimal is written in **standard form** (also called **standard notation**). Each of the 2's in 365.24219 has a different place value because of its position. The place value of the red 2 is two tenths. The place value of the blue 2 is two thousandths.

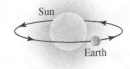

Sun

Earth

EXAMPLE 1   Consider the decimal number: 2,864.709531

a. What is the place value of the digit 5?

b. Which digit tells the number of millionths?

Strategy We will locate the decimal point in 2,864.709531. Then, moving to the right, we will name each column (tenths, hundredths, and so on) until we reach 5.

WHY It's easier to remember the names of the columns if you begin at the decimal point and move to the right.

Solution

a. 2,864.709531   Say "Tenths, hundredths, thousandths, ten-thousandths" as you move from column to column.

5 ten-thousandths is the place value of the digit 5.

b. 2,864.709531   Say "Tenths, hundredths, thousandths, ten-thousandths, hundred thousandths, millionths" as you move from column to column.

The digit 1 is in the millionths column.

> *Caution!* We *do not* separate groups of three digits on the right side of the decimal point with commas as we do on the left side. For example, it would be incorrect to write:
>
> 2,864.709,531

> **Self Check 1**
>
> Consider the decimal number: 56,081.639724
>
> **a.** What is the place value of the digit 9?
>
> **b.** Which digit tells the number of hundred-thousandths?
>
> *Now Try* **Problem 19**

We can write a whole number in decimal notation by placing a decimal point immediately to its right and then entering a zero, or zeros, to the right of the decimal point. For example,

$$99 \quad = \quad 99.0 \quad = \quad 99.00 \quad \text{Because } 99 = 99\tfrac{0}{10} = 99\tfrac{00}{100}.$$

A whole number   Place a decimal point here and enter a zero, or zeros, to the right of it.

When there is no whole-number part of a decimal, we can show that by entering a zero directly to the left of the decimal point. For example,

$$.83 \quad = \quad 0.83 \quad \text{Because } \tfrac{83}{100} = 0\tfrac{83}{100}.$$

No whole-number part   Enter a zero here, if desired.

Negative decimals are used to describe many situations that arise in everyday life, such as temperatures below zero and the balance in a checking account that is overdrawn. For example, the coldest natural temperature ever recorded on Earth was −128.6°F at the Russian Vostok Station in Antarctica on July 21, 1983.

© Les Welch/Icon SMI/Corbis

2 Write decimals in expanded form.

The decimal 4.458, entered in the place-value chart below, represents the time (in seconds) that it took women's record holder Melanie Troxel to cover a quarter mile in her top-fuel dragster. Notice that the place values of the columns for the whole-number part are 1, 10, 100, 1,000, and so on.

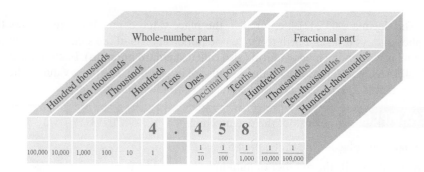

The place values of the columns for the fractional part of a decimal are $\frac{1}{10}$, $\frac{1}{100}$, $\frac{1}{1,000}$, and so on. Each of those columns has a value that is $\frac{1}{10}$ of the value of the place directly to its left. For example,

- The value of the tenths column is $\frac{1}{10}$ of the value of the ones column: $1 \cdot \frac{1}{10} = \frac{1}{10}$.
- The value of the hundredths column is $\frac{1}{10}$ of the value of the tenths column: $\frac{1}{10} \cdot \frac{1}{10} = \frac{1}{100}$.
- The value of the thousandths column is $\frac{1}{10}$ of the value of the hundredths column: $\frac{1}{100} \cdot \frac{1}{10} = \frac{1}{1,000}$.

The meaning of the decimal 4.458 becomes clear when we write it in **expanded form** (also called **expanded notation**).

4.458 = **4** ones + **4** tenths + **5** hundredths + **8** thousandths

which can be written as:

$$4.458 = 4 + \frac{4}{10} + \frac{5}{100} + \frac{8}{1,000}$$

> **The Language of Mathematics**   The word *decimal* comes from the Latin word *decima*, meaning a tenth part.

Self Check 2

Write the decimal number 1,277.9465 in expanded form.

Now Try **Problems 23 and 27**

EXAMPLE 2   Write the decimal number 592.8674 in expanded form.

Strategy Working from left to right, we will give the place value of each digit and combine them with + symbols.

WHY The term *expanded form* means to write the number as an addition of the place values of each of its digits.

Solution The expanded form of 592.8674 is:

5 hundreds + **9** tens + **2** ones + **8** tenths + **6** hundredths + **7** thousandths + **4** ten-thousandths

which can be written as

$$500 + 90 + 2 + \frac{8}{10} + \frac{6}{100} + \frac{7}{1,000} + \frac{4}{10,000}$$

3 Read decimals and write them in standard form.

To understand how to read a decimal, we will examine the expanded form of 4.458 in more detail. Recall that

$$4.458 = 4 + \frac{4}{10} + \frac{5}{100} + \frac{8}{1,000}$$

To add the fractions, we need to build $\frac{4}{10}$ and $\frac{5}{100}$ so that each has a denominator that is the LCD, 1,000.

$$4.458 = 4 + \frac{4}{10} \cdot \frac{\mathbf{100}}{\mathbf{100}} + \frac{5}{100} \cdot \frac{\mathbf{10}}{\mathbf{10}} + \frac{8}{1,000}$$

$$= 4 + \frac{400}{1,000} + \frac{50}{1,000} + \frac{8}{1,000}$$

$$= 4 + \frac{458}{1,000}$$

$$= 4\frac{458}{1,000}$$

We have found that $4.\underbrace{458}_{\text{Fractional part}}$ ⟵Whole-number part⟶ $= 4\frac{458}{1,000}$

We read 4.458 as "four and four hundred fifty-eight thousandths" because 4.458 is the same as $4\frac{458}{1,000}$. Notice that the last digit in 4.458 is in the thousandths place. This observation suggests the following method for reading decimals.

Reading a Decimal

To read a decimal:

1. Look to the left of the decimal point and say the name of the whole number.

2. The decimal point is read as "and."

3. Say the fractional part of the decimal as a whole number followed by the name of the last place-value column of the digit that is the farthest to the right.

We can use the steps for reading a decimal to write it in words.

EXAMPLE 3 Write each decimal in words and then as a fraction or mixed number. **You do not have to simplify the fraction.**

a. Sputnik, the first satellite launched into space, weighed 184.3 pounds.

b. Usain Bolt of Jamaica holds the men's world record in the 100-meter dash: 9.69 seconds.

c. A one-dollar bill is 0.0043 inch thick.

d. Liquid mercury freezes solid at −37.7°F.

Strategy We will identify the whole number to the left of the decimal point, the fractional part to its right, and the name of the place-value column of the digit the farthest to the right.

WHY We need to know those three pieces of information to read a decimal or write it in words.

Self Check 3

Write each decimal in words and then as a fraction or mixed number. **You do not have to simplify the fraction.**

a. The average normal body temperature is 98.6°F.

b. The planet Venus makes one full orbit around the sun every 224.7007 Earth days.

c. One gram is about 0.035274 ounce.

d. Liquid nitrogen freezes solid at −345.748°F.

Now Try Problems 31, 35, and 39

Solution

a.   184 . 3   The whole-number part is 184. The fractional part is 3.
                      The digit the farthest to the right, 3, is in the tenths place.

One hundred eighty-four and three tenths

Written as a mixed number, 184.3 is $184\frac{3}{10}$.

b.   9 . 69   The whole-number part is 9. The fractional part is 69.
                      The digit the farthest to the right, 9, is in the hundredths place.

Nine and sixty-nine hundredths

Written as a mixed number, 9.69 is $9\frac{69}{100}$.

c.   0 . 0043   The whole-number part is 0. The fractional part is 43.
                        The digit the farthest to the right, 3, is in the ten-thousandths place.

Forty-three ten-thousandths   Since the whole-number part is 0, we need not write it
                                 nor the word *and*.

Written as a fraction, 0.0043 is $\frac{43}{10,000}$.

d.   −37 . 7   This is a negative decimal.

Negative *thirty-seven and seven tenths.*

Written as a negative mixed number, −37.7 is $-37\frac{7}{10}$.

> **The Language of Mathematics**   Decimals are often read in an informal way.
> For example, we can read 184.3 as "one hundred eighty-four point three" and
> 9.69 as "nine point six nine."

The procedure for reading a decimal can be applied in reverse to convert from written-word form to standard form.

Self Check 4

Write each number in standard form:

a. *Eight hundred six and ninety-two hundredths*

b. *Twelve and sixty-seven ten-thousandths*

Now Try Problems 41, 45, and 47

EXAMPLE 4   Write each number in standard form:

a. *One hundred seventy-two and forty-three hundredths*

b. *Eleven and fifty-one thousandths*

Strategy We will locate the word *and* in the written-word form and translate the phrase that appears before it and the phrase that appears after it separately.

WHY The whole-number part of the decimal is described by the phrase that appears before the word *and*. The fractional part of the decimal is described by the phrase that follows the word *and*.

Solution

a.   **One hundred seventy-two**   **and**   **forty-three hundredths**

                            172.43

                                 └─This is the hundredths place-value column.

b. Sometimes, when changing from written-word form to standard form, we must insert placeholder 0's in the fractional part of a decimal so that that the last digit appears in the proper place-value column.

   Eleven   and   fifty-one thousandths

        11.051

              │ └─ This is the thousandths place-value column.
              └─ A place holder 0 must be inserted here so that the
                 last digit in 51 is in the thousandths column.

Caution! If a placeholder 0 is not written in 11.051, an incorrect answer of 11.51 (eleven and fifty-one *hundredths,* not *thousandths*) results.

4 Compare decimals using inequality symbols.

To develop a way to compare decimals, let's consider 0.3 and 0.271. Since 0.271 contains more digits, it may appear that 0.271 is greater than 0.3. However, the opposite is true. To show this, we write 0.3 and 0.271 in fraction form:

$$0.3 = \frac{3}{10} \qquad 0.271 = \frac{271}{1,000}$$

Now we build $\frac{3}{10}$ into an equivalent fraction so that it has a denominator of 1,000, like that of $\frac{271}{1,000}$.

$$0.3 = \frac{3}{10} \cdot \frac{100}{100} = \frac{300}{1,000}$$

Since $\frac{300}{1,000} > \frac{271}{1,000}$, it follows that $0.3 > 0.271$. This observation suggests a quicker method for comparing decimals.

Comparing Decimals

To compare two decimals:

1. Make sure both numbers have the same number of decimal places to the right of the decimal point. Write any additional zeros necessary to achieve this.

2. Compare the digits of each decimal, column by column, working from left to right.

3. *If the decimals are positive:* When two digits differ, the decimal with the greater digit is the greater number. *If the decimals are negative:* When two digits differ, the decimal with the smaller digit is the greater number.

EXAMPLE 5   Place an $<$ or $>$ symbol in the box to make a true statement:

a. 1.2679 ⬜ 1.2658   **b.** 54.9 ⬜ 54.929   **c.** -10.419 ⬜ -10.45

Strategy We will stack the decimals and then, working from left to right, we will scan their place-value columns looking for a difference in their digits.

WHY We need only look in that column to determine which digit is the greater.

Solution

a. Since both decimals have the same number of places to the right of the decimal point, we can immediately compare the digits, column by column.

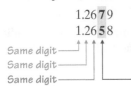

These digits are different: Since 7 is greater than 5, it follows that the first decimal is greater than the second.

Thus, 1.2679 is greater than 1.2658 and we can write $1.2679 > 1.2658$.

b. We can write two zeros after the 9 in 54.9 so that the decimals have the same number of digits to the right of the decimal point. This makes the comparison easier.

54.9**0 0**
54.9**2** 9

As we work from left to right, this is the first column in which the digits differ. Since $2 > 0$, it follows that 54.929 is greater than 54.9 (or 54.9 is less than 54.929) and we can write $54.9 < 54.929$.

Self Check 5

Place an $<$ or $>$ symbol in the box to make a true statement:

a. 3.4308 ⬜ 3.4312

b. 678.3409 ⬜ 678.34

c. -703.8 ⬜ -703.78

Now Try Problems 49, 55, and 59

Success Tip   Writing additional zeros *after the last digit to the right of the decimal point does not change the value of the decimal.* Also, deleting additional zeros after the last digit to the right of the decimal point does not change the value of the decimal. For example,

$$54.9 = 54.90 = 54.900$$

Because $54\frac{90}{100}$ and $54\frac{900}{1,000}$ in simplest form are equal to $54\frac{9}{10}$.

These additional zeros do not change the value of the decimal.

c. We are comparing two negative decimals. In this case, when two digits differ, the decimal with the smaller digit is the greater number.

$$-10.4\boxed{1}9$$
$$-10.4\boxed{5}0 \quad \text{Write a zero after 5 to help in the comparison.}$$

As we work from left to right, this is the first column in which the digits differ. Since $1 < 5$, it follows that -10.419 is greater than -10.45 and we can write $-10.419 > -10.45$.

5 Graph decimals on a number line.

Decimals can be shown by drawing points on a number line.

Self Check 6

Graph -1.1, -1.64, -0.8, and 1.9 on a number line.

Now Try **Problem 61**

EXAMPLE 6   Graph -1.8, -1.23, -0.3, and 1.89 on a number line.

Strategy We will locate the position of each decimal on the number line and draw a bold dot.

WHY To *graph a number* means to make a drawing that represents the number.

Solution The graph of each negative decimal is to the left of 0 and the graph of each positive decimal is to the right of 0. Since $-1.8 < -1.23$, the graph of -1.8 is to the left of -1.23.

6 Round decimals.

When we don't need exact results, we can approximate decimal numbers by **rounding.** To round the decimal part of a decimal number, we use a method similar to that used to round whole numbers.

Rounding a Decimal

1. To round a decimal to a certain decimal place value, locate the **rounding digit** in that place.
2. Look at the **test digit** directly to the right of the rounding digit.
3. If the test digit is 5 or greater, round up by adding 1 to the rounding digit and dropping all the digits to its right. If the test digit is less than 5, round down by keeping the rounding digit and dropping all the digits to its right.

EXAMPLE 7   *Chemistry* A student in a chemistry class uses a digital balance to weigh a compound in grams. Round the reading shown on the balance to the nearest thousandth of a gram.

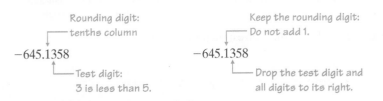

Strategy We will identify the digit in the thousandths column and the digit in the ten-thousandths column.

WHY To round to the nearest thousandth, the digit in the thousandths column is the rounding digit and the digit in the ten-thousandths column is the test digit.

Solution The rounding digit in the thousandths column is 8. Since the test digit 7 is 5 or greater, we round up.

Rounding digit: thousandths column
↓
15.2387
↑
Test digit: 7 is 5 or greater.

Add 1 to 8.
↓
15.2387
↑
Drop this digit.

The reading on the balance is approximately 15.239 grams.

Self Check 7
Round 24.41658 to the nearest ten-thousandth.

Now Try **Problems 65 and 69**

EXAMPLE 8   Round each decimal to the indicated place value:
a. −645.1358 to the nearest tenth   **b.** 33.096 to the nearest hundredth

Strategy In each case, we will first identify the rounding digit. Then we will identify the test digit and determine whether it is less than 5 or greater than or equal to 5.

WHY If the test digit is less than 5, we round down; if it is greater than or equal to 5, we round up.

Solution
a. Negative decimals are rounded in the same ways as positive decimals. The rounding digit in the tenths column is 1. Since the test digit 3 is less than 5, we round down.

Rounding digit:
tenths column
−645.1358
Test digit:
3 is less than 5.

Keep the rounding digit:
Do not add 1.
−645.1358
Drop the test digit and all digits to its right.

Thus, −645.1358 rounded to the nearest tenth is −645.1.

b. The rounding digit in the hundredths column is 9. Since the test digit 6 is 5 or greater, we round up.

Rounding digit:
hundredths column.
33.096
Test digit: 6 is 5 or greater.

Add 1. Since 9 + 1 = 10, write 0 in this column and carry 1 to the tenths column
33.096
Drop the test digit.

Thus, 33.096 rounded to the nearest hundredth is 33.10.

Caution! It would be incorrect to drop the 0 in the answer 33.10. If asked to round to a certain place value (in this case, thousandths), that place must have a digit, even if the digit is 0.

Self Check 8
Round each decimal to the indicated place value:

a. −708.522 to the nearest tenth

b. 9.1198 to the nearest thousandth

Now Try **Problems 73 and 77**

There are many situations in our daily lives that call for rounding amounts of money. For example, a grocery shopper might round the unit cost of an item to the nearest cent or a taxpayer might round his or her income to the nearest dollar when filling out an income tax return.

Self Check 9

a. Round $0.076601 to the nearest cent

b. Round $24,908.53 to the nearest dollar.

Now Try **Problems 85 and 87**

EXAMPLE 9

a. *Utility Bills*   A utility company calculates a homeowner's monthly electric bill by multiplying the unit cost of $0.06421 by the number of kilowatt hours used that month. Round the unit cost to the nearest cent.

b. *Annual Income*   A secretary earned $36,500.91 dollars in one year. Round her income to the nearest dollar.

Strategy In part a, we will round the decimal to the nearest hundredth. In part b, we will round the decimal to the ones column.

WHY Since there are 100 cents in a dollar, each cent is $\frac{1}{100}$ of a dollar. To round to the *nearest cent* is the same as rounding to the *nearest hundredth* of a dollar. To round to the *nearest dollar* is the same as rounding to the *ones place*.

Solution

a. The rounding digit in the hundredths column is 6. Since the test digit 4 is less than 5, we round down.

Thus, $0.06421 rounded to the nearest cent is $0.06.

b. The rounding digit in the ones column is 0. Since the test digit 9 is 5 or greater, we round up.

Thus, $36,500.91 rounded to the nearest dollar is $36,501.

7   Read tables and graphs involving decimals.

Year	Pounds
1960	2.68
1970	3.25
1980	3.66
1990	4.50
2000	4.64
2007	4.62

(Source: U.S. Environmental Protection Agency)

The table on the left is an example of the use of decimals. It shows the number of pounds of trash generated daily per person in the United States for selected years from 1960 through 2007.

When the data in the table is presented in the form of a **bar graph,** a trend is apparent. The amount of trash generated daily per person increased steadily until the year 2000. Since then, it appears to have remained about the same.

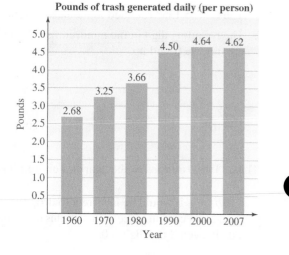

Pounds of trash generated daily (per person)

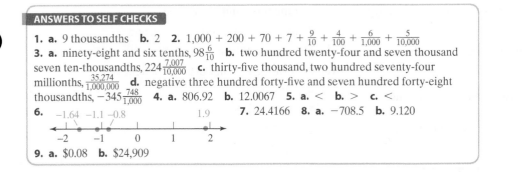

SECTION **2.7**   STUDY SET

VOCABULARY

Fill in the blanks.

1. Decimals are written by entering the digits 0, 1, 2, 3, 4, 5, 6, 7, 8, and 9 into place-value columns that are separated by a decimal _____.

2. The place-value columns to the left of the decimal point form the whole-number part of a decimal number and the place-value columns to the right of the decimal point form the _____ part.

3. We can show the value represented by each digit of the decimal 98.6213 by using _____ form:

$$98.6213 = 90 + 8 + \frac{6}{10} + \frac{2}{100} + \frac{1}{1,000} + \frac{3}{10,000}$$

4. When we don't need exact results, we can approximate decimal numbers by _____.

CONCEPTS

5. Write the name of each column in the following place-value chart.

4 , 7   8   9 . 0   2   6   5

6. Write the value of each column in the following place-value chart.

7	2	.	3	1	9	5	8

7. Fill in the blanks.

  a. The value of each place in the whole-number part of a decimal number is ____ times greater than the column directly to its right.

  b. The value of each place in the fractional part of a decimal number is ____ of the value of the place directly to its left.

8. Represent each situation using a signed number.

  a. A checking account overdrawn by \$33.45

  b. A river 6.25 feet above flood stage

  c. 3.9 degrees below zero

  d. 17.5 seconds after liftoff

9. a. Write a fraction and a decimal to describe what part of the rectangular region is shaded.

  b. Write a fraction and a decimal to describe what part of the square region is shaded.

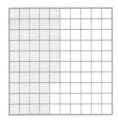

10. Shade 0.6 of each figure.

  a.

  b.

11. a. Write a fraction in simplest form to describe what part of the figure is shaded.

b. Write a fraction in simplest form to describe what part of the figure is *not* shaded.

c. Write a decimal to describe what part of the figure is shaded.

d. Write a decimal to describe what part of the figure is *not* shaded.

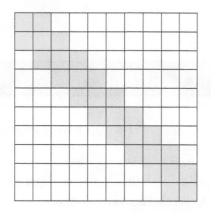

12. Write $400 + 20 + 8 + \frac{9}{10} + \frac{1}{100}$ as a decimal.

13. Fill in the blanks in the following illustration to label the *whole-number part* and the *fractional part*.

14. Fill in the blanks.

a. To round $0.13506 to the *nearest cent,* the rounding digit is ___ and the test digit is ___ .

b. To round $1,906.47 to the *nearest dollar,* the rounding digit is ___ and the test digit is ___ .

NOTATION

Fill in the blanks.

15. The columns to the right of the decimal point in a decimal number form its fractional part. Their place value names are similar to those in the whole-number part, but they end in the letters "____."

16. When reading a decimal, such as 2.37, we can read the decimal point as "____" or as "_____."

17. Write a decimal number that has . . .

6 in the ones column,

1 in the tens column,

0 in the tenths column,

8 in the hundreds column,

2 in the hundredths column,

9 in the thousands column,

4 in the thousandths column,

7 in the ten thousands column, and

5 in the ten-thousandths column.

18. Determine whether each statement is true or false.

a. $0.9 = 0.90$

b. $1.260 = 1.206$

c. $-1.2800 = -1.280$

d. $0.001 = .0010$

GUIDED PRACTICE

Answer the following questions about place value. See Example 1.

19. Consider the decimal number: 145.926

a. What is the place value of the digit 9?

b. Which digit tells the number of thousandths?

c. Which digit tells the number of tens?

d. What is the place value of the digit 5?

20. Consider the decimal number: 4.390762

a. What is the place value of the digit 6?

b. Which digit tells the number of thousandths?

c. Which digit tells the number of ten-thousandths?

d. What is the place value of the digit 4?

Write each decimal number in expanded form. See Example 2.

21. 37.89

22. 26.93

23. 124.575

24. 231.973

25. 7,498.6468

26. 1,946.7221

27. 6.40941

28. 8.70214

Write each decimal in words and then as a fraction or mixed number. See Example 3.

29. 0.3

30. 0.9

31. 50.41

32. 60.61

33. 19.529

34. 12.841

35. 304.0003

36. 405.0007

37. −0.00137   **38.** −0.00613

39. −1,072.499   **40.** −3,076.177

Write each number in standard form. **See Example 4.**

41. Six and one hundred eighty-seven thousandths

42. Four and three hundred ninety-two thousandths

43. Ten and fifty-six ten-thousandths

44. Eleven and eighty-six ten-thousandths

45. Negative sixteen and thirty-nine hundredths

46. Negative twenty-seven and forty-four hundredths

47. One hundred four and four millionths

48. Two hundred three and three millionths

Place an < or an > symbol in the box to make a true statement.
See Example 5.

49. 2.59   2.55   **50.** 5.17   5.14

51. 45.103   45.108   **52.** 13.874   13.879

53. 3.28724   3.2871   **54.** 8.91335   8.9132

55. 379.67   379.6088   **56.** 446.166   446.2

57. −23.45   −23.1   **58.** −301.98   −302.45

59. −0.065   −0.066   **60.** −3.99   −3.9888

Graph each number on a number line. **See Example 6.**

61. 0.8, −0.7, −3.1, 4.5, −3.9

$$\overset{\begin{array}{ccccccccccc} & & & & & & & & & & \\ -5 & -4 & -3 & -2 & -1 & 0 & 1 & 2 & 3 & 4 & 5 \end{array}}{\longleftrightarrow}$$

62. 0.6, −0.3, −2.7, 3.5, −2.2

$$\overset{\begin{array}{ccccccccccc} & & & & & & & & & & \\ -5 & -4 & -3 & -2 & -1 & 0 & 1 & 2 & 3 & 4 & 5 \end{array}}{\longleftrightarrow}$$

63. −1.21, −3.29, −4.25, 2.75, −1.84

$$\overset{\begin{array}{ccccccccccc} & & & & & & & & & & \\ -5 & -4 & -3 & -2 & -1 & 0 & 1 & 2 & 3 & 4 & 5 \end{array}}{\longleftrightarrow}$$

64. −3.19, −0.27, −3.95, 4.15, −1.66

$$\overset{\begin{array}{ccccccccccc} & & & & & & & & & & \\ -5 & -4 & -3 & -2 & -1 & 0 & 1 & 2 & 3 & 4 & 5 \end{array}}{\longleftrightarrow}$$

Round each decimal number to the indicated place value.
See Example 7.

65. 506.198 nearest tenth

66. 51.451 nearest tenth

67. 33.0832 nearest hundredth

68. 64.0059 nearest hundredth

69. 4.2341 nearest thousandth

70. 8.9114 nearest thousandth

71. 0.36563 nearest ten-thousandth

72. 0.77623 nearest ten-thousandth

Round each decimal number to the indicated place value.
See Example 8.

73. −0.137 nearest hundredth

74. −808.0897 nearest hundredth

75. −2.718218 nearest tenth

76. −3,987.8911 nearest tenth

77. 3.14959 nearest thousandth

78. 9.50966 nearest thousandth

79. 1.4142134 nearest millionth

80. 3.9998472 nearest millionth

81. 16.0995 nearest thousandth

82. 67.0998 nearest thousandth

83. 290.303496 nearest hundred-thousandth

84. 970.457297 nearest hundred-thousandth

Round each given dollar amount. **See Example 9.**

85. $0.284521 nearest cent

86. $0.312906 nearest cent

87. $27,841.52 nearest dollar

88. $44,633.78 nearest dollar

CONCEPT EXTENSIONS

Graph each number on the number line.

89. 3.275, 3.218, 3.291, 3.242

$$\overset{\begin{array}{ccc} | & | & | \\ 3.2 & & 3.3 \end{array}}{\longleftrightarrow}$$

90. −10.741, −10.787, −10.705, −10.752

$$\overset{\begin{array}{ccc} | & | & | \\ -10.8 & & -10.7 \end{array}}{\longleftrightarrow}$$

91. A large cube was constructed using 1,000 smaller cubes. Then some of the smaller cubes were removed, as shown on the next page.
   a. How many smaller cubes were removed?
   b. How many smaller cubes remain?
   c. Write a fraction and a decimal that describes what part of the large cube has been removed.

   d. Write a fraction and a decimal that describes what part of the large cube remains.

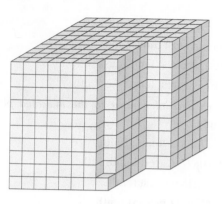

92. How many *tenths* of the figure below is shaded? Write your answer using a decimal.

APPLICATIONS

93. READING METERS To what decimal is the arrow pointing?

94. MEASUREMENT Estimate a length of 0.3 inch on the 1-inch-long line segment below.

_____

95. CHECKING ACCOUNTS Complete the check shown by writing in the amount, using a decimal.

Ellen Russell
455 Santa Clara Ave.
Parker, CO 25413

April 14 , 20 10

PAY TO THE ORDER OF ___ Citicorp ___ $ _____

One thousand twenty-five and $\frac{78}{100}$ ___ DOLLARS

BA Downtown Branch
P.O. Box 2456
Colorado Springs,CO 23712
MEMO Mortgage ___   Ellen Russell
45-828-02-33-4660

96. MONEY We use a decimal point when working with dollars, but the decimal point is not necessary when working with cents. For each dollar amount in the table, give the equivalent amount expressed as cents.

Dollars	Cents
$0.50	
$0.05	
$0.55	
$5.00	
$0.01	

97. INJECTIONS A syringe is shown below. Use an arrow to show to what point the syringe should be filled if a 0.38-cc dose of medication is to be given. ("cc" stands for "cubic centimeters.")

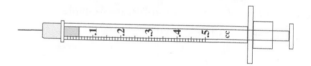

98. LASERS The laser used in laser vision correction is so precise that each pulse can remove 39 millionths of an inch of tissue in 12 billionths of a second. Write each of these numbers as a decimal.

99. NASCAR The closest finish in NASCAR history took place at the Darlington Raceway on March 16, 2003, when Ricky Craven beat Kurt Busch by a mere 0.002 seconds. Write the decimal in words and then as a fraction in simplest form. (Source: NASCAR)

100. THE METRIC SYSTEM The metric system is widely used in science to measure length (meters), weight (grams), and capacity (liters). Round each decimal to the nearest hundredth.

a. 1 ft is 0.3048 meter.

b. 1 mi is 1,609.344 meters.

c. 1 lb is 453.59237 grams.

d. 1 gal is 3.785306 liters.

101. UTILITY BILLS A portion of a homeowner's electric bill is shown below. Round each decimal dollar amount to the nearest cent.

Billing Period

From	To	Meter Number
06/05/10	07/05/10	10694435

The Gas Company

Next Meter Reading Date on or about Aug 03 2010

Summary of Charges

Customer Charge	30 Days	× $0.16438
Baseline	14 Therms	× $1.01857
Over Baseline	11 Therms	× $1.20091
State Regulatory Fee	25 Therms	× $0.00074
Public Purpose Surcharge	25 Therms	× $0.09910

102. INCOME TAX A portion of a W-2 tax form is shown below. Round each dollar amount to the nearest dollar.

Form **W-2** Wage and Tax Statement   **2010**

1 Wages, tips, other comp $35,673.79	2 Fed inc tax withheld $7,134.28	3 Social security wages $38,204.16
4 SS tax withheld $2,368.65	5 Medicare wages & tips $38,204.16	6 Medicare tax withheld $550.13
7 Social security tips	8 Allocated tips	9 Advance EIC payment
10 Depdnt care benefits	11 Nonqualified plans	12a

103. THE DEWEY DECIMAL SYSTEM When stacked on the shelves, the library books shown in the next column are to be in numerical order, least to greatest, *from left to right*. How should the titles be rearranged to be in the proper order?

104. 2008 OLYMPICS The top six finishers in the women's individual all-around gymnastic competition in the Beijing Olympic Games are shown below in alphabetical order. If the highest score wins, which gymnasts won the gold (1st place), silver (2nd place), and bronze (3rd place) medals?

	Name	Nation	Score
	Yuyuan Jiang	China	60.900
	Shawn Johnson	U.S.A.	62.725
	Nastia Liukin	U.S.A.	63.325
	Steliana Nistor	Romania	61.050
	Ksenia Semenova	Russia	61.925
	Yilin Yang	China	62.650

(Source: SportsIllustrated.cnn.com)

105. TUNE-UPS The six spark plugs from the engine of a Nissan Quest were removed, and the spark plug gap was checked. If vehicle specifications call for the gap to be from 0.031 to 0.035 inch, which of the plugs should be replaced?

Spark plug gap

Cylinder 1: 0.035 in.
Cylinder 2: 0.029 in.
Cylinder 3: 0.033 in.
Cylinder 4: 0.039 in.
Cylinder 5: 0.031 in.
Cylinder 6: 0.032 in.

106. GEOLOGY Geologists classify types of soil according to the grain size of the particles that make up the soil. The four major classifications of soil are shown below. Classify each of the samples (A, B, C, and D) in the table as clay, silt, sand, or granule.

Clay	Silt	Sand	Granule

0.00 in.   0.00008 in.   0.002 in.   0.08 in.   0.15 in.

Sample	Location found	Grain size (in.)	Classification
A	Riverbank	0.009	
B	Pond	0.0007	
C	NE corner	0.095	
D	Dry lake	0.00003	

107. MICROSCOPES A microscope used in a lab is capable of viewing structures that range in size from 0.1 to as small as 0.0001 centimeter. Which of the structures listed in the table would be visible through this microscope?

Structure	Size (cm)
Bacterium	0.00011
Plant cell	0.015
Virus	0.000017
Animal cell	0.00093
Asbestos fiber	0.0002

108. FASTEST CARS The graph below shows AutoWeek's list of fastest cars for 2009. Find the time it takes each car to accelerate from 0 to 60 mph.

LIONEL VADAM/Maxppp/Landov

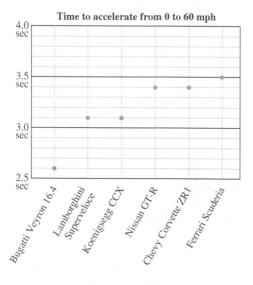

Time to accelerate from 0 to 60 mph

Bugatti Veyron 16.4, Lamborghini Superveloce, Koenigsegg CCX, Nissan GT-R, Chevy Corvette ZR1, Ferrari Scuderia

109. THE STOCK MARKET Refer to the graph below, which shows the earnings (and losses) in the value of one share of Goodyear Tire and Rubber Company stock over twelve quarters. (For accounting purposes, a year is divided into four quarters, each three months long.)

a. In what quarter, of what year, were the earnings per share the greatest? Estimate the gain.

b. In what quarter, of what year, was the loss per share the greatest? Estimate the loss.

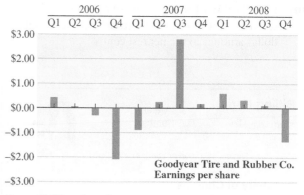

Goodyear Tire and Rubber Co. Earnings per share

(Source: Wall Street Journal)

110. GASOLINE PRICES Refer to the graph below.

a. In what month, of what year, was the retail price of a gallon of gasoline the lowest? Estimate the price.

b. In what month(s), of what year, was the retail price of a gallon of gasoline the highest? Estimate the price.

c. In what month of 2007 was the price of a gallon of gasoline the greatest? Estimate the price.

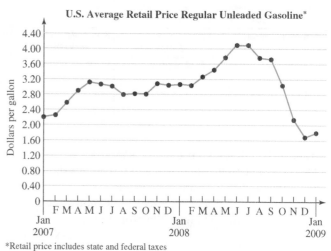

U.S. Average Retail Price Regular Unleaded Gasoline*

*Retail price includes state and federal taxes

(Source: EPA Short-Term Energy Outlook, March 2009)

▌ WRITING

111. Explain the difference between ten and one-tenth.

112. "The more digits a number contains, the larger it is." Is this statement true? Explain.

113. Explain why is it wrong to read 2.103 as "two and one hundred and three thousandths."

114. SIGNS

　a. A sign in front of a fast food restaurant had the cost of a hamburger listed as .99¢. Explain the error.

　b. The illustration below shows the unusual notation that some service stations use to express the price of a gallon of gasoline. Explain the error.

115. Write a definition for each of these words.

　　decade　　*decathlon*　　*decimal*

116. Show that in the decimal numeration system, each place-value column for the fractional part of a decimal is $\frac{1}{10}$ of the value of the place directly to its left.

SECTION **2.8**

Adding and Subtracting Decimals

Objectives

1 Add decimals.

2 Subtract decimals.

3 Add and subtract signed decimals.

4 Estimate sums and differences of decimals.

5 Solve application problems by adding and subtracting decimals.

ARE YOU READY?

The following problems review some basic skills that are needed when adding and subtracting decimals.

1. Add:

$$\begin{array}{r} 5{,}799 \\ +\ 6{,}879 \\ \hline \end{array}$$

2. Subtract:

$$\begin{array}{r} 2{,}470 \\ -\ 863 \\ \hline \end{array}$$

3. Add:

$5{,}576 + 649 + 1{,}922$

4. Subtract 1,249 from 50,009.

5. Evaluate:

　a. $-18 + 9$

　b. $-18 + (-9)$

　c. $18 - (-9)$

　d. $-18 - 9$

6. Round 3,608 to the nearest thousand.

To add or subtract objects, they must be similar. The federal income tax form shown below has a vertical line to make sure that dollars are added to dollars and cents added to cents. In this section, we show how decimal numbers are added and subtracted using this type of vertical form.

Form **1040EZ**	Department of the Treasury—Internal Revenue Service **Income Tax Return for Single and Joint Filers With No Dependents** **2010**			
Income **Attach Form(s) W-2 here.** Enclose, but do not attach, any payment.	1	Wages, salaries, and tips. This should be shown in box 1 of your Form(s) W-2. Attach your Form(s) W-2.	1	21,056	89
	2	Taxable interest. If the total is over $1,500, you cannot use Form 1040EZ.	2	42	06
	3	Unemployment compensation and Alaska Permanent Fund dividends (see page 11).	3	200	00
	4	Add lines 1, 2, and 3. This is your **adjusted gross income.**	4	21,298	95

1 Add decimals.

Adding decimals is similar to adding whole numbers. We use **vertical form** and stack the decimals with their corresponding place values and decimal points lined up. Then we add the digits in each column, working from right to left, making sure that hundredths are added to hundredths, tenths are added to tenths, ones are added to ones, and so on. We write the decimal point in the **sum** so that it lines up with the decimal points in the **addends.** For example, to find 4.21 + 1.23 + 2.45, we proceed as follows:

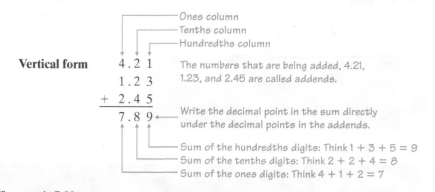

Ones column
Tenths column
Hundredths column

Vertical form

4 . 2 1
1 . 2 3
+ 2 . 4 5
─────────
7 . 8 9

The numbers that are being added, 4.21, 1.23, and 2.45 are called addends.

Write the decimal point in the sum directly under the decimal points in the addends.

Sum of the hundredths digits: Think 1 + 3 + 5 = 9
Sum of the tenths digits: Think 2 + 2 + 4 = 8
Sum of the ones digits: Think 4 + 1 + 2 = 7

The sum is 7.89.

In this example, each addend had two decimal places, tenths and hundredths. If the number of decimal places in the addends are different, we can insert additional zeros so that the number of decimal places match.

Adding Decimals

To add decimal numbers:

1. Write the numbers in vertical form with the decimal points lined up.

2. Add the numbers as you would add whole numbers, from right to left.

3. Write the decimal point in the result from Step 2 directly below the decimal points in the addends.

Like whole number addition, if the sum of the digits in any place-value column is greater than 9, we must **carry.**

Self Check 1

Add: 41.07 + 35 + 67.888 + 4.1
Now Try Problem 19

EXAMPLE 1   Add: 31.913 + 5.6 + 68 + 16.78

Strategy We will write the addition in vertical form so that the corresponding place values and decimal points of the addends are lined up. Then we will add the digits, column by column, working from right to left.

WHY We can only add digits with the same place value.

Solution To make the column additions easier, we will write two zeros after the 6 in the addend 5.6 and one zero after the 8 in the addend 16.78. Since whole numbers have an "understood" decimal point immediately to the right of their ones digit, we can write the addend 68 as 68.000 to help line up the columns.

31 . 913
  5 . 600   Insert two zeros after the 6.
 68 . 000   Insert a decimal point and three zeros: 68 = 68.000.
+ 16 . 780   Insert a zero after the 8.
─────────
             Line up the decimal points.

Now we add, right to left, as we would whole numbers, writing the sum from each column below the horizontal bar.

$$
\begin{array}{r}
\overset{\scriptstyle 2\,2}{31.913} \\
5.600 \\
68.000 \\
+\ 16.780 \\
\hline
122.293
\end{array}
$$

Carry a 2 (shown in blue) to the ones column.

Carry a 2 (shown in green) to the tens column.

Write the decimal point in the result directly below the decimal points in the addends.

The sum is 122.293.

Success Tip In Example 1, the digits in each place-value column were added from *top to bottom*. To check the answer, we can instead add from *bottom to top*. Adding down or adding up should give the same result. If it does not, an error has been made and you should re-add.

First add top to bottom

$$
\begin{array}{r}
\underline{122.293} \\
31.913 \\
5.600 \\
68.000 \\
+\ 16.780 \\
\hline
122.293
\end{array}
$$

To check, add bottom to top

Using Your CALCULATOR Adding Decimals

The bar graph on the right shows the number of grams of fiber in a standard serving of each of several foods. It is believed that men can significantly cut their risk of heart attack by eating at least 25 grams of fiber a day. Does this diet meet or exceed the 25-gram requirement?

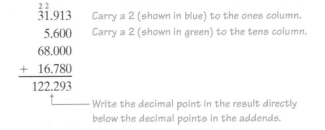

To find the total fiber intake, we add the fiber content of each of the foods. We can use a calculator to add the decimals.

3.1 $+$ 12.75 $+$ .9 $+$ 3.5 $+$ 1.1 $+$ 7.3 $=$ 　　　$\boxed{28.65}$

On some calculators, the $\boxed{\text{ENTER}}$ key is pressed to find the sum.

Since 28.65 > 25, this diet exceeds the daily fiber requirement of 25 grams.

---

2 Subtract decimals.

Subtracting decimals is similar to subtracting whole numbers. We use **vertical form** and stack the decimals with their corresponding place values and decimal points lined up so that we subtract similar objects—hundredths from hundredths, tenths from tenths, ones from ones, and so on. We write the decimal point in the **difference** so that it lines up with the decimal points in the **minuend** and **subtrahend.** For example, to find 8.59 − 1.27, we proceed as follows:

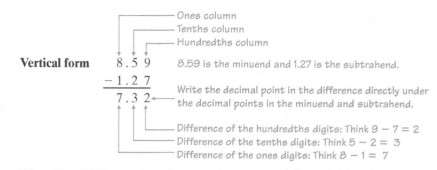

The difference is 7.32.

> ## Subtracting Decimals
>
> To subtract decimal numbers:
>
> **1.** Write the numbers in vertical form with the decimal points lined up.
>
> **2.** Subtract the numbers as you would subtract whole numbers from right to left.
>
> **3.** Write the decimal point in the result from Step 2 directly below the decimal points in the minued and the subtrahend.
>
> As with whole numbers, if the subtraction of the digits in any place-value column requires that we subtract a larger digit from a smaller digit, we must **borrow** or **regroup.**

Self Check 2

Subtract: 382.5 − 227.1

Now Try **Problem 27**

EXAMPLE 2   Subtract: 279.6 − 138.7

Strategy As we prepare to subtract in each column, we will compare the digit in the subtrahend (bottom number) to the digit directly above it in the minuend (top number).

WHY If a digit in the subtrahend is greater than the digit directly above it in the minuend, we must borrow (regroup) to subtract in that column.

Solution Since 7 in the tenths column of 138.7 is greater than 6 in the tenths column of 279.6, we cannot immediately subtract in that column because 6 − 7 is *not* a whole number. To subtract in the tenths column, we must regroup by borrowing as shown below.

$$
\begin{array}{r}
\overset{8\ \ 16}{279.\cancel{6}} \\
-\ 138.7 \\
\hline
140.9
\end{array}
$$

To subtract in the tenths column, borrow 1 one in the form of 10 tenths from the ones column. Add 10 to the 6 in the tenths column to get 16 (shown in blue).

Subtraction can be checked by addition. If a subtraction is done correctly, the sum of the difference and the subtrahend will equal the minuend: **Difference + subtrahend = minuend.**

Check:

$$
\begin{array}{r}
\overset{1}{1}40.9 \quad \text{Difference} \\
+\ 138.7 \quad \text{Subtrahend} \\
\hline
279.6 \quad \text{Minuend}
\end{array}
$$

Since the sum of the difference and the subtrahend is the minuend, the subtraction is correct.

Some subtractions require borrowing from two (or more) place-value columns.

EXAMPLE 3   Subtract 13.059 from 15.4.

Strategy We will translate the sentence to mathematical symbols and then perform the subtraction. As we prepare to subtract in each column, we will compare the digit in the subtrahend (bottom number) to the digit directly above it in the minuend (top number).

WHY If a digit in the subtrahend is greater than the digit directly above it in the minuend, we must borrow (regroup) to subtract in that column.

Solution Since 13.059 is the number to be subtracted, it is the subtrahend.

Subtract 13.059 from   15.4

$$15.4 - 13.059$$

To find the difference, we write the subtraction in vertical form. To help with the column subtractions, we write two zeros to the right of 15.4 so that both numbers have three decimal places.

$$
\begin{array}{r}
15.400 \\
- 13.059 \\
\end{array}
$$

Insert two zeros after the 4 so that the decimal places match.

Line up the decimal points.

Since 9 in the thousandths column of 13.059 is greater than 0 in the thousandths column of 15.400, we cannot immediately subtract. It is not possible to borrow from the digit 0 in the hundredths column of 15.400. We can, however, borrow from the digit 4 in the tenths column of 15.400.

$$
\begin{array}{r}
{}^{3\ 10}\\
15.\overset{}{4}00 \\
- 13.059 \\
\end{array}
$$

Borrow 1 tenth in the form of 10 hundredths from 4 in the tenths column. Add 10 to 0 in the hundredths column to get 10 (shown in blue).

Now we complete the two-column borrowing process by borrowing from the 10 in the hundredths column. Then we subtract, column-by-column, from the right to the left to find the difference.

$$
\begin{array}{r}
{}^{\quad 9}\\
{}^{3\ 10\ 10}\\
15.\overset{}{4}\,\overset{}{0}\,\overset{}{0} \\
- 13.059 \\
\hline
2.341 \\
\end{array}
$$

Borrow 1 hundredth in the form of 10 thousandths from 10 in the hundredths column. Add 10 to 0 in the thousandths column to get 10 (shown in green).

When 13.059 is subtracted from 15.4, the difference is 2.341.

Check:

$$
\begin{array}{r}
{}^{1\ 1}\\
2.341 \\
+ 13.059 \\
\hline
15.400 \\
\end{array}
$$

Since the sum of the difference and the subtrahend is the minuend, the subtraction is correct.

Self Check 3

Subtract 27.122 from 29.7.

Now Try **Problem 31**

Using Your CALCULATOR   **Subtracting Decimals**

A giant weather balloon is made of a flexible rubberized material that has an uninflated thickness of 0.011 inch. When the balloon is inflated with helium, the thickness becomes 0.0018 inch. To find the change in thickness, we need to subtract. We can use a calculator to subtract the decimals.

.011 $\boxed{-}$ .0018 $\boxed{=}$ $\boxed{0.0092}$

On some calculators, the $\boxed{\text{ENTER}}$ key is pressed to find the difference.

After the balloon is inflated, the rubberized material loses 0.0092 inch in thickness.

3   Add and subtract signed decimals.

To add signed decimals, we use the same rules that we used for adding integers.

> **Adding Two Decimals That Have the Same (Like) Signs**
>
> 1. To add two positive decimals, add them as usual. The final answer is positive.
> 2. To add two negative decimals, add their absolute values and make the final answer negative.

> **Adding Two Decimals That Have Different (Unlike) Signs**
>
> To add a positive decimal and a negative decimal, subtract the smaller absolute value from the larger.
>
> 1. If the positive decimal has the larger absolute value, the final answer is positive.
> 2. If the negative decimal has the larger absolute value, make the final answer negative.

Self Check 4

Add: $-5.04 + (-2.32)$

Now Try **Problem 35**

EXAMPLE 4   Add: $-6.1 + (-4.7)$

Strategy We will use the rule for adding two decimals that have the same sign.

WHY Both addends, -6.1 and -4.7, are negative.

Solution Find the absolute values: $|-6.1| = 6.1$ and $|-4.7| = 4.7$.

$$-6.1 + (-4.7) = -10.8$$ Add the absolute values, 6.1 and 4.7, to get 10.8. Then make the final answer negative.

$$\begin{array}{r} 6.1 \\ +\ 4.7 \\ \hline 10.8 \end{array}$$

Self Check 5

Add: $-21.4 + 16.75$

Now Try **Problem 39**

EXAMPLE 5   Add: $5.35 + (-12.9)$

Strategy We will use the rule for adding two integers that have different signs.

WHY One addend is positive and the other is negative.

Solution Find the absolute values: $|5.35| = 5.35$ and $|-12.9| = 12.9$.

$$5.35 + (-12.9) = -7.55$$ Subtract the smaller absolute value from the larger: 12.9 − 5.35 = 7.55. Since the negative number, −12.9, has the larger absolute value, make the final answer negative.

$$\begin{array}{r} \overset{8\ 10}{12.9\cancel{0}} \\ -\ 5.35 \\ \hline 7.55 \end{array}$$

The rule for subtraction can be used with signed decimals: *To subtract two decimals, add the first decimal to the opposite of the decimal to be subtracted.*

Self Check 6

Subtract: $-1.18 - 2.88$

Now Try **Problem 43**

EXAMPLE 6   Subtract: $-35.6 - 5.9$

Strategy We will apply the rule for subtraction: Add the first decimal to the opposite of the decimal to be subtracted.

WHY It is easy to make an error when subtracting signed decimals. We will probably be more accurate if we write the subtraction as addition of the opposite.

Solution The number to be subtracted is 5.9. Subtracting 5.9 is the same as adding its opposite, -5.9.

Change the subtraction to addition.

$$-35.6 - 5.9 = -35.6 + (-5.9) = -41.5$$

Change the number being subtracted to its opposite.

Use the rule for adding two decimals with the same sign. Make the final answer negative.

$$\begin{array}{r} \overset{1\,1}{35.6} \\ +\ 5.9 \\ \hline 41.5 \end{array}$$

EXAMPLE 7   Subtract: $-8.37 - (-16.2)$

Strategy We will apply the rule for subtraction: Add the first decimal to the opposite of the decimal to be subtracted.

WHY It is easy to make an error when subtracting signed decimals. We will probably be more accurate if we write the subtraction as addition of the opposite.

Solution The number to be subtracted is -16.2. Subtracting -16.2 is the same as adding its opposite, 16.2.

Add . . .

$$-8.37 - (-16.2) = -8.37 + 16.2 = 7.83$$

. . . the opposite

Use the rule for adding two decimals with different signs. Since 16.2 has the larger absolute value, the final answer is positive.

$$\begin{array}{r} \overset{1\,1}{} \\ \overset{5\ \cancel{6}\ 10}{1\cancel{6}.\cancel{2}\cancel{0}} \\ -\ 8.37 \\ \hline 7.83 \end{array}$$

Self Check 7
Subtract: $-2.56 - (-4.4)$
Now Try Problem 47

EXAMPLE 8   Evaluate: $-12.2 - (-14.5 + 3.8)$

Strategy We will perform the operation within the parentheses first.

WHY This is the first step of the order of operations rule.

Solution We perform the addition within the grouping symbols first.

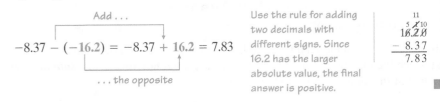

$$
\begin{aligned}
-12.2 - (-14.5 + 3.8) &= -12.2 - (-10.7) && \text{Perform the addition.} \\
&= -12.2 + 10.7 && \text{Add the opposite of } -10.7. \\
&= -1.5 && \text{Perform the addition.}
\end{aligned}
$$

$$\begin{array}{r} \overset{3\ 15}{1\cancel{4}.\cancel{5}} \\ -\ 3.8 \\ \hline 10.7 \end{array}$$

$$\begin{array}{r} \overset{1\ 12}{1\cancel{2}.\cancel{2}} \\ -10.7 \\ \hline 1.5 \end{array}$$

Self Check 8
Evaluate: $-4.9 - (-1.2 + 5.6)$
Now Try Problem 51

---

4   **Estimate sums and differences of decimals.**

Estimation can be used to determine whether an answer to a decimal addition or subtraction seems reasonable. There are several ways to estimate, but the objective is the same: Simplify the numbers in the problem so that the calculations can be made easily and quickly. One popular method or estimation is called **front-end rounding**.

EXAMPLE 9

a. Estimate the sum by rounding the addends to the nearest ten: $261.76 + 432.94$
b. Estimate the difference using front-end rounding: $381.77 - 57.01$

Strategy We will use rounding to approximate each addend, minuend, and subtrahend. Then we will find the sum or difference of the approximations.

WHY Rounding produces numbers that contain many 0's. Such numbers are easier to add or subtract.

Self Check 9
a. Estimate by rounding the addends to the nearest ten: $526.93 + 284.03$
b. Estimate using front-end rounding: $512.33 - 36.47$
Now Try Problems 55 and 57

Solution

a. $261.76 \rightarrow$ 260   *Round to the nearest ten.*

$\underline{+\ 432.94 \rightarrow \underline{+\ 430}}$ *Round to the nearest ten.*

690

The estimate is 690. If we compute $261.76 + 432.94$, the sum is 694.7. We can see that the estimate is close; it's just 4.7 less than 694.7.

b. We use front-end rounding. Each number is rounded to its largest place value so that all but its first digit is Zero.

$381.77 \rightarrow$ 400   *Round to the nearest hundred.*

$\underline{-\ \ 57.01 \rightarrow \underline{-\ \ 60}}$ *Round to the nearest ten.*

340

The estimate is 340. If we compute $381.77 - 57.01$, the difference is 324.76. We can see that the estimate is close; it's 15.24 more than 324.76.

> **Success Tip**   Estimates can be greater than or less than the exact answer. It depends on how often rounding up and rounding down occurs in the estimation.

5 Solve application problems by adding and subtracting decimals.

To make a profit, a merchant must sell an item for more than she paid for it. The price at which the merchant sells the product, called the **retail price,** is the *sum* of what the item **cost** the merchant plus the **markup.**

Retail price = cost + markup

Self Check 10

PRICING Find the retail price of a wool coat if a clothing outlet buys them for $109.95 each and then marks them up $99.95 to sell in its stores.

Now Try **Problem 95**

EXAMPLE 10   *Pricing*   Find the retail price of a Rubik's Cube if a game store owner buys them for $8.95 each and then marks them up $4.25 to sell in her store.

Solution It is helpful to list what we know and what we are to find.

Andrea Presazzi/Dreamstime.com

- Rubik's Cubes cost the store owner $8.95 each. *Given*
- She marks up the price $4.25. *Given*
- What is the retail price of a Rubik's Cube? *Find*

We translate the words of the problem to numbers and symbols.

The retail price	is equal to	the cost	plus	the markup.
The retail price	=	8.95	+	4.25

Use vertical form to perform decimal addition:

$$
\begin{array}{r}
\overset{1\ 1}{8.95} \\
+\ \ 4.25 \\
\hline
13.20
\end{array}
$$

The retail price of a Rubik's Cube is $13.20.

Check We can estimate to check the result. If we use $9 to approximate the cost of a Rubik's Cube to the store owner and $4 to be the approximate markup, then the retail price is about $9 + $4 = $13. The result, $13.20, seems reasonable.

EXAMPLE 11   *Kitchen Sinks* One model of kitchen sink is made of 18-gauge stainless steel that is 0.0500 inch thick. Another, less expensive, model is made from 20-gauge stainless steel that is 0.0375 inch thick. How much thicker is the 18-gauge?

Solution

- The 18-gauge stainless steel is 0.0500 inch thick.   *Given*
- The 20-gauge stainless steel is 0.0375 inch thick.   *Given*
- How much thicker is the 18-gauge stainless steel?   *Find*

Image copyright V. J. Matthew, 2009. Used under license from Shutterstock.com

Self Check 11

ALUMINUM How much thicker is 16-gauge aluminum that is 0.0508 inch thick than 22-gauge aluminum that is 0.0253 inch thick?

Now Try **Problem 101**

Phrases such as *how much older, how much longer,* and, in this case, *how much thicker,* indicate subtraction. We translate the words of the problem to numbers and symbols.

How much thicker	is equal to	the thickness of the 18-gauge stainless steel	minus	the thickness of the 20-gauge stainless steel.
How much thicker	=	0.0500	−	0.0375

Use vertical form to perform subtraction:

$$
\begin{array}{r}
\overset{9}{}\overset{4\;\;\cancel{10}\;\;10}{} \\
0.05\,\cancel{0}\,\cancel{0} \\
-\ 0.03\,7\,5 \\
\hline
0.01\,2\,5
\end{array}
$$

The 18-gauge stainless steel is 0.0125 inch thicker than the 20-gauge.

Check We can add to check the subtraction:

$$
\begin{array}{r}
\overset{1\ 1}{} \\
0.0125 \quad \text{Difference} \\
+\ 0.0375 \quad \text{Subtrahend} \\
\hline
0.0500 \quad \text{Minuend}
\end{array}
$$

The result checks.

Sometimes more than one operation is needed to solve a problem involving decimals.

EXAMPLE 12   *Conditioning Programs* A 350-pound football player lost 15.7 pounds during the first week of practice. During the second week, he gained 4.9 pounds. Find his weight after the first two weeks of practice.

Solution

- The football player's beginning weight was 350 pounds.   *Given*
- The first week he lost 15.7 pounds.   *Given*
- The second week he gained 4.9 pounds.   *Given*
- What was his weight after two weeks of practice?   *Find*

The word *lost* indicates subtraction. The word *gained* indicates addition. We translate the words of the problem to numbers and symbols.

The player's weight after two weeks of practice	is equal to	his beginning weight	minus	the first-week weight loss	plus	the second-week weight gain.
The player's weight after two weeks of practice	=	350	−	15.7	+	4.9

Self Check 12

WRESTLING A 195.5-pound wrestler had to lose 6.5 pounds to make his weight class. After the weigh-in, he gained back 3.7 pounds. What did he weigh then?

Now Try **Problem 107**

To evaluate $350 - 15.7 + 4.9$, we work from left to right and perform the subtraction first, then the addition.

$$
\begin{array}{r}
\overset{9}{}\\
\overset{4}{3}\overset{\cancel{10}}{\cancel{5}}\overset{10}{\cancel{0}}.\overset{}{\cancel{0}}\\
-\ \ 1\ 5\ .7\\
\hline
3\ 3\ 4\ .3
\end{array}
$$

Write the whole number 350 as 350.0 and use a two-column borrowing process to subtract in the tenths column.

This is the player's weight after one week of practice.

Next, we add the 4.9-pound gain to the previous result to find the player's weight after two weeks of practice.

$$
\begin{array}{r}
\overset{1}{3}34.3\\
+\ \ \ 4.9\\
\hline
339.2
\end{array}
$$

The player's weight was 339.2 pounds after two weeks of practice.

Check We can estimate to check the result. The player lost about 16 pounds the first week and then gained back about 5 pounds the second week, for a net loss of 11 pounds. If we subtract the approximate 11 pound loss from his beginning weight, we get $350 - 11 = 339$ pounds. The result, 339.2 pounds, seems reasonable.

ANSWERS TO SELF CHECKS

1. 148.058 **2.** 155.4 **3.** 2.578 **4.** −7.36 **5.** −4.65 **6.** −4.06 **7.** 1.84 **8.** −9.3 **9. a.** 810 **b.** 460 **10.** $209.90 **11.** 0.0255 in. **12.** 192.7 lb

---

SECTION 2.8   STUDY SET

VOCABULARY

Fill in the blanks.

1. In the addition problem shown below, label each *addend* and the *sum*.

$$
\begin{array}{r}
1.72 \leftarrow\\
4.68 \leftarrow\\
+\ 2.02 \leftarrow\\
\hline
8.42 \leftarrow
\end{array}
$$

2. When using the vertical form to add decimals, if the addition of the digits in any one column produces a sum greater than 9, we must _____.

3. In the subtraction problem shown below, label the *minuend, subtrahend,* and the *difference*.

$$
\begin{array}{r}
12.9 \leftarrow\\
-\ \ 4.3 \leftarrow\\
\hline
8.6 \leftarrow
\end{array}
$$

4. If the subtraction of the digits in any place-value column requires that we subtract a larger digit from a smaller digit, we must _____ or *regroup*.

5. To see whether the result of an addition is reasonable, we can round the addends and _____ the sum.

6. In application problems, phrases such as *how much older, how much longer,* and *how much thicker* indicate the operation of _____.

CONCEPTS

7. Check the following result. Use addition to determine if 15.2 is the correct difference.

$$
\begin{array}{r}
28.7\\
-\ 12.5\\
\hline
15.2
\end{array}
$$

8. Determine whether the *sign* of each result is positive or negative. *You do not have to find the sum.*

　a. $-7.6 + (-1.8)$

　b. $-24.99 + 29.08$

　c. $133.2 + (-400.43)$

9. Fill in the blank: To subtract signed decimals, add the _____ of the decimal that is being subtracted.

10. Apply the rule for subtraction and fill in the three blanks.

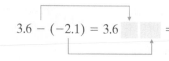

$$3.6 - (-2.1) = 3.6 \ \boxed{}\ \boxed{} = \boxed{}$$

11. Fill in the blanks to rewrite each subtraction as addition of the opposite of the number being subtracted.

a. $6.8 - 1.2 = 6.8 + ($ ____ $)$

b. $29.03 - (-13.55) = 29.03 +$ ____

c. $-5.1 - 7.4 = -5.1 + ($ ____ $)$

12. Fill in the blanks to complete the estimation.

$$
\begin{array}{rl}
567.7 \rightarrow & \text{____} \qquad \textit{Round to the nearest ten.} \\
+\,214.3 \rightarrow +\, & \text{____} \qquad \textit{Round to the nearest ten.} \\
\hline
782.0
\end{array}
$$

NOTATION

13. Copy the following addition problem. Insert a decimal point and additional zeros so that the number of decimal places in the addends match.

$$
\begin{array}{r}
46.6 \\
11 \\
+\,15.702 \\
\end{array}
$$

14. Refer to the subtraction problem below. Fill in the blanks: To subtract in the _____ column, we borrow 1 tenth in the form of 10 hundredths from the 3 in the _____ column.

$$
\begin{array}{r}
\overset{2\ 11}{29.3\,\cancel{1}} \\
-\,25.16 \\
\end{array}
$$

GUIDED PRACTICE

Add. See Objective 1.

15.
$$
\begin{array}{r}
32.5 \\
+\ 7.4 \\
\end{array}
$$

16.
$$
\begin{array}{r}
16.3 \\
+\ 3.5 \\
\end{array}
$$

17.
$$
\begin{array}{r}
3.04 \\
4.12 \\
+\ 1.43 \\
\end{array}
$$

18.
$$
\begin{array}{r}
2.11 \\
5.04 \\
+\ 2.72 \\
\end{array}
$$

Add. See Example 1.

19. $36.821 + 7.3 + 42 + 15.44$

20. $46.228 + 5.6 + 39 + 19.37$

21. $27.471 + 6.4 + 157 + 12.12$

22. $52.763 + 9.1 + 128 + 11.84$

Subtract. See Objective 2.

23.
$$
\begin{array}{r}
6.83 \\
-\ 3.52 \\
\end{array}
$$

24.
$$
\begin{array}{r}
9.47 \\
-\ 5.06 \\
\end{array}
$$

25.
$$
\begin{array}{r}
8.97 \\
-\ 6.22 \\
\end{array}
$$

26.
$$
\begin{array}{r}
7.56 \\
-\ 2.33 \\
\end{array}
$$

Subtract. See Example 2.

27.
$$
\begin{array}{r}
495.4 \\
-\ 153.7 \\
\end{array}
$$

28.
$$
\begin{array}{r}
977.6 \\
-\ 345.8 \\
\end{array}
$$

29.
$$
\begin{array}{r}
878.1 \\
-\ 174.6 \\
\end{array}
$$

30.
$$
\begin{array}{r}
767.2 \\
-\ 614.7 \\
\end{array}
$$

Perform the indicated operation. See Example 3.

31. Subtract 11.065 from 18.3.

32. Subtract 15.041 from 17.8.

33. Subtract 23.037 from 66.9.

34. Subtract 31.089 from 75.6.

Add. See Example 4.

35. $-6.3 + (-8.4)$

36. $-9.2 + (-6.7)$

37. $-9.5 + (-9.3)$

38. $-7.3 + (-5.4)$

Add. See Example 5.

39. $4.12 + (-18.8)$

40. $7.24 + (-19.7)$

41. $6.45 + (-12.6)$

42. $8.81 + (-14.9)$

Subtract. See Example 6.

43. $-62.8 - 3.9$

44. $-56.1 - 8.6$

45. $-42.5 - 2.8$

46. $-93.2 - 3.9$

Subtract. See Example 7.

47. $-4.49 - (-11.3)$

48. $-5.76 - (-13.6)$

49. $-6.78 - (-24.6)$

50. $-8.51 - (-27.4)$

Evaluate each expression. See Example 8.

51. $-11.1 - (-14.4 + 7.8)$

52. $-12.3 - (-13.6 + 7.9)$

53. $-16.4 - (-18.9 + 5.9)$

54. $-15.5 - (-19.8 + 5.7)$

Estimate each sum by rounding the addends to the nearest ten. See Example 9.

55. $510.65 + 279.19$

56. $424.08 + 169.04$

Estimate each difference by using front-end rounding. See Example 9.

57. $671.01 - 88.35$

58. $447.23 - 36.16$

Estimate each sum by using front end rounding. See Example 9.

59. $2,305.891 + 789.442 + 1,090.008 + 450.111$

60. $11,376.3 + 25,908.1 + 34,499.2$

Estimate each difference by rounding the numbers in the subtraction to the nearest hundred. See Example 9.

61. $45,787.16 - 33,422.02$

62. $1,805.4545 - 1,789.6301$

TRY IT YOURSELF

Perform the indicated operations.

63. $-45.6 + 34.7$

64. $-19.04 + 2.4$

65. $46.09 + (-7.8)$

66. $34.7 + (-30.1)$

67.
$$
\begin{array}{r}
21.88 \\
+\ 33.12 \\
\end{array}
$$

68.
$$
\begin{array}{r}
19.05 \\
+\ 31.95 \\
\end{array}
$$

69. $30.03 - (-17.88)$

70. $143.3 - (-64.01)$

71. $645 + 9.90005 + 0.12 + 3.02002$

72. $505.0103 + 23 + 0.989 + 12.0704$

73. Subtract 23.81 from 24.

74. Subtract 5.9 from 7.001.

75. $247.9 + 40 + 0.56$

76. $0.0053 + 1.78 + 6$

77.
$$\begin{array}{r} 78.1 \\ -\ 7.81 \end{array}$$

78.
$$\begin{array}{r} 202.234 \\ -\ 19.34 \end{array}$$

79. $-7.8 + (-6.5)$

80. $-5.78 + (-33.1)$

81. $16 - (67.2 + 6.27)$

82. $-43 - (0.032 - 0.045)$

83. Find the sum of *two and forty-three hundredths* and *five and six tenths.*

84. Find the difference of *nineteen hundredths* and *six thousandths.*

85. $|-14.1 + 6.9| + 8$

86. $15 - |-2.3 + (-2.4)|$

87. $5 - 0.023$

88. $30 - 11.98$

89. $-2.002 - (-4.6)$

90. $-0.005 - (-8)$

CONCEPT EXTENSIONS

The answer for each addition and subtraction shown below is missing a decimal point. Use estimation to determine where to place the decimal point in the answer.

91. a. $146.85 + 38.9 = 18575$
b. $14.685 - 3.89 = 10795$

92. a. $3,640.3 + 2,510.6 = 61509$
b. $364.03 - 251.06 = 11297$

93. a. Round to the nearest ten to estimate the sum: $305.29 + 102.89$
b. Is the estimate less than or greater than the actual sum?
c. By how much do the estimate and actual sum differ?

94. Two different decimals have the form ▮▮.▮▮▮, where the digit in the tens place and the digit in the hundredths place are not zeros. What two decimals of this form would have the greatest possible difference?

APPLICATIONS

95. RETAILING Find the retail price of each appliance listed in the table in the next column if a department store purchases it for the given cost and then marks it up as shown.

Appliance	Cost	Markup	Retail price
Refrigerator	$610.80	$205.00	
Washing machine	$389.50	$155.50	
Dryer	$363.99	$167.50	

96. PRICING Find the retail price of a Kenneth Cole two-button suit if a men's clothing outlet buys them for $210.95 each and then marks them up $144.95 to sell in its stores.

97. OFFSHORE DRILLING A company needs to construct a pipeline from an offshore oil well to a refinery located on the coast. Company engineers have come up with two plans for consideration, as shown. Use the information in the illustration to complete the table.

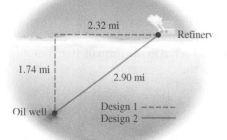

	Pipe underwater (mi)	Pipe underground (mi)	Total pipe (mi)
Design 1			
Design 2			

98. DRIVING DIRECTIONS Find the total distance of the trip using the information in the MapQuest printout shown below.

START 1:	Start out going EAST on SUNKIST AVE.	0.0 mi
2:	Turn LEFT onto MERCED AVE.	0.4 mi
3:	Turn Right onto PUENTE AVE.	0.3 mi
WEST 10 4:	Merge onto I-10 W toward LOS ANGELES.	2.2 mi
SOUTH 605 5:	Merge onto I-605 S.	10.6 mi
SOUTH 5 6:	Merge onto I-5 S toward SANTA ANA.	14.9 mi
110 A EXIT 7:	Take the HARBOR BLVD exit, EXIT 110A.	0.3 mi
8:	Turn RIGHT onto S HARBOR BLVD.	0.1 mi
END 9:	End at 1313 S Harbor Blvd Anaheim, CA.	

Total Distance: ___?___ miles   **MAPQUEST**®

99. PIPE (PVC) Find the *outside* diameter of the plastic sprinkler pipe shown below if the thickness of the pipe wall is 0.218 inch and the inside diameter is 1.939 inches.

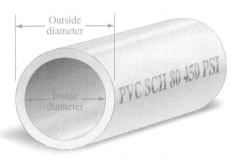

100. pH SCALE The pH scale shown below is used to measure the strength of acids and bases in chemistry. Find the difference in pH readings between

a. bleach and stomach acid.

b. ammonia and coffee.

c. blood and coffee.

Strong acid	Neutral	Strong base
0 1 2 3 4 5 6 7 8 9 10 11 12 13 14		

Stomach acid 1.75   Coffee 5.01   Blood 7.38   Ammonia 12.03   Bleach 12.7

101. RECORD HOLDERS The late Florence Griffith-Joyner of the United States holds the women's world record in the 100-meter sprint: 10.49 seconds. Libby Trickett of Australia holds the women's world record in the 100-meter freestyle swim: 52.88 seconds. How much faster did Griffith-Joyner run the 100 meters than Trickett swam it? (Source: *The World Almanac and Book of Facts,* 2009)

102. WEATHER REPORTS Barometric pressure readings are recorded on the weather map below. In a low-pressure area (L on the map), the weather is often stormy. The weather is usually fair in a high-pressure area (H). What is the difference in readings between the areas of highest and lowest pressure?

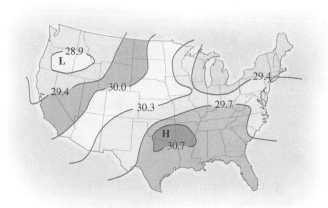

103. BANKING A businesswoman deposited several checks in her company's bank account, as shown on the deposit slip below. Find the *Subtotal* line on the slip by adding the amounts of the checks and total from the reverse side. If the woman wanted to get $25 in cash back from the teller, what should she write as the *Total deposit* on the slip?

Deposit slip

Cash		
Checks (properly endorsed)	116	10
	47	93
Total from reverse side	359	16
Subtotal		
Less cash	25	00
Total deposit		

104. SPORTS PAGES Decimals are often used in the sports pages of newspapers. Two examples are given below.

a. "German bobsledders set a world record today with a final run of 53.03 seconds, finishing ahead of the Italian team by only fourteen thousandths of a second." What was the time for the Italian bobsled team?

b. "The women's figure skating title was decided by only thirty-three hundredths of a point." If the winner's point total was 102.71, what was the second-place finisher's total? (*Hint:* The highest score wins in a figure skating contest.)

105. Suppose certain portions of a patient's morning (A.M.) temperature chart were not filled in. Use the given information to complete the chart below. (*Hint:* 98.6°F is considered normal.)

from Campus to Careers
Home Health Aide

Day of week	Patient's A.M. temperature	Amount above normal
Monday	99.7°	
Tuesday		2.5°
Wednesday	98.6°	
Thursday	100.0°	
Friday		0.9°

106. QUALITY CONTROL An electronics company has strict specifications for the silicon chips it uses in its computers. The company only installs chips that are within 0.05 centimeter of the indicated thickness. The table below gives that specifications for two types of chips. Fill in the blanks to complete the chart.

Chip type	Thickness specification	Acceptable range	
		Low	High
A	0.78 cm		
B	0.643 cm		

107. FLIGHT PATHS Estimate the added distance a plane must travel to avoid flying through the storm.

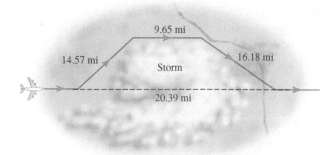

108. TELEVISION The following illustration shows the six most-watched television shows of all time (excluding Super Bowl games and the Olympics).

a. Estimate the combined total audience of all six shows?

b. How many more people watched the last episode of "MASH" than watched the last episode of "Seinfeld"?

c. How many more people would have had to watch the last "Seinfeld" to move it into a tie for fifth place?

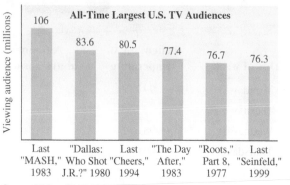

Source: Nielsen Media Research

109. THE HOME SHOPPING NETWORK The illustration shows a description of a cookware set that was sold on television.

a. Find the difference between the manufacturer's suggested retail price (MSRP) and the sale price.

b. Including shipping and handling (S & H), how much will the cookware set cost?

Item 229-442	
Continental 9-piece Cookware Set	
Stainless steel	
MSRP	$149.79
HSN Price	$59.85
On Sale	**$47.85**
S & H	$7.95

110. VEHICLE SPECIFICATIONS Certain dimensions of a compact car are shown. Find the wheelbase of the car.

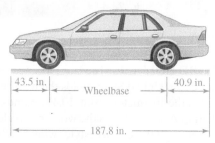

WRITING

111. Explain why we line up the decimal points and corresponding place-value columns when adding decimals.

112. Explain why we can write additional zeros to the right of a decimal such as 7.89 without affecting its value.

113. Explain what is wrong with the work shown below.

$$\begin{array}{r} 203.56 \\ 37 \\ +\;\;\;0.43 \\ \hline 204.36 \end{array}$$

114. Consider the following addition:

$$\begin{array}{r} \overset{2}{23.7} \\ 41.9 \\ +\;12.8 \\ \hline 78.4 \end{array}$$

Explain the meaning of the small red 2 written above the ones column.

115. Write a set of instructions that explains the two-column borrowing process shown below.

$$
\begin{array}{r}
\overset{\overset{9}{4\cancel{10}10}}{2.6\cancel{3}\cancel{0}\,\cancel{0}} \\
- \, 1.3\,2\,4\,6 \\
\hline
1.3\,2\,5\,4
\end{array}
$$

116. Explain why it is easier to add the decimals 0.3 and 0.17 than the fractions $\frac{3}{10}$ and $\frac{17}{100}$.

SECTION 2.9
Multiplying Decimals

Objectives

1 Multiply decimals.

2 Multiply decimals by powers of 10.

3 Multiply signed decimals.

4 Evaluate exponential expressions that have decimal bases.

5 Use the order of operations rule.

6 Evaluate formulas.

7 Estimate products of decimals.

8 Solve application problems by multiplying decimals.

ARE YOU READY?

▼ *The following problems review some basic skills that are needed when multiplying decimals.*

1. Multiply:

$$
\begin{array}{r}
846 \\
\times \; 79 \\
\hline
\end{array}
$$

2. Multiply:
$63 \cdot 1{,}000$

3. Evaluate:
  a. 9^2 **b.** $(-12)^2$

4. Evaluate:
$2(5) - 6(|-3|)^2$

5. Evaluate $2t^2 - 3(t - s)$ for $t = -2$ and $s = 4$

6. Round 351.724 to the nearest tenth.

Since decimal numbers are *base-ten* numbers, multiplication of decimals is similar to multiplication of whole numbers. However, when multiplying decimals, there is one additional step—we must determine where to write the decimal point in the product.

1 Multiply decimals.

To develop a rule for multiplying decimals, we will consider the multiplication $0.3 \cdot 0.17$ and find the product in a roundabout way. First, we write 0.3 and 0.17 as fractions and multiply them in that form. Then we express the resulting fraction as a decimal.

$$
\begin{aligned}
0.3 \cdot 0.17 &= \frac{3}{10} \cdot \frac{17}{100} \quad \text{Express the decimals 0.3 and 0.17 as fractions.} \\[2mm]
&= \frac{3 \cdot 17}{10 \cdot 100} \quad \begin{array}{l}\text{Multiply the numerators.}\\ \text{Multiply the denominators.}\end{array} \\[2mm]
&= \frac{51}{1{,}000} \\[2mm]
&= 0.051 \quad \text{Write the resulting fraction } \tfrac{51}{1{,}000} \text{ as a decimal.}
\end{aligned}
$$

From this example, we can make observations about multiplying decimals.

• The digits in the answer are found by multiplying 3 and 17.

$$
0.3 \;\; \cdot \;\; 0.17 \;\; = \;\; 0.051
$$

$$
3 \cdot 17 = 51
$$

- The answer has 3 decimal places. The *sum* of the number of decimal places in the factors 0.3 and 0.17 is also 3.

These observations illustrate the following rule for multiplying decimals.

Multiplying Decimals

To multiply two decimals:

1. Multiply the decimals as if they were whole numbers.
2. Find the total number of decimal places in both factors.
3. Insert a decimal point in the result from step 1 so that the answer has the same number of decimal places as the total found in step 2.

Self Check 1

Multiply: 2.7 · 4.3

Now Try Problem 9

EXAMPLE 1   Multiply: 5.9 · 3.4

Strategy We will ignore the decimal points and multiply 5.9 and 3.4 as if they were whole numbers. Then we will write a decimal point in that result so that the final answer has two decimal places.

WHY Since the factor 5.9 has 1 decimal place, and the factor 3.4 has 1 decimal place, the product should have 1 + 1 = 2 decimal places.

Solution We write the multiplication in vertical form and proceed as follows:

$$
\begin{array}{r}
\textbf{Vertical form} \qquad 5.9 \leftarrow \text{1 decimal place} \\
\times \quad 3.4 \leftarrow \text{1 decimal place} \\
\hline
236 \\
1770 \\
\hline
20.06
\end{array}
$$

The answer will have 1 + 1 = 2 decimal places.

Move 2 places from the right to the left and insert a decimal point in the answer.

Thus, 5.9 · 3.4 = 20.06.

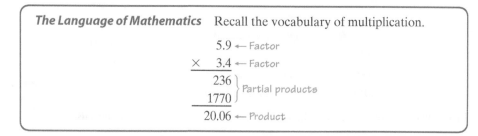

The Language of Mathematics   Recall the vocabulary of multiplication.

$$
\begin{array}{r}
5.9 \leftarrow \text{Factor} \\
\times \quad 3.4 \leftarrow \text{Factor} \\
\hline
\left.\begin{array}{r} 236 \\ 1770 \end{array}\right\} \text{Partial products} \\
\hline
20.06 \leftarrow \text{Product}
\end{array}
$$

Success Tip   When multiplying decimals, we do not need to line up the decimal points, as the next example illustrates.

EXAMPLE 2   Multiply: 1.3(0.005)

Self Check 2
Multiply: (0.0002)7.2
Now Try **Problem 13**

Strategy We will ignore the decimal points and multiply 1.3 and 0.005 as if they were whole numbers. Then we will write a decimal point in that result so that the final answer has four decimal places.

WHY Since the factor 1.3 has 1 decimal place, and the factor 0.005 has 3 decimal places, the product should have $1 + 3 = 4$ decimal places.

Solution Since many students find vertical form multiplication of decimals easier if the decimal with the smaller number of nonzero digits is written on the bottom, we will write 0.005 under 1.3.

$$
\begin{array}{r}
1.3 \leftarrow \text{1 decimal place} \\
\times \quad 0.005 \leftarrow \text{3 decimal places} \\
\hline
0.0065
\end{array}
\left.\begin{array}{l}
\text{The answer will have} \\
1 + 3 = 4 \text{ decimal places.}
\end{array}\right.
$$

Write 2 placeholder zeros in front of 6. Then move 4 places from the right to the left and insert a decimal point in the answer.

Thus, 1.3(0.005) = 0.0065.

EXAMPLE 3   Multiply: 234(5.1)

Self Check 3
Multiply: 178(4.7)
Now Try **Problem 17**

Strategy We will ignore the decimal point and multiply 234 and 5.1 as if they were whole numbers. Then we will write a decimal point in that result so that the final answer has one decimal place.

WHY Since the factor 234 has 0 decimal places, and the factor 5.1 has 1 decimal place, the product should have $0 + 1 = 1$ decimal place.

Solution We write the multiplication in vertical form, with 5.1 under 234.

$$
\begin{array}{r}
234 \leftarrow \text{No decimal places} \\
\times \quad 5.1 \leftarrow \text{1 decimal place} \\
\hline
23\,4 \\
1170\,0 \\
\hline
1193.4
\end{array}
\left.\begin{array}{l}
\text{The answer will have} \\
0 + 1 = 1 \text{ decimal place.}
\end{array}\right.
$$

Move 1 place from the right to the left and insert a decimal point in the answer.

Thus, 234(5.1) = 1,193.4.

Using Your CALCULATOR   **Multiplying Decimals**

When billing a household, a gas company converts the amount of natural gas used to units of heat energy called *therms*. The number of therms used by a household in one month and the cost per therm are shown below.

Customer charge . . . . 39 therms @ $0.72264

To find the total charges for the month, we multiply the number of therms by the cost per therm: 39 · 0.72264.

39 ⟨×⟩ .72264 ⟨=⟩ 28.18296

On some calculator models, the ⟨ENTER⟩ key is pressed to display the product.

$$
\boxed{28.18296}
$$

Rounding to the nearest cent, we see that the total charge is $28.18.

THINK IT THROUGH   *Overtime*

"Employees covered by the Fair Labor Standards Act must receive overtime pay for hours worked in excess of 40 in a workweek of at least 1.5 times their regular rates of pay."

United States Department of Labor

The map of the United States shown below is divided into nine regions. The average hourly wage for private industry workers in each region is also listed in the legend below the map. Find the average hourly wage for the region where you live. Then calculate the corresponding average hourly overtime wage for that region.

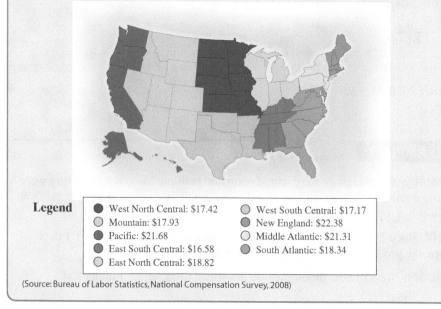

Legend	● West North Central: $17.42	○ West South Central: $17.17
	○ Mountain: $17.93	● New England: $22.38
	● Pacific: $21.68	○ Middle Atlantic: $21.31
	● East South Central: $16.58	○ South Atlantic: $18.34
	○ East North Central: $18.82	

(Source: Bureau of Labor Statistics, National Compensation Survey, 2008)

2   Multiply decimals by powers of 10.

The numbers 10, 100, and 1,000 are called **powers of 10,** because they are the results when we evaluate 10^1, 10^2, and 10^3. To develop a rule to find the product when multiplying a decimal by a power of 10, we multiply 8.675 by three different powers of 10.

Multiply: $8.675 \cdot 10$

$$
\begin{array}{r}
8.675 \\
\times \quad 10 \\
\hline
0000 \\
86750 \\
\hline
86.750
\end{array}
$$

Multiply: $8.675 \cdot 100$

$$
\begin{array}{r}
8.675 \\
\times \quad 100 \\
\hline
0000 \\
00000 \\
867500 \\
\hline
867.500
\end{array}
$$

Multiply: $8.675 \cdot 1{,}000$

$$
\begin{array}{r}
8.675 \\
\times \quad 1000 \\
\hline
0000 \\
00000 \\
000000 \\
8675000 \\
\hline
8675.000
\end{array}
$$

When we inspect the answers, the decimal point in the first factor 8.675 appears to be moved to the right by the multiplication process. The number of decimal places it moves depends on the power of 10 by which 8.675 is multiplied.

One zero in 10

$8.675 \cdot 10 = 86.75$

It moves 1 place to the right.

Two zeros in 100

$8.675 \cdot 100 = 867.5$

It moves 2 places to the right.

Three zeros in 1,000

$8.675 \cdot 1{,}000 = 8675$

It moves 3 places to the right.

These observations illustrate the following rule.

Multiplying a Decimal by 10, 100, 1,000, and So On

To find the product of a decimal and 10, 100, 1,000, and so on, move the decimal point to the right the same number of places as there are zeros in the power of 10.

EXAMPLE 4   Multiply: **a.** $2.81 \cdot 10$ **b.** $0.076(10,000)$

Strategy For each multiplication, we will identify the factor that is a power of 10, and count the number of zeros that it has.

WHY To find the product of a decimal and a power of 10 that is greater than 1, we move the decimal point to the right the same number of places as there are zeros in the power of 10.

Solution

a. $2.81 \cdot 10 = 28.1$ Since 10 has 1 zero, move the decimal point 1 place to the right.

b. $0.076(10,000) = 0760.$ Since 10,000 has 4 zeros, move the decimal point 4 places to the right. Write a placeholder zero (shown in blue).

   $= 760$

Self Check 4

Multiply:

a. $0.721 \cdot 100$

b. $6.08(1,000)$

Now Try **Problems 21 and 23**

Numbers such as 10, 100, and 1,000 are powers of 10 that are *greater than 1*. There are also powers of 10 that are *less than 1*, such as 0.1, 0.01, and 0.001. To develop a rule to find the product when multiplying a decimal by one tenth, one hundredth, one thousandth, and so on, we will consider three examples:

Multiply: $5.19 \cdot 0.1$

$$\begin{array}{r} 5.19 \\ \times \quad 0.1 \\ \hline 0.519 \end{array}$$

Multiply: $5.19 \cdot 0.01$

$$\begin{array}{r} 5.19 \\ \times \quad 0.01 \\ \hline 0.0519 \end{array}$$

Multiply: $5.19 \cdot 0.001$

$$\begin{array}{r} 5.19 \\ \times \quad 0.001 \\ \hline 0.00519 \end{array}$$

When we inspect the answers, the decimal point in the first factor 5.19 appears to be moved to the left by the multiplication process. The number of places that it moves depends on the power of ten by which it is multiplied.

These observations illustrate the following rule.

Multiplying a Decimal by 0.1, 0.01, 0.001, and So On

To find the product of a decimal and 0.1, 0.01, 0.001, and so on, move the decimal point to the left the same number of decimal places as there are in the power of 10.

EXAMPLE 5   Multiply: **a.** $145.8 \cdot 0.01$ **b.** $9.76(0.0001)$

Strategy For each multiplication, we will identify the factor of the form 0.1, 0.01, and 0.001, and count the number of decimal places that it has.

WHY To find the product of a decimal and a power of 10 that is less than 1, we move the decimal point to the left the same number of decimal places as there are in the power of 10.

Solution

a. $145.8 \cdot 0.01 = 1.458$ Since 0.01 has *two* decimal places, move the decimal point in 145.8 two places to the left.

b. $9.76(0.0001) = 0.000976$ Since 0.0001 has *four* decimal places, move the decimal point in 9.76 four places to the left. This requires that three placeholder zeros (shown in blue) be inserted in front of the 9.

Self Check 5

Multiply:

a. $0.1(129.9)$

b. $0.002 \cdot 0.00001$

Now Try **Problems 25 and 27**

Quite often, newspapers, websites, and television programs present large numbers in a shorthand notation that involves a decimal in combination with a place-value column name. For example,

- As of December 31, 2008, Sony had sold *21.3 million* Playstation 3 units worldwide. (Source: Sony Computer Entertainment)
- Boston's Big Dig was the most expensive single highway project in U.S. history. It cost about *$14.63 billion*. (Source: Roadtraffic-technology.com)
- The distance that light travels in one year is about *5.878 trillion* miles. (Source: Encyclopaedia Britannica)

We can use the rule for multiplying a decimal by a power of ten to write these large numbers in standard form.

Self Check 6

Write each number in standard notation:

a. 567.1 million

b. 50.82 billion

c. 4.133 trillion

Now Try Now Try Problems 29, 31, and 33

EXAMPLE 6 Write each number in standard notation:
a. 21.3 million **b.** 14.63 billion **c.** 5.9 trillion

Strategy We will express each of the large numbers as the product of a decimal and a power of 10.

WHY Then we can use the rule for multiplying a decimal by a power of 10 to find their product. The result will be in the required standard form.

Solution

a. 21.3 million = 21.3 · **1 million**

= 21.3 · **1,000,000**   Write 1 million in standard form.

= 21,300,000   Since 1,000,000 has six zeros, move the decimal point in 21.3 six places to the right.

b. 14.63 billion = 14.63 · **1 billion**

= 14.63 · 1,000,000,000   Write 1 billion in standard form.

= 14,630,000,000   Since 1,000,000,000 has nine zeros, move the decimal point in 14.63 nine places to the right.

c. 5.9 trillion = 5.9 · **1 trillion**

= 5.9 · 1,000,000,000,000   Write 1 trillion in standard form.

= 5,900,000,000,000   Since 1,000,000,000,000 has twelve zeros, move the decimal point in 5.9 twelve places to the right.

3 Multiply signed decimals.

The rules for multiplying integers also hold for multiplying signed decimals. The product of two decimals with like signs is positive, and the product of two decimals with unlike signs is negative.

Self Check 7

Multiply:

a. 6.6(−5.5)

b. −44.968(−100)

Now Try Problems 37 and 41

EXAMPLE 7 Multiply: **a.** −1.8(4.5) **b.** (−1,000)(−59.08)

Strategy In part a, we will use the rule for multiplying signed decimals that have different (unlike) signs. In part b, we will use the rule for multiplying signed decimals that have the same (like) signs.

WHY In part a, one factor is negative and one is positive. In part b, both factors are negative.

Solution

a. Find the absolute values: $|-1.8| = 1.8$ and $|4.5| = 4.5$. Since the decimals have unlike signs, their product is negative.

$$-1.8(4.5) = -8.1$$

Multiply the absolute values, 1.8 and 4.5, to get 8.1. Then make the final answer negative.

$$\begin{array}{r} 1.8 \\ \times\ 4.5 \\ \hline 90 \\ 720 \\ \hline 8.10 \end{array}$$

b. Find the absolute values: $|-1{,}000| = 1{,}000$ and $|-59.08| = 59.08$. Since the decimals have like signs, their product is positive.

$$(-1{,}000)(-59.08) = 1{,}000(59.08)$$
$$= 59{,}080$$

Multiply the absolute values, 1,000 and 59.08. Since 1,000 has 3 zeros, move the decimal point in 59.08 3 places to the right. Write a placeholder zero. The answer is positive.

4 Evaluate exponential expressions that have decimal bases.

We have evaluated exponential expressions that have whole number bases, integer bases, and fractional bases. The base of an exponential expression can also be a positive or a negative decimal.

EXAMPLE 8 Evaluate: **a.** $(2.4)^2$ **b.** $(-0.05)^2$

Strategy We will write each exponential expression as a product of repeated factors, and then perform the multiplication. This requires that we identify the base and the exponent.

WHY The exponent tells the number of times the base is to be written as a factor.

Solution

a. $(2.4)^2 = 2.4 \cdot 2.4$ The base is 2.4 and the exponent is 2. Write the base as a factor 2 times.

$= 5.76$ Multiply the decimals.

$$\begin{array}{r} 2.4 \\ \times\ 2.4 \\ \hline 96 \\ 480 \\ \hline 5.76 \end{array}$$

b. $(-0.05)^2 = (-0.05)(-0.05)$ The base is -0.05 and the exponent is 2. Write the base as a factor 2 times.

$= 0.0025$ Multiply the decimals. The product of two decimals with like signs is positive.

$$\begin{array}{r} 0.05 \\ \times\ 0.05 \\ \hline 0.0025 \end{array}$$

Self Check 8

Evaluate:

a. $(-1.3)^2$

b. $(0.09)^2$

Now Try **Problems 45 and 47**

5 Use the order of operations rule.

Recall that the order of operations rule is used to evaluate expressions that involve more than one operation.

EXAMPLE 9 Evaluate: $-(0.6)^2 + 5|-3.6 + 1.9|$

Strategy The absolute value bars are grouping symbols. We will perform the addition within them first.

WHY By the order of operations rule, we must perform all calculations within parentheses and other grouping symbols (such as absolute value bars) first.

Self Check 9

Evaluate:
$-2|-4.4 + 5.6| + (-0.8)^2$

Now Try **Problem 49**

Solution

$-(0.6)^2 + 5|-3.6 + 1.9|$

$= -(0.6)^2 + 5|-1.7|$ Do the addition within the absolute value symbols. Use the rule for adding two decimals with different signs.

$= -(0.6)^2 + 5(1.7)$ Simplify: $|-1.7| = 1.7$.

$= -0.36 + 5(1.7)$ Evaluate: $(0.6)^2 = 0.36$.

$= -0.36 + 8.5$ Do the multiplication: $5(1.7) = 8.5$.

$= 8.14$ Use the rule for adding two decimals with different signs.

$$\begin{array}{r} \overset{2}{\cancel{3}}.\overset{16}{\cancel{6}} \\ -\ 1.9 \\ \hline 1.7 \end{array}$$

$$\begin{array}{r} \overset{3}{1}.7 \\ \times\ \ 5 \\ \hline 8.5 \end{array}$$

$$\begin{array}{r} \overset{4\ 10}{8.\cancel{5}\cancel{0}} \\ -0.36 \\ \hline 8.14 \end{array}$$

6 Evaluate formulas.

Recall that to evaluate a formula, we replace the letters (called **variables**) with specific numbers and then use the order of operations rule.

Self Check 10

Evaluate $V = 1.3\pi r^3$ for $\pi = 3.14$ and $r = 3$.

Now Try Problem 53

EXAMPLE 10   Evaluate the formula $S = 6.28r(h + r)$ for $h = 3.1$ and $r = 6$.

Strategy In the given formula, we will replace the letter r with 6 and h with 3.1.

WHY Then we can use the order of operations rule to find the value of the expression on the right side of the = symbol.

Solution

$S = 6.28r(h + r)$ $6.28r(h + r)$ means $6.28 \cdot r \cdot (h + r)$.

$= 6.28(6)(3.1 + 6)$ Replace r with 6 and h with 3.1.

$= 6.28(6)(9.1)$ Do the addition within the parentheses.

$= 37.68(9.1)$ Do the multiplication: $6.28(6) = 37.68$.

$= 342.888$ Do the multiplication.

$$\begin{array}{r} 37.68 \\ \times\ \ 9.1 \\ \hline 3768 \\ 339120 \\ \hline 342.888 \end{array}$$

7 Estimate products of decimals.

Estimation can be used to determine whether the answer to a decimal multiplication is reasonable. There are several ways to estimate, but the objective is the same: Simplify the numbers in the problem so that the calculations can be made easily and quickly.

Self Check 11

a. Estimate using front-end rounding: $4.337 \cdot 65$

b. Estimate by rounding the factors to the nearest tenth: $3.092 \cdot 11.642$

c. Estimate by rounding: $0.7899(985.34)$

Now Try Problems 61 and 63

EXAMPLE 11

a. Estimate using front-end rounding: $27 \cdot 6.41$

b. Estimate by rounding each factor to the nearest tenth: $13.91 \cdot 5.27$

c. Estimate by rounding: $0.1245(101.4)$

Strategy We will use rounding to approximate the factors. Then we will find the product of the approximations.

WHY Rounding produces factors that contain fewer digits. Such numbers are easier to multiply.

Solution

a. To estimate $27 \cdot 6.41$ by front-end rounding, we begin by rounding both factors to their *largest* place value.

$$\begin{array}{rcl} 27 & \longrightarrow & 30 \quad \text{Round to the nearest ten.} \\ \times\ 6.41 & \longrightarrow & \times\ \ 6 \quad \text{Round to the nearest one.} \\ \hline & & 180 \end{array}$$

The estimate is 180. If we calculate 27 · 6.41, the product is exactly 173.07. The estimate is close: It's about 7 more than 173.07.

b. To estimate 13.91 · 5.27, we will round both decimals to the nearest tenth.

$$
\begin{array}{r}
13.91 \longrightarrow \quad 13.9 \\
\times\ 5.27 \longrightarrow \times\ \underline{5.3} \\
417 \\
\underline{6950} \\
73.67
\end{array}
$$

Round to the nearest tenth.
Round to the nearest tenth.

The estimate is 73.67. If we calculate 13.91 · 5.27, the product is exactly 73.3057. The estimate is close: It's just slightly more than 73.3057.

c. Since 101.4 is approximately 100, we can estimate 0.1245(**101.4**) using 0.1245(**100**).

$$0.1245(100) = 12.45$$

Since 100 has two zeros, move the decimal point in 0.1245 two places to the right.

The estimate is 12.45. If we calculate 0.1245(101.4), the product is exactly 12.6243. Note that the estimate is close: It's slightly less than 12.6243.

8   Solve application problems by multiplying decimals.

Application problems that involve repeated addition are often more easily solved using multiplication.

EXAMPLE 12   *Coins* Banks wrap pennies in rolls of 50 coins. If a penny is 1.55 millimeters thick, how tall is a stack of 50 pennies?

Solution

- There are 50 pennies in a stack.   *Given*
- A penny is 1.55 millimeters thick.   *Given*
- How tall is a stack of 50 pennies?   *Find*

The height (in millimeters) of a stack of 50 pennies, each of which is 1.55 thick, is the sum of fifty 1.55's. This repeated addition can be calculated more simply by multiplication.

The height of a stack of pennies	is equal to	the thickness of one penny	times	the number of pennies in the stack.
The height of stack of pennies	=	1.55	·	50

Use vertical form to perform the multiplication:

$$
\begin{array}{r}
1.55 \\
\times\ \underline{50} \\
000 \\
\underline{7750} \\
77.50
\end{array}
$$

A stack of 50 pennies is 77.5 millimeters tall.

Check We can estimate to check the result. If we use 2 millimeters to approximate the thickness of one penny, then the height of a stack of 50 pennies is about 2 · 50 millimeters = 100 millimeters. The result, 77.5 mm, seems reasonable.

Self Check 12

COINS Banks wrap nickels in rolls of 40 coins. If a nickel is 1.95 millimeters thick, how tall is a stack of 40 nickels?

Now Try **Problem 101**

Sometimes more than one operation is needed to solve a problem involving decimals.

Self Check 13

WEEKLY EARNINGS A pharmacy assistant's basic workweek is 40 hours. After her daily shift is over, she can work overtime at a rate of 1.5 times her regular rate of $15.90 per hour. How much money will she earn in a week if she works 4 hours of overtime?

Now Try **Problem 117**

EXAMPLE 13   *Weekly Earnings*   A cashier's basic workweek is 40 hours. After his daily shift is over, he can work overtime at a rate 1.5 times his regular rate of $13.10 per hour. How much money will he earn in a week if he works 6 hours of overtime?

Solution

- A cashier's basic workweek is 40 hours.   *Given*
- His overtime pay rate is 1.5 times his regular rate of $13.10 per hour. *Given*
- How much money will he earn in a week if he works his regular shift and 6 hours overtime?   *Find*

To find the cashier's overtime pay rate, we multiply 1.5 times his regular pay rate, $13.10.

$$\begin{array}{r} 13.10 \\ \times 1.5 \\ \hline 6550 \\ 13100 \\ \hline 19.650 \end{array}$$

The cashier's overtime pay rate is $19.65 per hour.
We now translate the words of the problem to numbers and symbols.

The total amount the cashier earns in a week	is equal to	40 hours	times	his regular pay rate	plus	the number of overtime hours	times	his overtime rate.
The total amount the cashier earns in a week	=	40	·	$13.10	+	6	·	$19.65

We will use the rule for the order of operations to evaluate the expression:

$$40 \cdot 13.10 + 6 \cdot 19.65 = 524.00 + 117.90 \quad \text{Do the multiplication first.}$$
$$= 641.90 \quad\quad\quad\quad\quad \text{Do the addition.}$$

$$\begin{array}{r} 13.10 \\ \times 40 \\ \hline 0000 \\ 52400 \\ \hline 524.00 \end{array}$$

$$\begin{array}{r} {}^{53\ 3} \\ 19.65 \\ \times 6 \\ \hline 117.90 \end{array}$$

$$\begin{array}{r} {}^{1} \\ 524.00 \\ + 117.90 \\ \hline 641.90 \end{array}$$

The cashier will earn a total of $641.90 for the week.

Check We can use estimation to check. The cashier works 40 hours per week for approximately $13 per hour to earn about 40 · $13 = $520. His 6 hours of overtime at approximately $20 per hour earns him about 6 · $20 = $120. His total earnings that week are about $520 + $120 = $640. The result, $641.90, seems reasonable. ∎

SECTION 2.9   STUDY SET

VOCABULARY

Fill in the blanks.

1. In the multiplication problem shown below, label each *factor,* the *partial products,* and the *product.*

$$\begin{array}{r} 3.4 \leftarrow \\ \times\ 2.6 \leftarrow \\ \hline 204 \leftarrow \\ 680 \leftarrow \\ \hline 8.84 \leftarrow \end{array}$$

2. Numbers such as 10, 100, and 1,000 are called _____ of 10.

CONCEPTS

Fill in the blanks.

3. Insert a decimal point in the correct place for each product shown below. Write placeholder zeros, if necessary.

a. $\begin{array}{r} 3.8 \\ \times\ 0.6 \\ \hline 228 \end{array}$ b. $\begin{array}{r} 1.79 \\ \times\ 8.1 \\ \hline 179 \\ 14320 \\ \hline 14499 \end{array}$

c. $\begin{array}{r} 2.0 \\ \times\ 7 \\ \hline 140 \end{array}$ d. $\begin{array}{r} 0.013 \\ \times\ 0.02 \\ \hline 0026 \end{array}$

4. Fill in the blanks.
   a. To find the product of a decimal and 10, 100, 1,000, and so on, move the decimal point to the _____ the same number of places as there are zeros in the power of 10.
   b. To find the product of a decimal and 0.1, 0.01, 0.001, and so on, move the decimal point to the _____ the same number of places as there are in the power of 10.

5. Determine whether the *sign* of each result is positive or negative. *You do not have to find the product.*
   a. −7.6(−1.8)
   b. −4.09 · 2.274

6. a. When we move its decimal point to the right, does a decimal number get larger or smaller?
   b. When we move its decimal point to the left, does a decimal number get larger or smaller?

NOTATION

7. a. List the first five powers of 10 that are greater than 1.
   b. List the first five powers of 10 that are less than 1.

8. Write each number in standard notation.
   a. one million
   b. one billion
   c. one trillion

GUIDED PRACTICE

Multiply. See Example 1.

9. 4.8 · 6.2   10. 3.5 · 9.3
11. 5.6(8.9)   12. 7.2(8.4)

Multiply. See Example 2.

13. 0.003(2.7)   14. 0.002(2.6)
15. $\begin{array}{r} 5.8 \\ \times\ 0.009 \end{array}$ 16. $\begin{array}{r} 8.7 \\ \times\ 0.004 \end{array}$

Multiply. See Example 3.

17. 179(6.3)   18. 225(4.9)
19. $\begin{array}{r} 316 \\ \times\ 7.4 \end{array}$ 20. $\begin{array}{r} 527 \\ \times\ 3.7 \end{array}$

Multiply. See Example 4.

21. 6.84 · 100   22. 2.09 · 100
23. 0.041(10,000)   24. 0.034(10,000)

Multiply. See Example 5.

25. $647.59 \cdot 0.01$ **26.** $317.09 \cdot 0.01$

27. $1.15(0.001)$ **28.** $2.83(0.001)$

Write each number in standard notation. See Example 6.

29. 14.2 million   **30.** 33.9 million

31. 98.2 billion   **32.** 80.4 billion

33. 1.421 trillion   **34.** 3.056 trillion

35. 657.1 billion   **36.** 422.7 billion

Multiply. See Example 7.

37. $-1.9(7.2)$ **38.** $-5.8(3.9)$

39. $-3.3(-1.6)$ **40.** $-4.7(-2.2)$

41. $(-10,000)(-44.83)$ **42.** $(-10,000)(-13.19)$

43. $678.231(-1,000)$ **44.** $491.565(-1,000)$

Evaluate each expression. See Example 8.

45. $(3.4)^2$ **46.** $(5.1)^2$

47. $(-0.03)^2$ **48.** $(-0.06)^2$

Evaluate each expression. See Example 9.

49. $-(-0.2)^2 + 4|-2.3 + 1.5|$

50. $-(-0.3)^2 + 6|-6.4 + 1.7|$

51. $-(-0.8)^2 + 7|-5.1 - 4.8|$

52. $-(-0.4)^2 + 6|-6.2 - 3.5|$

Evaluate each formula. See Example 10.

53. $A = P + Prt$ for $P = 85.50, r = 0.08,$ and $t = 5$

54. $A = P + Prt$ for $P = 99.95, r = 0.05,$ and $t = 10$

55. $A = lw$ for $l = 5.3$ and $w = 7.2$

56. $A = 0.5bh$ for $b = 7.5$ and $h = 6.8$

57. $P = 2l + 2w$ for $l = 3.7$ and $w = 3.6$

58. $P = a + b + c$ for $a = 12.91, b = 19,$ and $c = 23.6$

59. $C = 2\pi r$ for $\pi = 3.14$ and $r = 2.5$

60. $A = \pi r^2$ for $\pi = 3.14$ and $r = 4.2$

Estimate each product using front-end rounding. See Example 11.

61. $46 \cdot 5.3$ **62.** $37 \cdot 4.29$

Estimate each product by rounding the factors to the nearest tenth. See Example 11.

63. $17.11 \cdot 3.85$ **64.** $18.33 \cdot 6.46$

Estimate each product by rounding the factors to the nearest one. See Example 11.

65. $34.89 \cdot 12.07$

66. $503.4 \cdot 6.88$

Estimate each product by rounding the factors to the nearest hundredth. See Example 11.

67. $0.0256(0.0671)$

68. $0.00911(0.0684)$

▎TRY IT YOURSELF

Perform the indicated operations.

69. $-0.56 \cdot 0.33$ **70.** $-0.64 \cdot 0.79$

71. $(-0.7 - 0.5)(2.4 - 3.1)$

72. $(-8.1 - 7.8)(0.3 + 0.7)$

73. $\begin{array}{r} 0.008 \\ \times\, 0.09 \\ \hline \end{array}$ **74.** $\begin{array}{r} 0.003 \\ \times\, 0.09 \\ \hline \end{array}$

75. $(-5.6)(-2.2)$ **76.** $(-7.1)(-4.1)$

77. $-4.6(23.4 - 19.6)$ **78.** $6.9(9.8 - 8.9)$

79. $(-4.9)(-0.001)$ **80.** $(-0.001)(-7.09)$

81. $(-0.2)^2 + 2(7.1)$ **82.** $(-6.3)(3) - (-1.2)^2$

83. $\begin{array}{r} 2.13 \\ \times\, 4.05 \\ \hline \end{array}$ **84.** $\begin{array}{r} 3.06 \\ \times\, 1.82 \\ \hline \end{array}$

85. $-7(8.1781)$

86. $-5(4.7199)$

87. $-1,000(0.02239)$

88. $-100(0.0897)$

89. $(0.5 + 0.6)^2(-3.2)$

90. $(-5.1)(4.9 - 3.4)^2$

91. $-0.2(306)(-0.4)$

92. $-0.3(417)(-0.5)$

93. $-0.01(|-2.6 - 6.7|)^2$

94. $-0.01(|-8.16 + 9.9|)^2$

Complete each table.

95.

Decimal	Its square
0.1	
0.2	
0.3	
0.4	
0.5	
0.6	
0.7	
0.8	
0.9	

96.

Decimal	Its cube
0.1	
0.2	
0.3	
0.4	
0.5	
0.6	
0.7	
0.8	
0.9	

CONCEPT EXTENSIONS

The answer for each multiplication shown below is missing a decimal point. Use estimation to determine where to place the decimal point in the answer.

97. $7.436(5.89) = 4379804$

98. $1.45 \cdot 8.9 = 12905$

99. a. Round each factor to the nearest tenth to estimate the product: $4.68 \cdot 3.72$
 b. Is the estimate greater than or less than the actual product?
 c. By how much do the estimate and actual product differ?

100. a. Find two decimals (each less than 1) such that their product contains exactly three nonzero digits to the right of the decimal point.
 b. Find two decimals (each greater than 1) such that their product contains exactly four nonzero digits to the right of the decimal point.

APPLICATIONS

101. REAMS OF PAPER Find the thickness of a 500-sheet ream of copier paper if each sheet is 0.0038 inch thick.

102. MILEAGE CLAIMS Each month, a salesman is reimbursed by his company for any work-related travel that he does in his own car at the rate of $0.445 per mile. How much will the salesman receive if he traveled a total of 120 miles in his car on business in the month of June?

103. SALARIES Use the following formula and estimate the annual salary of a recording engineer who works 38 hours per week at a rate of $37.35 per hour.

$$\frac{\text{Annual}}{\text{salary}} = \frac{\text{hourly}}{\text{rate}} \cdot \frac{\text{hours}}{\text{per week}} \cdot 52.2 \text{ weeks}$$

104. PAYCHECKS If you are paid every other week, your monthly gross income is your gross income from one paycheck times 2.17. Find the monthly gross income of a supermarket clerk who earns $1,095.70 every two weeks. Round the result to the nearest cent.

105. BAKERY SUPPLIES A bakery buys various types of nuts as ingredients for cookies. Complete the table by filling in the cost of each purchase.

Type of nut	Price per pound	Pounds	Cost
Almonds	$5.95	16	
Walnuts	$4.95	25	

106. NEW HOMES
 a. Estimate the cost to build the home shown below if construction costs are $92.55 per square foot.
 b. What would be the exact cost?

House Plan #DP-2203					
Square Feet:	**2,291 Sq Ft.**	Width:	**70'70"**	Bedrooms:	**3**
Stories:	**Single Story**	Depth:	**64'0"**	Bathrooms:	**3**
				Garage Bays:	**2**

107. BIOLOGY Cells contain DNA. In humans, it determines such traits as eye color, hair color, and height. A model of DNA appears below. If 1 Å (angstrom) = 0.000000004 inch, find the dimensions of 34 Å, 3.4 Å, and 10 Å, shown in the illustration.

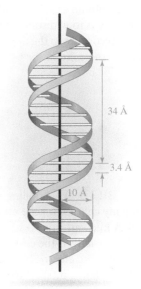

108. TACHOMETERS
 a. Estimate the decimal number to which the tachometer needle points in the illustration below.
 b. What engine speed (in rpm) does the tachometer indicate?

109. CITY PLANNING The streets shown in blue on the city map below are 0.35 mile apart. Find the distance of each trip between the two given locations.

a. The airport to the Convention Center

b. City Hall to the Convention Center

c. The airport to the Convention Center and then to City Hall

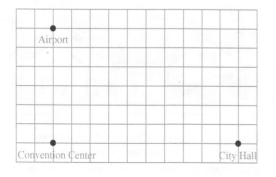

110. RETROFITS The illustration below shows the current widths of the three columns of a freeway overpass. A computer analysis indicated that the width of each column should actually be 1.4 times what it currently is to withstand the stresses of an earthquake. According to the analysis, how wide should each of the columns be?

111. ELECTRIC BILLS When billing a household, a utility company charges for the number of kilowatt-hours used. A kilowatt-hour (kwh) is a standard measure of electricity. If the cost of 1 kwh is $0.14277, what is the electric bill for a household that uses 719 kwh in a month? Round the answer to the nearest cent.

112. UTILITY TAXES Some gas companies are required to tax the number of therms used each month by the customer. What are the taxes collected on a monthly usage of 31 therms if the tax rate is $0.00566 per therm? Round the answer to the nearest cent.

113. Write each highlighted number in standard form.

a. CONSERVATION The *19.6-million acre* Arctic National Wildlife Refuge is located in the northeast corner of Alaska. (Source: National Wildlife Federation)

b. POPULATION According to projections by the International Programs Center at the U.S. Census Bureau, at 7:16 P.M. eastern time on Saturday, February 25, 2006, the population of the Earth hit *6.5 billion* people.

c. DRIVING The U.S. Department of Transportation estimated that Americans drove a total of *3.026 trillion miles* in 2008. (Source: Federal Highway Administration)

114. Write each highlighted number in standard form.

a. MILEAGE Irv Gordon, of Long Island, New York, has driven a record *2.6 million miles* in his 1966 Volvo P-1800. (Source: autoblog.com)

b. E-COMMERCE Online spending during the 2008 holiday season (November 1 through December 23) was about *$25.5 billion.* (Source: pcmag.com)

c. FEDERAL DEBT On March 27, 2009, the U.S. national debt was *$11.073 trillion.* (Source: National Debt Clock)

115. SOCCER A soccer goal is rectangular and measures 24 feet wide by 8 feet high. Major league soccer officials are proposing to increase its width by 1.5 feet and increase its height by 0.75 foot.

a. What is the area of the goal opening now?

b. What would the area be if the proposal is adopted?

c. How much area would be added?

116. SALT INTAKE Studies done by the Centers for Disease Control and Prevention found that the average American eats 3.436 grams of salt each day. The recommended amount is 1.5 grams per day. How many more grams of salt does the average American eat in one week compared with what the Center recommends?

117. CONCERT SEATING Two types of tickets were sold for a concert. Floor seating costs $12.50 a ticket, and balcony seats cost $15.75.

a. Complete the following table and find the receipts from each type of ticket.

b. Find the total receipts from the sale of both types of tickets.

Ticket type	Price	Number sold	Receipts
Floor		1,000	
Balcony		100	

118. PLUMBING BILLS A corner of the invoice for plumbing work is torn. What is the labor charge for the 4 hours of work? What is the total charge (standard service charge, parts, labor)?

Carter Plumbing 100 W. Dalton Ave.		Invoice #210
Standard service charge	$	25.75
Parts	$	38.75
Labor: 4 hr @ $40.55/hr	$	
Total charges	$	

119. WEIGHTLIFTING The barbell is evenly loaded with iron plates. How much plate weight is loaded on the barbell?

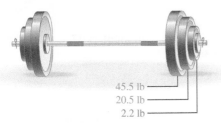

45.5 lb
20.5 lb
2.2 lb

120. SWIMMING POOLS Long bricks, called *coping*, can be used to outline the edge of a swimming pool. How many meters of coping will be needed in the construction of the swimming pool shown?

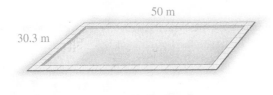

50 m

30.3 m

121. STORM DAMAGE After a rainstorm, the saturated ground under a hilltop house began to give way. A survey team noted that the house dropped 0.57 inch initially. In the next three weeks, the house fell 0.09 inch per week. How far did the house fall because of the rain?

122. WATER USAGE In May, the water level of a reservoir reached its high mark for the year. During the summer months, as water usage increased, the level dropped. In the months of May and June, it fell 4.3 feet each month. In August and September, because of high temperatures, it fell another 8.7 feet each month. By the beginning of October, how far below the year's high mark had the water level fallen?

WRITING

123. Explain how to determine where to place the decimal point in the answer when multiplying two decimals.

124. List the similarities and differences between whole-number multiplication and decimal multiplication.

125. Explain how to multiply a decimal by a power of 10 that is greater than 1, and by a power of ten that is less than 1.

126. Is it easier to multiply the decimals 0.4 and 0.16 or the fractions $\frac{4}{10}$ and $\frac{16}{100}$? Explain why.

127. Why do we have to line up the decimal points when adding, but we do not have to when multiplying?

128. Which vertical form for the following multiplication do you like better? Explain why.

$$\begin{array}{r} 0.000003 \\ \times \quad 2.7 \end{array} \qquad \begin{array}{r} 2.7 \\ \times\ 0.000003 \end{array}$$

SECTION 2.10

Applications Introduction: Estimation with Decimals

In Sections 2.8 and 2.9, we studied estimation methods for decimal addition, subtraction, and multiplication. We used two types of rounding to find approximations of sums, differences, and products. The procedure to estimate the quotient of a decimal division requires a bit more insight. With this method, we round the divisor and the dividend so that they divide exactly (no remainder). This often requires the use of the concept of *multiple*.

Recall that the **multiples of a number** are the products of that number and 1, 2, 3, 4, 5, and so on. For example, the first 10 multiples of 8 are 8, 16, 24, 32, 40, 48, 56, 64, 72, and 80.

$8 \cdot 1 = 8$	$8 \cdot 6 = 48$
$8 \cdot 2 = 16$	$8 \cdot 7 = 56$
$8 \cdot 3 = 24$	$8 \cdot 8 = 64$
$8 \cdot 4 = 32$	$8 \cdot 9 = 72$
$8 \cdot 5 = 40$	$8 \cdot 10 = 80$

To estimate quotients, we begin by rounding the divisor and dividend in such a way that the dividend is a *multiple of the divisor*. If possible, round both numbers up or both numbers down. After rounding, you will see that division with the approximations is much easier to perform and results in a whole-number quotient.

EXAMPLE 1   Estimate 5,562.184 ÷ 71.9

Strategy We will round the dividend (5,562.184) and the divisor (71.9) up and find 5,600 ÷ 80.

WHY The estimation is easier if the dividend and the divisor end with zeros. Also, 80 divides 5,600 exactly because 5,600 is a multiple of 80.

Solution

The dividend is approximately

$$5,562.184 \div 71.9 \qquad 5,600 \div 80 = 70$$

The divisor is approximately

To divide, drop one zero from 5,600 and from 80, and find 560 ÷ 8.

The estimate is 70.

If we calculate 5,562.184 ÷ 71.9, the exact quotient is 77.36. Note that the estimate is close: it's 7.36 less than 77.36.

Objectives

1. Divide a decimal by a whole number.

2. Divide a decimal by a decimal.

3. Round a decimal quotient.

4. Estimate quotients of decimals.

5. Divide decimals by powers of 10.

6. Divide signed decimals.

7. Use the order of operations rule.

8. Evaluate formulas.

9. Solve application problems by dividing decimals.

SECTION 2.10
Dividing Decimals

ARE YOU READY?

The following problems review some basic skills that are needed when dividing decimals.

1. Divide: $9\overline{)1,962}$

2. Divide: $28\overline{)19,712}$

3. Divide: $\dfrac{125,000}{5,000}$

4. Divide: $\dfrac{-12}{-4}$

5. Evaluate: $\dfrac{-4(-5) - 2}{3 - 3^2}$

6. Round 54.0912 to the nearest hundredth.

We use a process called long division to divide whole numbers.

Long division form

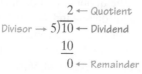

$$
\begin{array}{r}
2 \leftarrow \text{Quotient} \\
\text{Divisor} \rightarrow 5\overline{)10} \leftarrow \text{Dividend} \\
\underline{10} \\
0 \leftarrow \text{Remainder}
\end{array}
$$

In this section, we consider division problems in which the divisor, the dividend, or both are decimals.

1   Divide a decimal by a whole number.

To develop a rule for decimal division, let's consider the problem $47 \div 10$. If we rewrite the division as $\frac{47}{10}$, we can use the long division method for changing an improper fraction to a mixed number to find the answer:

Here the result is written in $quotient + \dfrac{remainder}{divisor}$ form.

To perform this same division using decimals, we write 47 as 47.0 and divide as we would divide whole numbers.

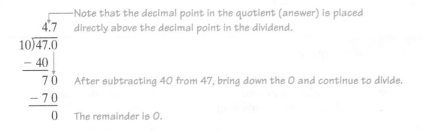

Note that the decimal point in the quotient (answer) is placed directly above the decimal point in the dividend.

After subtracting 40 from 47, bring down the 0 and continue to divide.

The remainder is 0.

Since $4\frac{7}{10} = 4.7$, either method gives the same answer. This result suggests the following method for dividing a decimal by a whole number.

Dividing a Decimal by a Whole Number

To divide a decimal by a whole number:

1.   Write the problem in long division form and place a decimal point in the quotient (answer) directly above the decimal point in the dividend.
2.   Divide as if working with whole numbers.
3.   If necessary, additional zeros can be written to the right of the last digit of the dividend to continue the division.

EXAMPLE 1   Divide: $42.6 \div 6$. Check the result.

Strategy Since the divisor, 6, is a whole number, we will write the problem in long division form and place a decimal point directly above the decimal point in 42.6. Then we will divide as if the problem was $426 \div 6$.

WHY To divide a decimal by a whole number, we divide as if working with whole numbers.

Solution
Step 1

Place a decimal point in the quotient that lines up with the decimal point in the dividend.

$$6\overline{)42.6}$$

Step 2 Now divide using the four-step division process: **estimate, multiply, subtract, and bring down.**

Self Check 1

Divide: $20.8 \div 4$. Check the result.

Now Try Problem 15

```
      7.1
  6)42.6      Ignore the decimal points and divide as if working with whole numbers.
  − 42
    0 6       After subtracting 42 from 42, bring down the 6 and continue to divide.
  −  6
     0        The remainder is 0.
```

Decimal division is checked in the same way: *The product of the quotient and the divisor should be the dividend.*

```
   7.1  ← Quotient        7.1
 ×   6  ← Divisor       6)42.6
  42.6  ← Dividend
```

The check confirms that $42.6 \div 6 = 7.1$.

Self Check 2

Divide: $101.44 \div 32$

Now Try Problem 19

EXAMPLE 2   Divide: $71.68 \div 28$

Strategy Since the divisor is a whole number, 28, we will write the problem in long division form and place a decimal point directly above the decimal point in 71.68. Then we will divide as if the problem was $7,168 \div 28$.

WHY To divide a decimal by a whole number, we divide as if working with whole numbers.

Solution

Write the decimal point in the quotient (answer) directly above the decimal point in the dividend.

```
      2.56      Ignore the decimal points and divide as if working
  28)71.68      with whole numbers.
  − 56
    15 6        After subtracting 56 from 71, bring down the 6
  − 14 0        and continue to divide.
     1 68       After subtracting 140 from 156, bring down the 8
   − 1 68       and continue to divide.
       0        The remainder is 0.
```

We can use multiplication to check this result.

```
    2.56
  ×   28              2.56
    2048          28)71.68
    5120
   71.68
```

The check confirms that $71.68 \div 28 = 2.56$.

Self Check 3

Divide: $42.8 \div 8$

Now Try Problem 23

EXAMPLE 3   Divide: $19.2 \div 5$

Strategy We will write the problem in long division form, place a decimal point directly above the decimal point in 19.2, and divide. If necessary, we will write additional zeros to the right of the 2 in 19.2.

WHY Writing additional zeros to the right of the 2 allows us to continue the division process until we obtain a remainder of 0 or the digits in the quotient repeat in a pattern.

Solution

$$
\begin{array}{r}
3.8 \\
5\overline{)19.2} \\
-15 \downarrow \\
\hline
4\,2 \\
-4\,0 \\
\hline
2
\end{array}
$$

After subtracting 15 from 19, bring down the 2 and continue to divide.

All the digits in the dividend have been used, but the remainder is not 0.

We can write a zero to the right of 2 in the dividend and continue the division process. Recall that writing additional zeros to the right of the decimal point does not change the value of the decimal. That is, $19.2 = 19.20$.

$$
\begin{array}{r}
3.84 \\
5\overline{)19.20} \\
-15 \\
\hline
4\,2 \\
-4\,0\downarrow \\
\hline
20 \\
-20 \\
\hline
0
\end{array}
$$

Write a zero to the right of the 2 and bring it down.

Continue to divide.

The remainder is 0.

Check:

$$
\begin{array}{r}
3.84 \\
\times 5 \\
\hline
19.20
\end{array}
$$
← Since this is the dividend, the result checks.

2   Divide a decimal by a decimal.

To develop a rule for division involving a decimal divisor, let's consider the problem $0.36\overline{)0.2592}$, where the divisor is the decimal 0.36. First, we express the division in fraction form.

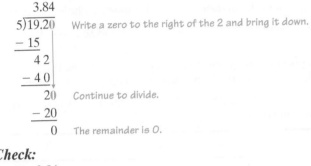

$0.36\overline{)0.2592}$ can be represented by $\dfrac{0.2592}{0.36}$

Divisor

To be able to use the rule for dividing decimals by a *whole number* discussed earlier, we need to move the decimal point in the divisor 0.36 two places to the right. This can be accomplished by multiplying it by 100. However, if the denominator of the fraction is multiplied by 100, the numerator must also be multiplied by 100 so that the fraction maintains the same value. It follows that $\frac{100}{100}$ is the form of 1 that we should use to build $\frac{0.2592}{0.36}$.

$$
\begin{aligned}
\frac{0.2592}{0.36} &= \frac{0.2592}{0.36} \cdot \frac{100}{100} && \text{Multiply by a form of 1.} \\[2mm]
&= \frac{0.2592 \cdot 100}{0.36 \cdot 100} && \begin{array}{l}\text{Multiply the numerators.} \\ \text{Multiply the denominators.}\end{array} \\[2mm]
&= \frac{25.92}{36} && \begin{array}{l}\text{Multiplying both decimals by 100 moves} \\ \text{their decimal points two places to the right.}\end{array}
\end{aligned}
$$

This fraction represents the division problem $36\overline{)25.92}$. From this result, we have the following observations.

- The division problem $0.36\overline{)0.2592}$ is equivalent to $36\overline{)25.92}$; that is, they have the same answer.

• The decimal points in *both* the divisor and the dividend of the first division problem have been moved two decimal places to the right to create the second division problem.

$$0.36\overline{)0.2592} \qquad \text{becomes} \qquad 36\overline{)25.92}$$

These observations illustrate the following rule for division with a decimal divisor.

Division with a Decimal Divisor

To divide with a decimal divisor:

1. Write the problem in long division form.
2. Move the decimal point of the divisor so that it becomes a whole number.
3. Move the decimal point of the dividend the same number of places to the right.
4. Write the decimal point in the quotient (answer) directly above the decimal point in the dividend. Divide as if working with whole numbers.
5. If necessary, additional zeros can be written to the right of the last digit of the dividend to continue the division.

Self Check 4

Divide: $\dfrac{0.6045}{0.65}$

Now Try Problem 27

EXAMPLE 4 Divide: $\dfrac{0.2592}{0.36}$

Strategy We will move the decimal point of the divisor, 0.36, two places to the right and we will move the decimal point of the dividend, 0.2592, the same number of places to the right.

WHY We can then use the rule for dividing a decimal by a *whole number*.

Solution We begin by writing the problem in long division form.

0 36$\overline{)0\ 25\ .\ 92}$ *Move the decimal point two places to the right in the divisor and the dividend. Write the decimal point in the quotient (answer) directly above the decimal point in the dividend.*

Since the divisor is now a whole number, we can use the rule for dividing a decimal by a whole number to find the quotient.

$$
\begin{array}{r}
0.72 \\
36\overline{)25.92} \\
-25\ 2 \\
\hline
72 \\
-72 \\
\hline
0
\end{array}
$$

Now divide as with whole numbers.

Check:

$$
\begin{array}{r}
0.72 \\
\times\ \ \ 36 \\
\hline
432 \\
2160 \\
\hline
25.92
\end{array}
$$

Since this is the dividend, the result checks.

Success Tip When dividing decimals, moving the decimal points the same number of places to the right in *both* the divisor and the dividend does not change the answer.

3 Round a decimal quotient.

In Example 4, the division process stopped after we obtained a 0 from the second subtraction. Sometimes when we divide, the subtractions never give a zero remainder, and the division process continues forever. In such cases, we can round the result.

EXAMPLE 5 Divide: $\dfrac{9.35}{0.7}$. Round the quotient to the nearest hundredth.

Strategy We will use the methods of this section to divide to the thousandths column.

WHY To round to the hundredths column, we need to continue the division process for one more decimal place, which is the thousandths column.

Solution We begin by writing the problem in long division form.

$$0\,7)\overline{93\,.\,5}$$

To write the divisor as a whole number, move the decimal point one place to the right. Do the same for the dividend. Place the decimal point in the quotient (answer) directly above the decimal point in the dividend.

We need to write two zeros to the right of the last digit of the dividend so that we can divide to the thousandths column.

$$7)\overline{93.500}$$

After dividing to the thousandths column, we round to the hundredths column.

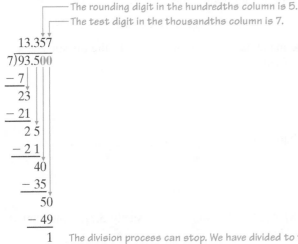

The rounding digit in the hundredths column is 5.
The test digit in the thousandths column is 7.

Since the test digit 7 is 5 or greater, we will round 13.357 up to approximate the quotient to the nearest hundredth.

$$\frac{9.35}{0.7} \approx 13.36 \qquad \text{Read} \approx \text{as "is approximately equal to."}$$

Check:

```
    13.36  ← The approximation of the quotient
×    0.7   ← The original divisor
  9.352    ← Since this is close to the original dividend, 9.35, the result seems reasonable.
```

Success Tip To round a quotient to a certain decimal place value, continue the division process one more column to its right to find the *test digit.*

Self Check 5

Divide: $12.82 \div 0.9$. Round the quotient to the nearest hundredth.

Now Try **Problem 33**

Using Your **CALCULATOR**   **Dividing Decimals**

The nucleus of a cell contains vital information about the cell in the form of DNA. The nucleus is very small: A typical animal cell has a nucleus that is only 0.00023622 inch across. How many nuclei (plural of *nucleus*) would have to be laid end to end to extend to a length of 1 inch?

To find how many 0.00023622-inch lengths there are in 1 inch, we must use division: 1 ÷ 0.00023622.

1 ÷ .00023622 = $\boxed{4233.3418}$

On some calculators, we press the $\boxed{\text{ENTER}}$ key to display the quotient.

It would take approximately 4,233 nuclei laid end to end to extend to a length of 1 inch.

4 Estimate quotients of decimals.

There are many ways to make an error when dividing decimals. Estimation is a helpful tool that can be used to determine whether or not an answer seems reasonable.

To estimate quotients, we use a method that approximates both the dividend and the divisor so that they divide easily. There is one rule of thumb for this method: If possible, round both numbers up or both numbers down.

Self Check 6

Estimate the quotient:
6,229.249 ÷ 68.9

Now Try **Problems 35 and 39**

EXAMPLE 6   Estimate the quotient: 248.687 ÷ 43.1

Strategy We will round the dividend and the divisor down and find 240 ÷ 40.

WHY The division can be made easier if the dividend and the divisor end with zeros. Also, 40 divides 240 exactly.

Solution

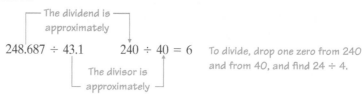

The estimate is 6.

If we calculate 248.687 ÷ 43.1, the quotient is exactly 5.77. Note that the estimate is close: It's just 0.23 more than 5.77.

5 Divide decimals by powers of 10.

To develop a set of rules for division of decimals by a power of 10, we consider the problems 8.13 ÷ 10 and 8.13 ÷ 0.1.

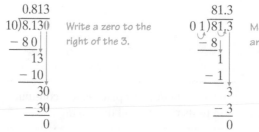

Note that the quotients, 0.813 and 81.3, and the dividend, 8.13, are the same except for the location of the decimal points. The first quotient, 0.813, can be easily obtained by moving the decimal point of the dividend one place to the left. The second quotient, 81.3, is easily obtained by moving the decimal point of the dividend one place to the right. These observations illustrate the following rules for dividing a decimal by a power of 10.

Dividing a Decimal by 10, 100, 1,000, and So On

To find the quotient of a decimal and 10, 100, 1,000, and so on, move the decimal point to the left the same number of places as there are zeros in the power of 10.

Dividing a Decimal by 0.1, 0.01, 0.001, and So On

To find the quotient of a decimal and 0.1, 0.01, 0.001, and so on, move the decimal point to the right the same number of decimal places as there are in the power of 10.

EXAMPLE 7   Find each quotient:

a. $16.74 \div 10$ **b.** $8.6 \div 10,000$ **c.** $\dfrac{290.623}{0.01}$

Strategy We will identify the divisor in each division. If it is a power of 10 greater than 1, we will count the number of zeros that it has. If it is a power of 10 less than 1, we will count the number of decimal places that it has.

WHY Then we will know how many places to the right or left to move the decimal point in the dividend to find the quotient.

Solution

a. $16.74 \div 10 = 1.674$ Since the divisor 10 has one zero, move the decimal point one place to the left.

b. $8.6 \div 10,000 = .00086$ Since the divisor 10,000 has four zeros, move the decimal point four places to the left. Write three placeholder zeros (shown in blue).

$\qquad\qquad\quad = 0.00086$

c. $\dfrac{290.623}{0.01} = 29062.3$ Since the divisor 0.01 has two decimal places, move the decimal point in 290.623 two places to the right.

Self Check 7

Find each quotient:

a. $721.3 \div 100$

b. $\dfrac{1.07}{1,000}$

c. $19.4407 \div 0.0001$

Now Try Problems 43 and 49

6 Divide signed decimals.

The rules for dividing integers also hold for dividing signed decimals. The quotient of two decimals with *like signs* is positive, and the quotient of two decimals with *unlike signs* is negative.

EXAMPLE 8   Divide: **a.** $-104.483 \div 16.3$ **b.** $\dfrac{-38.677}{-0.1}$

Strategy In part a, we will use the rule for dividing signed decimals that have different (unlike) signs. In part b, we will use the rule for dividing signed decimals that have the same (like) signs.

WHY In part a, the divisor is positive and the dividend is negative. In part b, both the dividend and divisor are negative.

Self Check 8

Divide:

a. $-100.624 \div 15.2$

b. $\dfrac{-23.9}{-0.1}$

***Now Try* Problems 51 and 55**

Solution

a. First, we find the absolute values: $|-104.483| = 104.483$ and $|16.3| = 16.3$. Then we divide the absolute values, 104.483 by 16.3, using the methods of this section.

$$
\begin{array}{r}
6.41 \\
163\overline{)1044.83} \\
-978 \\
\hline
66\,8 \\
-65\,20 \\
\hline
1\,63 \\
-1\,63 \\
\hline
0
\end{array}
$$

Move the decimal point in the divisor and the dividend one place to the right.

Write the decimal point in the quotient (answer) directly above the decimal point in the dividend.

Divide as if working with whole numbers.

Since the signs of the original dividend and divisor are unlike, we make the final answer negative. Thus,

$$-104.483 \div 16.3 = -6.41$$

Check the result using multiplication.

b. We can use the rule for dividing a decimal by a power of 10 to find the quotient.

$$\frac{-38.677}{-0.1} = 386.77$$

Since the divisor 0.1 has one decimal place, move the decimal point in 38.677 one place to the right. Since the dividend and divisor have like signs, the quotient is positive.

7 Use the order of operations rule.

Recall that the order of operations rule is used to evaluate expressions that involve more than one operation.

Self Check 9

Evaluate: $\dfrac{2.7756 + 3(-0.63)}{0.4 - 1.2}$

***Now Try* Problem 59**

EXAMPLE 9   Evaluate: $\dfrac{2(0.351) + 0.5592}{0.2 - 0.6}$

Strategy We will evaluate the expression above and the expression below the fraction bar separately. Then we will do the indicated division, if possible.

WHY Fraction bars are grouping symbols. They group the numerator and denominator.

Solution

$$\frac{2(0.351) + 0.5592}{0.2 - 0.6}$$

$$= \frac{0.702 + 0.5592}{-0.4}$$

In the numerator, do the multiplication.
In the denominator, do the subtraction.

$$= \frac{1.2612}{-0.4}$$

In the numerator, do the addition.

$$= -3.153$$

Do the division indicated by the fraction bar. The quotient of two numbers with unlike signs is negative.

$$
\begin{array}{r}
\overset{1}{0.351} \\
\times \quad 2 \\
\hline
0.702
\end{array}
\qquad
\begin{array}{r}
\overset{1}{0.7}\overset{1}{0}20 \\
+ 0.5592 \\
\hline
1.2612
\end{array}
$$

$$
\begin{array}{r}
3.153 \\
4\overline{)12.612} \\
-12 \\
\hline
6 \\
-4 \\
\hline
21 \\
-20 \\
\hline
12 \\
-12 \\
\hline
0
\end{array}
$$

8 Evaluate formulas.

EXAMPLE 10   Evaluate the formula $b = \dfrac{2A}{h}$ for $A = 15.36$ and $h = 6.4$.

Strategy In the given formula, we will replace the letter A with 15.36 and h with 6.4.

WHY Then we can use the order of operations rule to find the value of the expression on the right side of the = symbol.

Solution

$b = \dfrac{2A}{h}$ This is the given formula.

$= \dfrac{2(15.36)}{6.4}$ Replace A with 15.36 and h with 6.4.

$= \dfrac{30.72}{6.4}$ In the numerator, do the multiplication.

$= 4.8$ Do the division indicated by the fraction bar.

$$\begin{array}{r} \overset{1}{1}\overset{1}{5}.36 \\ \times \quad 2 \\ \hline 30.72 \end{array}$$

$$\begin{array}{r} 4.8 \\ 64\overline{)307.2} \\ -256 \\ \hline 51\,2 \\ -51\,2 \\ \hline 0 \end{array}$$

Self Check 10

Evaluate the formula $l = \dfrac{A}{w}$ for $A = 5.511$ and $w = 1.002$.

Now Try **Problem 63**

9 Solve application problems by dividing decimals.

Recall that application problems that involve forming equal-sized groups can be solved by division.

EXAMPLE 11   *French Bread* A bread slicing machine cuts 25-inch-long loaves of French bread into 0.625-inch-thick slices. How many slices are there in one loaf?

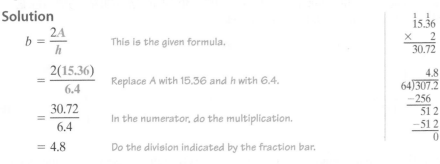

Solution

- 25-inch-long loaves of French bread are cut into slices.   Given
- Each slice is 0.625-inch thick.   Given
- How many slices are there in one loaf?   Find

Self Check 11

FRUIT CAKES A 9-inch-long fruit-cake loaf is cut into 0.25-inch-thick slices. How many slices are there in one fruitcake?

Now Try **Problem 99**

Cutting a loaf of French bread into equally thick slices indicates division. We translate the words of the problem to numbers and symbols.

The number of slices in a loaf of French bread	is equal to	the length of the loaf of French bread	divided by	the thickness of one slice.
The number of slices in a loaf of French bread	=	25	÷	0.625

When we write $25 \div 0.625$ in long division form, we see that the divisor is a decimal.

$0.625\overline{)25.000}$ To write the divisor as a whole number, move the decimal point three places to the right. To move the decimal point three places to the right in the dividend, three placeholder zeros must be inserted (shown in blue).

Now that the divisor is a whole number, we can perform the division.

$$
\begin{array}{r}
40 \\
625\overline{)25000} \\
-2500 \\
\hline
00 \\
-0 \\
\hline
0
\end{array}
$$

There are 40 slices in one loaf of French bread.

Check The multiplication below verifies that 40 slices, each 0.625-inch thick, makes a 25-inch-long loaf. The result checks.

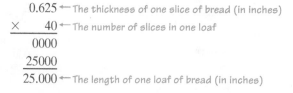

Recall that the **arithmetic mean,** or **average,** of several numbers is a value around which the numbers are grouped. We use addition and division to find the mean (average).

Self Check 12

U.S. NATIONAL PARKS Use the following data to determine the average number of visitors per year to the national parks for the years 2004 through 2008. (Source: National Park Service)

Year	Visitors (millions)
2008	2.749
2007	2.756
2006	2.726
2005	2.735
2004	2.769

Now Try Problem 107

EXAMPLE 12   *Comparison Shopping*   An online shopping website, Shopping.com, listed the four best prices for an automobile GPS receiver as shown below. What is the mean (average) price of the GPS?

Strategy We will add 169.99, 182.65, 194.84, and 204.48 and divide the sum by 4.

WHY To find the mean (average) of a set of values, we divide the sum of the values by the number of values.

Solution

$$
\text{Mean} = \frac{169.99 + 182.65 + 194.84 + 204.48}{4}
$$
Since there are 4 prices, divide the sum by 4.

$$
= \frac{751.96}{4}
$$
In the numerator, do the addition.

$$
= 187.99
$$
Do the indicated division.

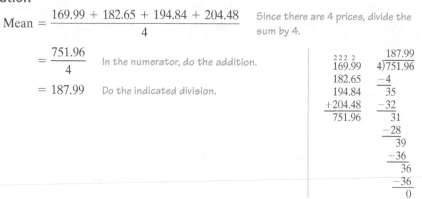

The mean (average) price of the GPS receiver is $187.99.

THINK IT THROUGH   *GPA*

"In considering all of the factors that are important to employers as they recruit students in colleges and universities nationwide, college major, grade point average, and work-related experience usually rise to the top of the list."

Mary D. Feduccia, Ph.D., Career Services Director, Louisiana State University

A grade point average (GPA) is a weighted average based on the grades received and the number of units (credit hours) taken. A GPA for one semester (or term) is defined as

the quotient of the sum of the grade points earned for each class and the sum of the number of units taken. The number of grade points earned for a class is the product of the number of units assigned to the class and the value of the grade received in the class.

1. Use the table of grade values below to compute the GPA for the student whose semester grade report is shown. Round to the nearest hundredth.

Grade	Value
A	4
B	3
C	2
D	1
F	0

Class	Units	Grade
Geology	4	C
Algebra	5	A
Psychology	3	C
Spanish	2	B

2. If you were enrolled in school last semester (or term), list the classes taken, units assigned, and grades received like those shown in the grade report above. Then calculate your GPA.

ANSWERS TO SELF CHECKS

1. 5.2   **2.** 3.17   **3.** 5.35   **4.** 0.93   **5.** 14.24   **6.** $6,300 \div 70 = 630 \div 7 = 90$
7. a. 7.213   **b.** 0.00107   **c.** 194,407   **8. a.** -6.62 **b.** 239   **9.** -1.107 **10.** 5.5
11. 36 slices   **12.** 2.747 million visitors

SECTION 2.10   STUDY SET

▌VOCABULARY

Fill in the blanks.

1. In the division problem shown below, label the *dividend,* the *divisor,* and the *quotient.*

$$3.17 \leftarrow \boxed{}$$
$$\boxed{} \rightarrow 5\overline{)15.85} \leftarrow \boxed{}$$

2. To perform the division $2.7\overline{)9.45}$, we move the decimal point of the divisor so that it becomes the _____ number 27.

▌CONCEPTS

3. A decimal point is missing in each of the following quotients. Write a decimal point in the proper position.

a. $\dfrac{526}{4\overline{)21.04}}$ **b.** $\dfrac{0008}{3\overline{)0.024}}$

4. a. How many places to the right must we move the decimal point in 6.14 so that it becomes a whole number?

b. When the decimal point in 49.8 is moved three places to the right, what is the resulting number?

5. Move the decimal point in the divisor and the dividend the same number of places so that the divisor becomes a whole number. *You do not have to find the quotient.*

 a. $1.3\overline{)10.66}$

 b. $3.71\overline{)16.695}$

6. Fill in the blanks: To divide with a decimal divisor, write the problem in _____ division form. Move the decimal point of the divisor so that it becomes a _____ number. Then move the decimal point of the dividend the same number of places to the _____. Write the decimal point in the quotient directly _____ the decimal point in the dividend and divide as working with whole _____.

7. To perform the division $7.8\overline{)14.562}$, the decimal points in the divisor and dividend are moved 1 place to the right. This is equivalent to multiplying $\frac{14.562}{7.8}$ by what form of 1?

8. Use multiplication to check the following division. Is the result correct?

$$\frac{1.917}{0.9} = 2.13$$

9. When rounding a decimal to the hundredths column, to what other column must we look at first?

10. a. When 9.545 is divided by 10, is the answer smaller or larger than 9.545?

 b. When 9.545 is divided by 0.1, is the answer smaller or larger than 9.545?

11. Fill in the blanks.

 a. To find the quotient of a decimal and 10, 100, 1,000, and so on, move the decimal point to the _____ the same number of places as there are zeros in the power of 10.

 b. To find the quotient of a decimal and 0.1, 0.01, 0.001, and so on, move the decimal point to the _____ the same number of decimal places as there are in the power of 10.

12. Determine whether the *sign* of each result is positive or negative. *You do not have to find the quotient.*

 a. $-15.25 \div (-0.5)$

 b. $\dfrac{-25.92}{3.2}$

█ NOTATION

13. Explain what the red arrows are illustrating in the division problem below.

$467\overline{)3208.7}$

14. The division shown below is not finished. Why was the red 0 written after the 7 in the dividend?

$$\begin{array}{r} 2.3 \\ 2\overline{)4.70} \\ -4 \\ \hline 07 \\ -6 \\ \hline 1 \end{array}$$

█ GUIDED PRACTICE

Divide. Check the result. **See Example 1.**

15. $12.6 \div 6$ **16.** $40.8 \div 8$

17. $3\overline{)27.6}$ **18.** $4\overline{)28.8}$

Divide. Check the result. **See Example 2.**

19. $98.21 \div 23$ **20.** $190.96 \div 28$

21. $37\overline{)320.05}$ **22.** $32\overline{)125.12}$

Divide. Check the result. **See Example 3.**

23. $13.4 \div 4$ **24.** $38.3 \div 5$

25. $5\overline{)22.8}$ **26.** $6\overline{)28.5}$

Divide. Check the result. **See Example 4.**

27. $\dfrac{0.1932}{0.42}$ **28.** $\dfrac{0.2436}{0.29}$

29. $0.29\overline{)0.1131}$ **30.** $0.58\overline{)0.1566}$

Divide. Round the quotient to the nearest hundredth. Check the result. **See Example 5.**

31. $\dfrac{11.83}{0.6}$ **32.** $\dfrac{16.43}{0.9}$

33. $\dfrac{17.09}{0.7}$ **34.** $\dfrac{13.07}{0.6}$

Estimate each quotient. **See Example 6.**

35. $289.842 \div 72.1$

36. $284.254 \div 91.4$

37. $383.76 \div 7.8$

38. $348.84 \div 5.7$

39. $3,883.284 \div 48.12$

40. $5,556.521 \div 67.89$

41. $6.1\overline{)15,819.74}$

42. $9.2\overline{)19,460.76}$

Find each quotient. **See Example 7.**

43. $451.78 \div 100$ **44.** $991.02 \div 100$

45. $\dfrac{30.09}{10,000}$ **46.** $\dfrac{27.07}{10,000}$

47. $1.25 \div 0.1$ **48.** $8.62 \div 0.01$

49. $\dfrac{545.2}{0.001}$ **50.** $\dfrac{67.4}{0.001}$

Divide. See Example 8.

51. $-110.336 \div 12.8$

52. $-121.584 \div 14.9$

53. $-91.304 \div (-22.6)$

54. $-66.126 \div (-32.1)$

55. $\dfrac{-20.3257}{-0.001}$

56. $\dfrac{-48.8933}{-0.001}$

57. $0.003 \div (-100)$

58. $0.008 \div (-100)$

Evaluate each expression. See Example 9.

59. $\dfrac{2(0.614) + 2.3854}{0.2 - 0.9}$

60. $\dfrac{2(1.242) + 0.8932}{0.4 - 0.8}$

61. $\dfrac{5.409 - 3(1.8)}{(0.3)^2}$

62. $\dfrac{1.674 - 5(0.222)}{(0.1)^2}$

Evaluate each formula. See Example 10.

63. $t = \dfrac{d}{r}$ for $d = 211.75$ and $r = 60.5$

64. $h = \dfrac{2A}{b}$ for $A = 9.62$ and $b = 3.7$

65. $r = \dfrac{d}{t}$ for $d = 219.375$ and $t = 3.75$

66. $\pi = \dfrac{C}{d}$ for $C = 14.4513$ and $d = 4.6$ (Round to the nearest hundredth.)

TRY IT YOURSELF

Perform the indicated operations. Round the result to the specified decimal place, when indicated.

67. $4.5\overline{)11.97}$

68. $4.1\overline{)14.637}$

69. $\dfrac{75.04}{10}$

70. $\dfrac{22.32}{100}$

71. $8\overline{)0.036}$

72. $4\overline{)0.073}$

73. $9\overline{)2.889}$

74. $6\overline{)3.378}$

75. $\dfrac{-3(0.2) - 2(3.3)}{30(0.4)^2}$

76. $\dfrac{(-1.3)^2 + 9.2}{-2(0.2) - 0.5}$

77. Divide 1.2202 by -0.01.

78. Divide -0.4531 by -0.001.

79. $-5.714 \div 2.4$ (nearest tenth)

80. $-21.21 \div 3.8$ (nearest tenth)

81. $-39 \div (-4)$

82. $-26 \div (-8)$

83. $7.8915 \div .00001$

84. $23.025 \div 0.0001$

85. $\dfrac{0.0102}{0.017}$

86. $\dfrac{0.0092}{0.023}$

87. $12.243 \div 0.9$ (nearest hundredth)

88. $13.441 \div 0.6$ (nearest hundredth)

89. $1,000\overline{)34.8}$

90. $10,000\overline{)678.9}$

91. $\dfrac{40.7(3 - 8.3)}{0.4 - 0.61}$ (nearest hundredth)

92. $\dfrac{(0.5)^2 - (0.3)^2}{0.005 + 0.1}$ (nearest hundredth)

93. Divide 0.25 by 1.6

94. Divide 1.2 by 0.64

CONCEPT EXTENSIONS

The answer for each division shown below is missing a decimal point. Use estimation to determine where to place the decimal point in the answer.

95. $\dfrac{29.25}{4.5} = 65$

96. $0.052\overline{)0.23712} = 456$

97. Suppose you know that $26\overline{)146.38} = 5.63$. Use that result to determine the answer to each of the following problems *without* doing the division.

 a. $2.6\overline{)146.38}$

 b. $0.26\overline{)146.38}$

 c $26\overline{)1.4638}$

 d $0.026\overline{)0.0014638}$

98. What is the divisor in the division problem:
$\dfrac{65.428}{\overline{)49.071}}$?

APPLICATIONS

99. BUTCHER SHOPS A meat slicer trims 0.05-inch-thick pieces from a sausage. If the sausage is 14 inches long, how many slices are there in one sausage?

100. ELECTRONICS The volume control on a computer is shown to the right. If the distance between the Low and High settings is 21 cm, how far apart are the equally spaced volume settings?

VOLUME CONTROL
Low

High

101. COMPUTERS A computer can do an arithmetic calculation in 0.00003 second. How many of these calculations could it do in 60 seconds?

102. THE LOTTERY In December of 2008, fifteen city employees of Piqua, Ohio, who had played the Mega Millions Lottery as a group, won the jackpot. They were awarded a total of $94.5 million. If the money was split equally, how much did each person receive? (Source: pal-item.com)

103. SPRAY BOTTLES Each squeeze of the trigger of a spray bottle emits 0.017 ounce of liquid. How many squeezes are there in an 8.5-ounce bottle?

104. CAR LOANS See the loan statement below. How many more monthly payments must be made to pay off the loan?

American Finance Company	June
Monthly payment:	Paid to date: $547.30
$42.10	Loan balance: $631.50

105. HIKING Refer to the illustration below to determine how long it will take the person shown to complete the hike. Then determine at what time of the day she will complete the hike.

Departure A.M.   Arrival

The hiker walks 2.5 miles each hour.

Start   27.5-mile hike   Finish

106. HOURLY PAY The graph below shows the average hours worked and the average weekly earnings of U.S. production workers in manufacturing for the years 1998 and 2008. What did the average production worker in manufacturing earn per hour

   a. in 1998?   **b.** in 2008?

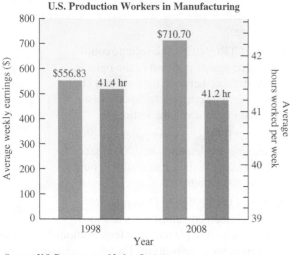

U.S. Production Workers in Manufacturing

$710.70
$556.83   41.4 hr   41.2 hr

1998   2008
Year

Source: *U.S. Department of Labor Statistic*

107. TRAVEL The illustration in the next column shows the annual number of person-trips of 50 miles or more (one way) for the years 2002–2007, as estimated by the Travel Industry Association of America. Find the average number of trips per year for this period of time.

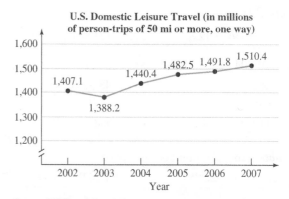

U.S. Domestic Leisure Travel (in millions of person-trips of 50 mi or more, one way)

1,407.1   1,388.2   1,440.4   1,482.5   1,491.8   1,510.4

2002   2003   2004   2005   2006   2007
Year

Source: *U.S. Travel Association*

108. OIL WELLS Geologists have mapped out the types of soil through which engineers must drill to reach an oil deposit. See the illustration below.

Surface

Silt	0.68 mi
Rock	0.36 mi
Sand	0.44 mi
Oil	

  a. How far below the surface is the oil deposit?

  b. What is the average depth that must be drilled each week if the drilling is to be a four-week project?

109. REFLEXES An online reaction time test is shown below. When the stop light changes from red to green, the participant is to immediately click on the large green button. The program then displays the participant's reaction time in the table. After the participant takes the test five times, the *average* reaction time is found. Determine the average reaction time for the results shown below.

Test Number	Reaction Time (in seconds)	The stoplight to watch.	The button to click.
1	0.219		
2	0.233		Click here on green light
3	0.204		
4	0.297		
5	0.202		
AVG.	?		

110. INDY 500 Driver Scott Dixon, of New Zealand, had the fastest average qualifying speed for the 2008 Indianapolis 500-mile race. This earned him the *pole position* to begin the race. The speeds for each of his four qualifying laps are shown below. What was his average qualifying speed?

| Lap 1: 226.598 mph |
| Lap 2: 226.505 mph |
| Lap 3: 226.303 mph |
| Lap 4: 226.058 mph |

(Source: indianapolismotorspeedway.com)

112. Explain why we must sometimes use rounding when we write the answer to a division problem.

113. The division $0.5\overline{)2.005}$ is equivalent to $5\overline{)20.05}$. Explain what equivalent means in this case.

114. In $3\overline{)0.7}$, why can additional zeros be placed to the right of 0.7 without affecting the result?

115. Explain how to estimate the following quotient: $0.75\overline{)2.415}$

116. Explain why multiplying $\frac{4.86}{0.2}$ by the form of 1 shown below moves the decimal points in the dividend, 4.86, and the divisor, 0.2, one place to the right.

$$\frac{4.86}{0.2} = \frac{4.86}{0.2} \cdot \frac{10}{10}$$

WRITING

111. Explain the process used to divide two numbers when both the divisor and the dividend are decimals. Give an example.

SECTION 2.11

Fractions and Decimals

Objectives

1 Write fractions as equivalent terminating decimals.

2 Write fractions as equivalent repeating decimals.

3 Round repeating decimals.

4 Graph fractions and decimals on a number line.

5 Compare fractions and decimals.

6 Evaluate expressions containing fractions and decimals.

7 Solve application problems involving fractions and decimals.

ARE YOU READY?

The following problems review some basic skills that are needed when working with decimals and fractions.

Fill in the blanks:

1. $\frac{21}{7}$ means ___ ÷ ___ .

2. $\frac{3}{4} \cdot \frac{25}{25} =$ ___

3. $6\frac{5}{9} =$ ___ + ___

4. Write an < or an > symbol in the box: 0.623 ___ 0.632

In this section, we continue to explore the relationship between fractions and decimals.

1 Write fractions as equivalent terminating decimals.

A fraction and a decimal are said to be **equivalent** if they name the same number. Every fraction can be written in an equivalent decimal form by dividing the numerator by the denominator, as indicated by the fraction bar.

Writing a Fraction as a Decimal

To write a fraction as a decimal, divide the numerator of the fraction by its denominator.

Self Check 1

Write each fraction as a decimal.

a. $\dfrac{1}{2}$

b. $\dfrac{3}{16}$

c. $\dfrac{9}{2}$

Now Try **Problems 15, 17, and 21**

EXAMPLE 1   Write each fraction as a decimal.

a. $\dfrac{3}{4}$ b. $\dfrac{5}{8}$ c. $\dfrac{7}{2}$

Strategy We will divide the numerator of each fraction by its denominator. We will continue the division process until we obtain a zero remainder.

WHY We divide the numerator by the denominator because a fraction bar indicates division.

Solution

a. $\frac{3}{4}$ means $3 \div 4$. To find $3 \div 4$, we begin by writing it in long division form as $4)\overline{3}$. To proceed with the division, we must write the dividend 3 with a decimal point and some additional zeros. Then we use the procedure for dividing a decimal by a whole number.

$$
\begin{array}{r}
0.75 \\
4\overline{)3.00} \\
-2\,8\downarrow \\
\hline
20 \\
-20 \\
\hline
0
\end{array}
$$
Write a decimal point and two additional zeros to the right of 3.

The remainder is 0.

Thus, $\frac{3}{4} = 0.75$. We say that the **decimal equivalent** of $\frac{3}{4}$ is 0.75.

We can check the result by writing 0.75 as a fraction in simplest form:

$$0.75 = \frac{75}{100}$$ *0.75 is seventy-five hundredths.*

$$= \frac{3 \cdot \overset{1}{\cancel{25}}}{4 \cdot \underset{1}{\cancel{25}}}$$ *To simplify the fraction, factor 75 as $3 \cdot 25$ and 100 as $4 \cdot 25$ and remove the common factor of 25.*

$$= \frac{3}{4}$$ *This is the original fraction.*

b. $\frac{5}{8}$ means $5 \div 8$.

$$
\begin{array}{r}
0.625 \\
8\overline{)5.000} \\
-4\,8\downarrow \\
\hline
20 \\
-16 \\
\hline
40 \\
-40 \\
\hline
0
\end{array}
$$
Write a decimal point and three additional zeros to the right of 5.

The remainder is 0.

Thus, $\frac{5}{8} = 0.625$.

c. $\frac{7}{2}$ means $7 \div 2$.

$$
\begin{array}{r}
3.5 \\
2\overline{)7.0} \\
-6\downarrow \\
\hline
1\,0 \\
-1\,0 \\
\hline
0
\end{array}
$$
Write a decimal point and one additional zero to the right of 7.

The remainder is 0.

Thus, $\frac{7}{2} = 3.5$.

Caution! A common error when finding a decimal equivalent for a fraction is to *incorrectly divide the denominator by the numerator.* An example of this is shown on the right, where the decimal equivalent of $\frac{5}{8}$ (a number less than 1) is incorrectly found to be 1.6 (a number greater than 1).

$$\begin{array}{r} 1.6 \\ 5\overline{)8.0} \\ -5 \\ \hline 3\,0 \\ -3\,0 \\ \hline 0 \end{array}$$

In parts a, b, and c of Example 1, the division process ended because a remainder of 0 was obtained. When such a division *terminates* with a remainder of 0, we call the resulting decimal a **terminating decimal.** Thus, 0.75, 0.625, and 3.5 are three examples of terminating decimals.

The Language of Mathematics To *terminate* means to bring to an end. In the movie *The Terminator,* actor Arnold Schwarzenegger plays a heartless machine sent to Earth to bring an end to his enemies.

2 Write fractions as equivalent repeating decimals.

Sometimes, when we are finding a decimal equivalent of a fraction, the division process never gives a remainder of 0. In this case, the result is a **repeating decimal.** Examples of repeating decimals are 0.4444 ... and 1.373737 .... The three dots tell us that a block of digits repeats in the pattern shown. Repeating decimals can also be written using a bar over the repeating block of digits. For example, 0.4444 ... can be written as $0.\overline{4}$, and 1.373737 ... can be written as $1.\overline{37}$.

Caution! When using an **overbar** to write a repeating decimal, use the least number of digits necessary to show the repeating block of digits.

$0.333 \ldots = 0.\overline{333}$ $6.7454545 \ldots = 6.7\overline{454}$

$0.333 \ldots = 0.\overline{3}$ $6.7454545 \ldots = 6.7\overline{45}$

Some fractions can be written as decimals using an alternate approach. If the denominator of a fraction in simplified form has factors of only 2's or 5's, or a combination of both, it can be written as a decimal by multiplying it by a form of 1. The objective is to write the fraction in an equivalent form with a denominator that is a power of 10, such as 10, 100, 1,000, and so on.

EXAMPLE 2 Write each fraction as a decimal using multiplication by a form of 1:   **a.** $\frac{4}{5}$ **b.** $\frac{11}{40}$

Strategy We will multiply $\frac{4}{5}$ by $\frac{2}{2}$ and we will multiply $\frac{11}{40}$ by $\frac{25}{25}$.

WHY The result of each multiplication will be an equivalent fraction with a denominator that is a power of 10. Such fractions are then easy to write in decimal form.

Self Check 2

Write each fraction as a decimal using multiplication by a form of 1:

a. $\frac{2}{5}$

b. $\frac{8}{25}$

Now Try Problems 27 and 29

Solution

a. Since we need to multiply the denominator of $\frac{4}{5}$ by 2 to obtain a denominator of 10, it follows that $\frac{2}{2}$ should be the form of 1 that is used to build $\frac{4}{5}$.

$$\frac{4}{5} = \frac{4}{5} \cdot \frac{2}{2} \qquad \text{Multiply } \tfrac{4}{5} \text{ by 1 in the form of } \tfrac{2}{2}.$$

$$= \frac{8}{10} \qquad \begin{array}{l}\text{Multiply the numerators.}\\ \text{Multiply the denominators.}\end{array}$$

$$= 0.8 \qquad \text{Write the fraction as a decimal.}$$

b. Since we need to multiply the denominator of $\frac{11}{40}$ by 25 to obtain a denominator of 1,000, it follows that $\frac{25}{25}$ should be the form of 1 that is used to build $\frac{11}{40}$.

$$\frac{11}{40} = \frac{11}{40} \cdot \frac{25}{25} \qquad \text{Multiply } \tfrac{11}{40} \text{ by 1 in the form of } \tfrac{25}{25}.$$

$$= \frac{275}{1,000} \qquad \begin{array}{l}\text{Multiply the numerators.}\\ \text{Multiply the denominators.}\end{array}$$

$$= 0.275 \qquad \text{Write the fraction as a decimal.}$$

Mixed numbers can also be written in decimal form.

Self Check 3

Write the mixed number $3\frac{17}{20}$ in decimal form.

Now Try Problem 37

EXAMPLE 3   Write the mixed number $5\frac{7}{16}$ in decimal form.

Strategy We need only find the decimal equivalent for the fractional part of the mixed number.

WHY The whole-number part in the decimal form is the same as the whole-number part in the mixed number form.

Solution To write $\frac{7}{16}$ as a fraction, we find $7 \div 16$.

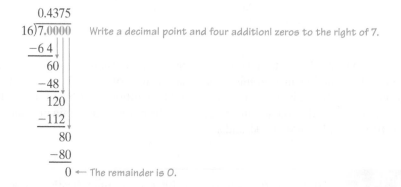

Since the whole-number part of the decimal must be the same as the whole-number part of the mixed number, we have:

$$5\frac{7}{16} = 5.4375$$

We would have obtained the same result if we changed $5\frac{7}{16}$ to the improper fraction $\frac{87}{16}$ and divided 87 by 16.

EXAMPLE 4 Write $\frac{5}{12}$ as a decimal.

Self Check 4
Write $\frac{1}{12}$ as a decimal.
Now Try **Problem 41**

Strategy We will divide the numerator of the fraction by its denominator and watch for a repeating pattern of nonzero remainders.

WHY Once we detect a repeating pattern of remainders, the division process can stop.

Solution $\frac{5}{12}$ means $5 \div 12$.

```
        0.4166
   12)5.0000       Write a decimal point and four additional zeros to the right of 5.
     −4 8
        20
       −12
        80
       −72
        80        It is apparent that 8 will continue to reappear as the remainder. Therefore,
       −72        6 will continue to reappear in the quotient. Since the repeating pattern is
         8        now clear, we can stop the division.
```

We can use three dots to show that a repeating pattern of 6's appears in the quotient:

$$\frac{5}{12} = 0.416666\ldots$$

Or, we can use an overbar to indicate the repeating part (in this case, only the 6), and write the decimal equivalent in more compact form:

$$\frac{5}{12} = 0.41\overline{6}$$

EXAMPLE 5 Write $-\frac{6}{11}$ as a decimal.

Self Check 5
Write $-\frac{13}{33}$ as a decimal.
Now Try **Problem 47**

Strategy To find the decimal equivalent for $-\frac{6}{11}$, we will first find the decimal equivalent for $\frac{6}{11}$. To do this, we will divide the numerator of $\frac{6}{11}$ by its denominator and watch for a repeating pattern of nonzero remainders.

WHY Once we detect a repeating pattern of remainders, the division process can stop.

Solution $\frac{6}{11}$ means $6 \div 11$.

```
        0.54545
   11)6.00000      Write a decimal point and five additional zeros to the right of 6.
     − 5 5
        50
       − 44
        60
       − 55
        50
       − 44
        60        It is apparent that 6 and 5 will continue to reappear as remainders.
       − 55        Therefore, 5 and 4 will continue to reappear in the quotient. Since the
         5        repeating pattern is now clear, we can stop the division process.
```

We can use three dots to show that a repeating pattern of 5 and 4 appears in the quotient:

$$\frac{6}{11} = 0.545454\ldots \text{ and therefore, } -\frac{6}{11} = -0.545454\ldots$$

Or, we can use an overbar to indicate the repeating part (in this case, 54), and write the decimal equivalent in more compact form:

$$\frac{6}{11} = 0.\overline{54} \text{ and therefore, } -\frac{6}{11} = -0.\overline{54}$$

The repeating part of the decimal equivalent of some fractions is quite long. Here are some examples:

$$\frac{9}{37} = 0.\overline{243} \qquad \text{A block of three digits repeats.}$$

$$\frac{13}{101} = 0.\overline{1287} \qquad \text{A block of four digits repeats.}$$

$$\frac{6}{7} = 0.\overline{857142} \qquad \text{A block of six digits repeats.}$$

Every fraction can be written as either a terminating decimal or a repeating decimal. For this reason, the set of fractions (**rational numbers**) form a subset of the set of decimals called the set of **real numbers.** The set of real numbers corresponds to all points on a number line.

Not all decimals are terminating or repeating decimals. For example,

$$0.2020020002\ldots$$

does not terminate, and it has no repeating block of digits. This decimal cannot be written as a fraction with an integer numerator and a nonzero integer denominator. Thus, it is not a rational number. It is an example from the set of **irrational numbers.**

3 Round repeating decimals.

When a fraction is written in decimal form, the result is either a terminating or a repeating decimal. Repeating decimals are often rounded to a specified place value.

Self Check 6

Write $\frac{4}{9}$ as a decimal and round to the nearest hundredth.

Now Try **Problem 51**

EXAMPLE 6 Write $\frac{1}{3}$ as a decimal and round to the nearest hundredth.

Strategy We will use the methods of this section to divide to the thousandths column.

WHY To round to the hundredths column, we need to continue the division process for one more decimal place, which is the thousandths column.

Solution $\frac{1}{3}$ means $1 \div 3$.

$$
\begin{array}{r}
0.333 \\
3\overline{)1.000} \\
\underline{-9} \\
10 \\
\underline{-9} \\
10 \\
\underline{-9} \\
1
\end{array}
$$

Write a decimal point and three additional zeros to the right of 1.

The division process can stop. We have divided to the thousandths column.

After dividing to the thousandths column, we round to the hundredths column.

The rounding digit in the hundredths column is 3.
The test digit in the thousandths column is 3.

0.333 . . .

Since 3 is less than 5, we round down, and we have

$\frac{1}{3} \approx 0.33$ *Read ≈ as "is approximately equal to."*

EXAMPLE 7   Write $\frac{2}{7}$ as a decimal and round to the nearest thousandth.

Strategy We will use the methods of this section to divide to the ten-thousandths column.

WHY To round to the thousandths column, we need to continue the division process for one more decimal place, which is the ten-thousandths column.

Solution $\frac{2}{7}$ means $2 \div 7$.

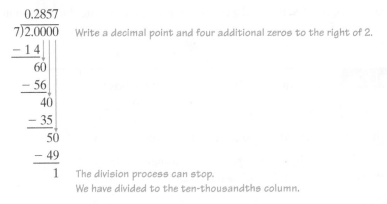

Write a decimal point and four additional zeros to the right of 2.

The division process can stop.
We have divided to the ten-thousandths column.

After dividing to the ten-thousandths column, we round to the thousandths column.

The rounding digit in the thousandths column is 5.
The test digit in the ten-thousandths column is 7.

0.2857

Since 7 is greater than 5, we round up, and $\frac{2}{7} \approx 0.286$.

Self Check 7
Write $\frac{7}{24}$ as a decimal and round to the nearest thousandth.

Now Try **Problem 61**

Using Your CALCULATOR   **The Fixed-Point Key**

After performing a calculation, a scientific calculator can round the result to a given decimal place. This is done using the *fixed-point key*. As we did in Example 7, let's find the decimal equivalent of $\frac{2}{7}$ and round to the nearest thousandth. This time, we will use a calculator.

First, we set the calculator to round to the third decimal place (thousandths) by pressing 2nd FIX 3. Then we press 2 ÷ 7 =   `0.286`

Thus, $\frac{2}{7} \approx 0.286$. To round to the nearest tenth, we would fix 1; to round to the nearest hundredth, we would fix 2; and so on. After using the FIX feature, don't forget to remove it and return the calculator to the normal mode.

Graphing calculators can also round to a given decimal place. See the owner's manual for the required keystrokes.

4 Graph fractions and decimals on a number line.

A number line can be used to show the relationship between fractions and their decimal equivalents. On the number line below, sixteen equally spaced marks are used to scale from 0 to 1. Some commonly used fractions that have terminating decimal equivalents are shown. For example, we see that $\frac{1}{8} = 0.125$ and $\frac{13}{16} = 0.8125$.

On the next number line, six equally spaced marks are used to scale from 0 to 1. Some commonly used fractions and their repeating decimal equivalents are shown.

5 Compare fractions and decimals.

To compare the size of a fraction and a decimal, it is helpful to write the fraction in its equivalent decimal form.

Place an $<$, $>$, or an $=$ symbol in the box to make a true statement:

a. $\dfrac{3}{8}$ ☐ 0.305

b. $0.7\overline{6}$ ☐ $\dfrac{7}{9}$

c. $\dfrac{11}{4}$ ☐ 2.75

Now Try **Problems 67, 69, and 71**

EXAMPLE 8   Place an $<$, $>$, or an $=$ symbol in the box to make a true

statement: **a.** $\dfrac{4}{5}$ ☐ 0.91   **b.** $0.3\overline{5}$ ☐ $\dfrac{1}{3}$ **c.** $\dfrac{9}{4}$ ☐ 2.25

Strategy In each case, we will write the given fraction as a decimal.

WHY Then we can use the procedure for comparing two decimals to determine which number is the larger and which is the smaller.

Solution

a. To write $\frac{4}{5}$ as a decimal, we divide 4 by 5.

$$
\begin{array}{r}
0.8 \\
5\overline{)4.0} \quad \text{\small \textit{Write a decimal point and one additional zero to the right of 4.}}\\
-4\,0 \\
\hline
0
\end{array}
$$

Thus, $\frac{4}{5} = 0.8$.

To make the comparison of the decimals easier, we can write one zero after 8 so that they have the same number of digits to the right of the decimal point.

$0.8\,0$ *This is the decimal equivalent for $\frac{4}{5}$.*

$0.9\,1$
$\quad\uparrow$

As we work from left to right, this is the first column in which the digits differ. Since $8 < 9$, it follows that $0.80 = \frac{4}{5}$ is less than 0.91, and we can write $\frac{4}{5} < 0.91$.

b. In Example 6, we saw that $\frac{1}{3} = 0.3333\ldots$. To make the comparison of these repeating decimals easier, we write them so that they have the same number of digits to the right of the decimal point.

$0.3\,5\,55\ldots$ *This is $0.3\overline{5}$.*

$0.3\,3\,33\ldots$ *This is $\frac{1}{3}$.*
$\quad\;\uparrow$

As we work from left to right, this is the first column in which the digits differ. Since $5 > 3$, it follows that $0.3555\ldots = 0.3\overline{5}$ is greater than $0.3333\ldots = \frac{1}{3}$, and we can write $0.3\overline{5} > \frac{1}{3}$.

c. To write $\frac{9}{4}$ as a decimal, we divide 9 by 4.

$$
\begin{array}{r}
2.25 \\
4\overline{)9.00} \\
-8 \\
\hline
1\,0 \\
-8 \\
\hline
20 \\
-20 \\
\hline
0
\end{array}
$$

Write a decimal point and two additional zeros to the right of 9.

From the division, we see that $\frac{9}{4} = 2.25$.

EXAMPLE 9   Write the numbers in order from smallest to largest: $2.168,\ 2\frac{1}{6},\ \frac{20}{9}$

Strategy   We will write $2\frac{1}{6}$ and $\frac{20}{9}$ in decimal form.

WHY   Then we can do a column-by-column comparison of the numbers to determine the largest and smallest.

Solution   From the number line on page 158, we see that $\frac{1}{6} = 0.1\overline{6}$. Thus, $2\frac{1}{6} = 2.1\overline{6}$. To write $\frac{20}{9}$ as a decimal, we divide 20 by 9.

$$
\begin{array}{r}
2.222 \\
9\overline{)20.000} \\
-18 \\
\hline
20 \\
-18 \\
\hline
20 \\
-18 \\
\hline
20 \\
-18 \\
\hline
2
\end{array}
$$

Write a decimal point and three additional zeros to the right of 20.

Thus, $\frac{20}{9} = 2.222\ldots$.

To make the comparison of the three decimals easier, we stack them as shown below.

$$
\begin{array}{l}
2.1680 \qquad \text{This is 2.168 with an additional 0.} \\
2.1666\ldots \quad \text{This is } 2\frac{1}{6} = 2.1\overline{6}. \\
2.2222\ldots \quad \text{This is } \frac{20}{9}.
\end{array}
$$

Working from left to right, this is the first column in which the digits differ. Since $2 > 1$, it follows that $2.222\ldots = \frac{20}{9}$ is the largest of the three numbers.

Working from left to right, this is the first column in which the top two numbers differ. Since $8 > 6$, it follows that 2.168 is the next largest number and that $2.1\overline{6} = 2\frac{1}{6}$ is the smallest.

Written in order from smallest to largest, we have :

$$2\frac{1}{6},\ 2.168,\ \frac{20}{9}$$

Self Check 9

Write the numbers in order from smallest to largest: $1.832,\ \frac{9}{5},\ 1\frac{5}{6}$

Now Try   **Problem 75**

6 Evaluate expressions containing fractions and decimals.

Expressions can contain both fractions and decimals. In the following examples, we show two methods that can be used to evaluate expressions of this type. With the first method we find the answer by working in terms of fractions.

Self Check 10

Evaluate by working in terms of fractions: $0.53 + \frac{1}{6}$

Now Try Problem 79

EXAMPLE 10   Evaluate $\frac{1}{3} + 0.27$ by working in terms of fractions.

Strategy We will begin by writing 0.27 as a fraction.

WHY Then we can use the methods of Chapter 3 for adding fractions with unlike denominators to find the sum.

Solution To write 0.27 as a fraction, it is helpful to read it aloud as "twenty-seven hundredths."

$$\frac{1}{3} + 0.27 = \frac{1}{3} + \frac{27}{100} \qquad \text{Replace 0.27 with } \frac{27}{100}.$$

$$= \frac{1}{3} \cdot \frac{100}{100} + \frac{27}{100} \cdot \frac{3}{3} \qquad \begin{array}{l}\text{The LCD for } \frac{1}{3} \text{ and } \frac{27}{100} \text{ is 300. To build each}\\ \text{fraction so that its denominator is 300,}\\ \text{multiply by a form of 1.}\end{array}$$

$$= \frac{100}{300} + \frac{81}{300} \qquad \begin{array}{l}\text{Multiply the numerators.}\\ \text{Multiply the denominators.}\end{array}$$

$$= \frac{181}{300} \qquad \begin{array}{l}\text{Add the numerators and write the sum over}\\ \text{the common denominator 300.}\end{array}$$

Now we will evaluate the expression from Example 10 by working in terms of decimals.

Self Check 11

Estimate the result by working in terms of decimals: $0.53 - \frac{1}{6}$

Now Try Problem 87

EXAMPLE 11   Estimate $\frac{1}{3} + 0.27$ by working in terms of decimals.

Strategy Since 0.27 has two decimal places, we will begin by finding a decimal approximation for $\frac{1}{3}$ to two decimal places.

WHY Then we can use the methods of this chapter for adding decimals to find the sum.

Solution We have seen that the decimal equivalent of $\frac{1}{3}$ is the repeating decimal 0.333 . . . . Rounded to the nearest hundredth: $\frac{1}{3} \approx 0.33$.

$$\frac{1}{3} + 0.27 \approx 0.33 + 0.27 \qquad \text{Approximate } \frac{1}{3} \text{ with the decimal 0.33.}$$

$$\approx 0.60 \qquad \text{Do the addition.}$$

$$\begin{array}{r}\overset{1}{0.33}\\ +0.27\\ \hline 0.60\end{array}$$

In Examples 10 and 11, we evaluated $\frac{1}{3} + 0.27$ in different ways. In Example 10, we obtained the exact answer, $\frac{181}{300}$. In Example 11, we obtained an approximation, 0.6. The results seem reasonable when we write $\frac{181}{300}$ in decimal form: $\frac{181}{300} = 0.60333 \ldots .$

EXAMPLE 12 Evaluate: $\left(\dfrac{4}{5}\right)(1.35) + (0.5)^2$

Strategy We will find the decimal equivalent of $\dfrac{4}{5}$ and then evaluate the expression in terms of decimals.

WHY Its easier to perform multiplication and addition with the given decimals than it would be converting them to fractions.

Solution We use division to find the decimal equivalent of $\dfrac{4}{5}$.

$$
\begin{array}{r}
0.8 \\
5\overline{)4.0} \\
-4\,0 \\
\hline
0
\end{array}
$$
Write a decimal point and one additional zero to the right of the 4.

Now we use the order of operation rule to evaluate the expression.

$\left(\dfrac{4}{5}\right)(1.35) + (0.5)^2$

$= (\mathbf{0.8})(1.35) + (0.5)^2$ *Replace $\frac{4}{5}$ with its decimal equivalent, 0.8.*

$= (0.8)(1.35) + 0.25$ *Evaluate: $(0.5)^2 = 0.25$.*

$= 1.08 + 0.25$ *Do the multiplication: $(0.8)(1.35) = 1.08$.*

$= 1.33$ *Do the addition.*

$$
\begin{array}{r}
\overset{2}{0.5} \\
\times\ 0.5 \\
\hline
0.25
\end{array}
$$

$$
\begin{array}{r}
\overset{2\ 4}{1.35} \\
\times\ \ 0.8 \\
\hline
1.080
\end{array}
$$

$$
\begin{array}{r}
\overset{1}{1.08} \\
+0.25 \\
\hline
1.33
\end{array}
$$

Self Check 12
Evaluate: $(-0.6)^2 + (2.3)\left(\dfrac{1}{8}\right)$

Now Try **Problem 99**

7 **Solve application problems involving fractions and decimals.**

EXAMPLE 13 **Shopping** A shopper purchased $\dfrac{3}{4}$ pound of fruit, priced at \$0.88 a pound, and $\dfrac{1}{3}$ pound of fresh-ground coffee, selling for \$6.60 a pound. Find the total cost of these items.

Solution

- $\dfrac{3}{4}$ pound of fruit was purchased at \$0.88 per pound.   *Given*
- $\dfrac{1}{3}$ pound of coffee was purchased at \$6.60 per pound.   *Given*
- What was the total cost of the items?   *Find*

Form To find the total cost of each item, multiply the number of pounds purchased by the price per pound.

The total cost of the items	is equal to	the number of pounds of fruit	times	the price per pound	plus	the number of pounds of coffee	times	the price per pound
The total cost of the items	$=$	$\dfrac{3}{4}$	$\cdot$	\$0.88	$+$	$\dfrac{1}{3}$	$\cdot$	\$6.60

Because 0.88 is divisible by 4 and 6.60 is divisible by 3, we can work with the decimals and fractions in this form; no conversion is necessary.

$\dfrac{3}{4} \cdot 0.88 + \dfrac{1}{3} \cdot 6.60$

$= \dfrac{3}{4} \cdot \dfrac{0.88}{1} + \dfrac{1}{3} \cdot \dfrac{6.60}{1}$ *Express 0.88 as $\frac{0.88}{1}$ and 6.60 as $\frac{6.60}{1}$.*

$$
\begin{array}{r}
\overset{2}{0.88} \\
\times\ \ \ 3 \\
\hline
2.64
\end{array}
$$

Self Check 13

DELICATESSENS A shopper purchased $\frac{2}{3}$ pound of Swiss cheese, priced at $2.19 per pound, and $\frac{3}{4}$ pound of sliced turkey, selling for $6.40 per pound. Find the total cost of these items.

Now Try Problem 111

$$= \frac{2.64}{4} + \frac{6.60}{3}$$ Multiply the numerators.
Multiply the denominators.

$$= 0.66 + 2.20$$ Do each division.

$$= 2.86$$ Do the addition.

$$\begin{array}{r} 0.66 \\ 4\overline{)2.64} \\ -2\,4 \\ \hline 24 \\ -24 \\ \hline 0 \end{array}$$ $$\begin{array}{r} 2.20 \\ 3\overline{)6.60} \\ -6 \\ \hline 06 \\ -6 \\ \hline 00 \\ -0 \\ \hline 0 \end{array}$$

$$\begin{array}{r} 0.66 \\ +2.20 \\ \hline 2.86 \end{array}$$

The total cost of the items is $2.86.

Check If approximately 1 pound of fruit, priced at approximately $1 per pound, was purchased, then about $1 was spent on fruit. If exactly $\frac{1}{3}$ of a pound of coffee, priced at approximately $6 per pound, was purchased, then about $\frac{1}{3} \cdot$ $6, or $2, was spent on coffee. Since the approximate cost of the items $1 + $2 = $3, is close to the result, $2.86, the result seems reasonable.

> **ANSWERS TO SELF CHECKS**
>
> **1. a.** 0.5 **b.** 0.1875 **c.** 4.5 **2. a.** 0.4 **b.** 0.32 **3.** 3.85 **4.** 0.08$\overline{3}$ **5.** $-0.\overline{39}$ **6.** 0.44
> **7.** 0.292 **8. a.** > **b.** < **c.** = **9.** $\frac{9}{5}$, 1.832, $1\frac{5}{6}$ **10.** $\frac{209}{300}$ **11.** approximately 0.36
> **12.** 0.6475 **13.** $6.26

SECTION 2.11   STUDY SET

VOCABULARY

Fill in the blanks.

1. A fraction and a decimal are said to be _____ if they name the same number.

2. The _____ equivalent of $\frac{3}{4}$ is 0.75.

3. 0.75, 0.625, and 3.5 are examples of _____ decimals.

4. 0.3333 . . . and 1.666 . . . are examples of _____ decimals.

CONCEPTS

Fill in the blanks.

5. $\frac{7}{8}$ means 7 ☐ 8.

6. To write a fraction as a decimal, divide the _____ of the fraction by its denominator.

7. To perform the division shown below, a decimal point and two additional _____ were written to the right of 3.

    $$4\overline{)3.00}$$

8. Sometimes, when finding the decimal equivalent of a fraction, the division process ends because a remainder of 0 is obtained. We call the resulting decimal a _____ decimal.

9. Sometimes, when we are finding the decimal equivalent of a fraction, the division process never gives a remainder of 0. We call the resulting decimal a _____ decimal.

10. If the denominator of a fraction in simplified form has factors of only 2's or 5's, or a combination of both, it can be written as a decimal by multiplying it by a form of ☐.

11. **a.** Round 0.3777 . . . to the nearest hundredth.

    b. Round 0.212121 . . . to the nearest thousandth.

12. **a.** When evaluating the expression $0.25 + \left(2.3 + \frac{2}{5}\right)^2$, would it be easier to work in terms of fractions or decimals?

    b. What is the first step that should be performed to evaluate the expression?

NOTATION

13. Write each decimal in fraction form.

    a. 0.7   **b.** 0.77

14. Write each repeating decimal in simplest form using an overbar.

    a. 0.888 . . .   **b.** 0.323232 . . .

    c. 0.56333 . . .   **d.** 0.8898989 . . .

GUIDED PRACTICE

Write each fraction as a decimal. See Example 1.

15. $\frac{1}{2}$

16. $\frac{1}{4}$

17. $\frac{7}{8}$

18. $\frac{3}{8}$

19. $\frac{11}{20}$

20. $\frac{17}{20}$

21. $\frac{13}{5}$

22. $\frac{15}{2}$

23. $\frac{9}{16}$

24. $\frac{3}{32}$

25. $-\frac{17}{32}$

26. $-\frac{15}{16}$

Write each fraction as a decimal using multiplication by a form of 1. See Example 2.

27. $\frac{3}{5}$

28. $\frac{13}{25}$

29. $\frac{9}{40}$

30. $\frac{7}{40}$

31. $\frac{19}{25}$

32. $\frac{21}{50}$

33. $\frac{1}{500}$

34. $\frac{1}{250}$

Write each mixed number in decimal form. See Example 3.

35. $3\frac{3}{4}$

36. $5\frac{4}{5}$

37. $12\frac{11}{16}$

38. $32\frac{9}{16}$

Write each fraction as a decimal. Use an overbar in your answer. See Example 4.

39. $\frac{1}{9}$

40. $\frac{8}{9}$

41. $\frac{7}{12}$

42. $\frac{11}{12}$

43. $\frac{7}{90}$

44. $\frac{1}{99}$

45. $\frac{1}{60}$

46. $\frac{1}{66}$

Write each fraction as a decimal. Use an overbar in your answer. See Example 5.

47. $-\frac{5}{11}$

48. $-\frac{7}{11}$

49. $-\frac{20}{33}$

50. $-\frac{16}{33}$

Write each fraction in decimal form. Round to the nearest hundredth. See Example 6.

51. $\frac{7}{30}$

52. $\frac{8}{9}$

53. $\frac{22}{45}$

54. $\frac{17}{45}$

55. $\frac{24}{13}$

56. $\frac{34}{11}$

57. $-\frac{13}{12}$

58. $-\frac{25}{12}$

Write each fraction in decimal form. Round to the nearest thousandth. See Example 7.

59. $\frac{5}{33}$

60. $\frac{5}{24}$

61. $\frac{10}{27}$

62. $\frac{17}{21}$

Graph the given numbers on a number line. See Objective 4.

63. $1\frac{3}{4}$, -0.75, $0.\overline{6}$, $-3.8\overline{3}$

64. $2\frac{7}{8}$, -2.375, $0.\overline{3}$, $4.1\overline{6}$

65. 3.875, $-3.\overline{5}$, $0.\overline{2}$, $-1\frac{4}{5}$

66. 1.375, $-4\frac{1}{7}$, $0.\overline{1}$, $-2.\overline{7}$

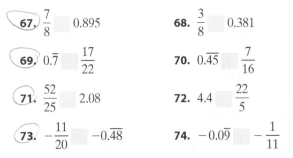

Place an <, >, or an = symbol in the box to make a true statement. See Example 8.

67. $\frac{7}{8}$ ☐ 0.895

68. $\frac{3}{8}$ ☐ 0.381

69. $0.\overline{7}$ ☐ $\frac{17}{22}$

70. $0.\overline{45}$ ☐ $\frac{7}{16}$

71. $\frac{52}{25}$ ☐ 2.08

72. 4.4 ☐ $\frac{22}{5}$

73. $-\frac{11}{20}$ ☐ $-0.\overline{48}$

74. $-0.0\overline{9}$ ☐ $-\frac{1}{11}$

Write the numbers in order from smallest to largest.
See Example 9.

75. $6\frac{1}{2}$, 6.25, $\frac{19}{3}$

76. $7\frac{3}{8}$, 7.08, $\frac{43}{6}$

77. $-0.\overline{81}$, $-\frac{8}{9}$, $-\frac{6}{7}$

78. $-0.\overline{19}$, $-\frac{1}{11}$, -0.1

Evaluate each expression. Work in terms of fractions.
See Example 10.

79. $\frac{1}{9} + 0.3$

80. $\frac{2}{3} + 0.1$

81. $0.9 - \frac{7}{12}$

82. $0.99 - \frac{5}{6}$

83. $\frac{5}{11}(0.3)$

84. $(0.9)\left(\frac{1}{27}\right)$

85. $\frac{1}{4}(0.25) + \frac{15}{16}$

86. $\frac{2}{5}(0.02) - (0.04)$

Estimate the value of each expression. Work in terms of decimals. See Example 11.

87. $0.24 + \frac{1}{3}$

88. $0.02 + \frac{5}{6}$

89. $5.69 - \frac{5}{12}$

90. $3.19 - \frac{2}{3}$

91. $0.43 - \frac{1}{12}$

92. $0.27 + \frac{5}{12}$

93. $\frac{1}{15} - 0.55$

94. $\frac{7}{30} - 0.84$

Evaluate each expression. Work in terms of decimals.
See Example 12.

95. $(3.5 + 6.7)\left(-\frac{1}{4}\right)$

96. $\left(-\frac{5}{8}\right)\left(5.3 - 3\frac{9}{10}\right)$

97. $\left(\frac{1}{5}\right)^2(1.7)$

98. $(2.35)\left(\frac{2}{5}\right)^2$

99. $7.5 - (0.78)\left(\frac{1}{2}\right)^2$

100. $8.1 - \left(\frac{3}{4}\right)^2(0.12)$

101. $\frac{3}{8}(3.2) + \left(4\frac{1}{2}\right)\left(-\frac{1}{4}\right)$

102. $(-0.8)\left(\frac{1}{4}\right) + \left(\frac{1}{5}\right)(0.39)$

CONCEPT EXTENSIONS

103. a. Find the perimeter of the figure below. Express the answer using a decimal.

    b. Find the area of the figure below. Express the answer using a mixed number.

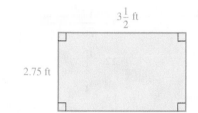

104. a. Find the perimeter of the figure below. Express the answer using a mixed number.

    b. Find the area of the figure below. Express the answer using a decimal.

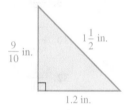

105. a. Find the decimal equivalent of each fraction:
$\frac{7}{9}$, $\frac{7}{99}$, and $\frac{7}{999}$.

    b. Use you answers to part a to predict the decimal equivalent of $\frac{7}{9,999}$.

106. a. Without dividing, determine whether the decimal equivalent of $\frac{92}{179}$ is greater than or less than the decimal equivalent of $\frac{93}{179}$.

    b. Without dividing, determine whether the decimal equivalent of $\frac{139}{643}$ is greater than or less than the decimal equivalent of $\frac{139}{644}$.

APPLICATIONS

107. DRAFTING The architect's scale shown on the next page has several measuring edges. The edge marked 16 divides each inch into 16 equal parts. Find the decimal form for each fractional part of 1 inch that is highlighted with a red arrow.

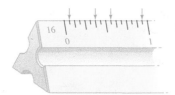

108. MILEAGE SIGNS The freeway sign shown below gives the number of miles to the next three exits. Convert the mileages to decimal notation.

Barranca Ave.	$\frac{3}{4}$ mi
210 Freeway	$2\frac{1}{4}$ mi
Ada St.	$3\frac{1}{2}$ mi

109. GARDENING Two brands of replacement line for a lawn trimmer shown below are labeled in different ways. On one package, the line's thickness is expressed as a decimal; on the other, as a fraction. Which line is thicker?

NYLON LINE
Thickness: 0.065 in.

TRIMMER LINE
$\frac{3}{40}$ in. thick

110. AUTO MECHANICS While doing a tune-up, a mechanic checks the gap on one of the spark plugs of a car to be sure it is firing correctly. The owner's manual states that the gap should be $\frac{2}{125}$ inch. The gauge the mechanic uses to check the gap is in decimal notation; it registers 0.025 inch. Is the spark plug gap too large or too small?

111. HORSE RACING In thoroughbred racing, the time a horse takes to run a given distance is measured using fifths of a second. For example, :23^2 (read "twenty-three and two") means $23\frac{2}{5}$ seconds. The illustration below lists four split times for a horse named *Speedy Flight* in a $1\frac{1}{16}$-mile race. Express each split time in decimal form.

Speedy Flight	Turfway Park, Ky		3-year-old
	17 May 2010		$1\frac{1}{16}$ mile
	Splits	:23^2 :23^4 :24^1 :32^3	

112. GEOLOGY A geologist weighed a rock sample at the site where it was discovered and found it to weigh $17\frac{7}{8}$ lb. Later, a more accurate digital scale in the laboratory gave the weight as 17.671 lb. What is the difference in the two measurements?

113. WINDOW REPLACEMENTS The amount of sunlight that comes into a room depends on the area of the windows in the room. What is the area of the window shown below? (*Hint:* Use the formula $A = \frac{1}{2}bh$.)

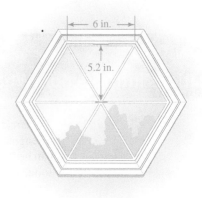

6 in.

5.2 in.

114. FORESTRY A command post asked each of three fire crews to estimate the length of the fire line they were fighting. Their reports came back in different forms, as shown. Find the perimeter of the fire. Round to the nearest tenth.

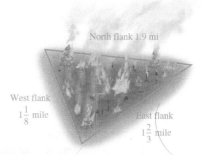

North flank 1.9 mi

West flank $1\frac{1}{8}$ mile

East flank $1\frac{2}{3}$ mile

115. DELICATESSENS A shopper purchased $\frac{2}{3}$ pound of green olives, priced at $4.14 per pound, and $\frac{3}{4}$ pound of smoked ham, selling for $5.68 per pound. Find the total cost of these items.

116. CHOCOLATE A shopper purchased $\frac{3}{4}$ pound of dark chocolate, priced at $8.60 per pound, and $\frac{1}{3}$ pound of milk chocolate, selling for $5.25 per pound. Find the total cost of these items.

WRITING

117. Explain the procedure used to write a fraction in decimal form.

118. How does the terminating decimal 0.5 differ from the repeating decimal $0.\overline{5}$?

119. A student represented the repeating decimal 0.1333... as $0.1\overline{333}$. Is this the best form? Explain why or why not.

120. Is 0.10100100010000... a repeating decimal? Explain why or why not.

121. A student divided 19 by 25 to find the decimal equivalent of $\frac{19}{25}$ to be 0.76. Explain how she can check this result.

122. Explain the error in the following work to find the decimal equivalent for $\frac{5}{6}$.

$$
\begin{array}{r}
1.2 \\
5\overline{)\,6.0} \\
-5 \\
\hline
10 \\
-10 \\
\hline
0
\end{array}
$$

Thus, $\frac{5}{6} \ne 1.2$.

SECTION **2.12**

Applications Introduction: What is π?

The *circle* is one of the most important of all human discoveries. Circles are a basic tool of engineers, designers, artists, jewelers, architects, and many other professions. They can be seen in wheels, pulleys, gears, flowers, eyes, the movement of planets, sprinklers, food, and thousands of other examples.

To be specific, a **circle** is a closed curve in a plane. All of its points are an equal distance from its center. A **diameter** of a circle is a line segment that has both of its endpoints on the circle and passes through the center. The distance around a circle is called its **circumference.** In this activity, you will discover an important relationship between the circumference and diameter of a circle.

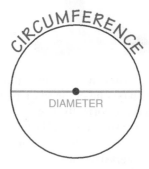

WHAT IS π?

Overview In this activity, you will discover an important fact about the ratio of the circumference to the diameter of a circle.

Instructions Form groups of 2 or 3 students. With a piece of string or a cloth tape measure, find the circumference and the diameter of objects that are circular in shape. You can measure anything that is round: for example, a coin, the top of a can, a tire, or a wastepaper basket. Enter your results in a table, as shown below. Convert each measurement to a decimal, and then use a calculator to determine a decimal approximation of the ratio of the circumference C to the diameter d.

Object	Circumference	Diameter	$\frac{C}{d}$ (approx.)
A quarter	$2\frac{15}{16}$ in. = 2.9375 in.	$\frac{15}{16}$ in. = 0.9375 in.	3.13333

Since early history, mathematicians have known that the ratio of the circumference to the diameter of a circle is the same for any size circle, approximately 3. Today, following centuries of study, we know that this ratio is exactly 3.141592653589. ...

$$\frac{C}{d} = 3.141592653589 \ldots$$

The Greek letter π (pi) is used to represent the ratio of circumference to diameter:

$$\pi = \frac{C}{d} \quad \text{where } \pi = 3.141592653589 \ldots$$

Are the ratios in your table numerically close to π? Give some reasons why they aren't exactly 3.141592653589. . . in each case.

Some interesting facts about π

1. As of 2012, Japanese systems engineer Shigeru Kondo and US computer scientist Alexander Yee held the world record for calculating π. The pair used a custom-made computer and 191 days of computational power to reach and amazing *ten trillion* digits. (Source: numberworld.org)

2. In 2006, Akira Haraguchi, a Japanese mental health counselor, recited π to 100,000 decimal places from memory. (Source: foxnews.com)

3. *Pi Day* is an unofficial holiday that recognizes the mathematical constant π. It is celebrated every year on March 14, which is 3/14 in month/day form.

4. π occurs in hundreds of formulas from science and mathematics that are used to mathematically describe DNA, rainbows, wave motion, gambling, fluid force, heat transfer, and magnetism.

For more interesting facts about π, visit the website: *facts.randomhistory.com/2009/07/03_pi.html.*

SECTION 2.12

Circles

Objectives

1 Define circle, radius, chord, diameter, and arc.

2 Find the circumference of a circle.

3 Find the area of a circle.

ARE YOU READY?

The following problems review some basic skills that are needed when working with circles.

Fill in the blanks.

1. A _____ is an equation that states a mathematical relationship between two or more variables.

2. The distance around a plane (flat) geometric figure is called its _____, and the amount of surface that it encloses is called its _____.

3. Area is measured in _____ units such as ft^2, yd^2, and $in.^2$.

4. The formula for the area of a triangle is $A = $ _____ .

In this section, we will discuss the circle, one of the most useful geometric figures of all. In fact, the discoveries of fire and the circular wheel are two of the most important events in the history of the human race. We will begin our study by introducing some basic vocabulary associated with circles.

1 Define circle, radius, chord, diameter, and arc.

Circle

A **circle** is the set of all points in a plane that lie a fixed distance from a point called its **center.**

A segment drawn from the center of a circle to a point on the circle is called a **radius.** (The plural of *radius* is *radii.*) From the definition, it follows that all radii of the same circle are the same length.

A **chord** of a circle is a line segment that connects two points on the circle. A **diameter** is a chord that passes through the center of the circle. Since a diameter D of a circle is twice as long as a radius r, we have

$$D = 2r$$

Each of the previous definitions is illustrated in figure (a) below, in which O is the center of the circle.

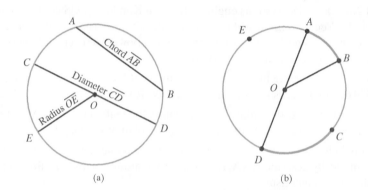

(a)   (b)

Any part of a circle is called an **arc.** In figure (b) above, the part of the circle from point A to point B that is highlighted in blue is $\overset{\frown}{AB}$, read as "arc AB." $\overset{\frown}{CD}$ is the part of the circle from point C to point D that is highlighted in green. An arc that is half of a circle is a **semicircle.**

Semicircle

A **semicircle** is an arc of a circle whose endpoints are the endpoints of a diameter.

If point O is the center of the circle in figure (b), $\overline{AD}$ is a diameter and $\overset{\frown}{AED}$ is a semicircle. The middle letter E distinguishes semicircle $\overset{\frown}{AED}$ (the part of the circle from point A to point D that includes point E) from semicircle $\overset{\frown}{ABD}$ (the part of the circle from point A to point D that includes point B).

An arc that is shorter than a semicircle is a **minor arc.** An arc that is longer than a semicircle is a **major arc.** In figure (b),

$\overset{\frown}{AE}$ is a minor arc   and $\overset{\frown}{ABE}$ is a major arc.

> ***Success Tip***   It is often possible to name a major arc in more than one way. For example, in figure (b), major arc $\overset{\frown}{ABE}$ is the part of the circle from point A to point E that includes point B. Two other names for the same major arc are $\overset{\frown}{ACE}$ and $\overset{\frown}{ADE}$.

2 Find the circumference of a circle.

Since early history, mathematicians have known that the ratio of the distance around a circle (the **circumference**) divided by the length of its diameter is approximately 3. First Kings, Chapter 7, of the Bible describes a round bronze tank that was 15 feet from brim to brim and 45 feet in circumference, and $\frac{45}{15} = 3$. Today, we use a more precise value for this ratio, known as π (pi). If C is the circumference of a circle and D is the length of its diameter, then

$$\pi = \frac{C}{D} \quad \text{where } \pi = 3.141592653589\ldots \quad \tfrac{22}{7} \text{ and 3.14 are often used as estimates of } \pi.$$

If we multiply both sides of $\pi = \frac{C}{D}$ by D, we have the following formula.

Circumference of a Circle

The circumference of a circle is given by the formula

$$C = \pi D \quad \text{where } C \text{ is the circumference and } D \text{ is the length of the diameter}$$

Since a diameter of a circle is twice as long as a radius r, we can substitute $2r$ for D in the formula $C = \pi D$ to obtain another formula for the circumference C:

$$C = 2\pi r \quad \text{The notation } 2\pi r \text{ means } 2 \cdot \pi \cdot r.$$

EXAMPLE 1   Find the circumference of the circle shown on the right. Give the exact answer and an approximation.

Strategy We will substitute 5 for r in the formula $C = 2\pi r$ and evaluate the right side.

WHY The variable C represents the unknown circumference of the circle.

Solution

$C = 2\pi r$	This is the formula for the circumference of a circle.
$C = 2\pi(5)$	Substitute 5 for r, the radius.
$C = 2(5)\pi$	When a product involves π, we usually rewrite it so that π is the last factor.
$C = 10\pi$	Do the first multiplication: 2(5) = 10. This is the exact answer.

The circumference of the circle is exactly 10π cm. If we replace π with 3.14, we get an approximation of the circumference.

$C = 10\pi$	
$C \approx 10(3.14)$	
$C \approx 31.4$	To multiply by 10, move the decimal point in 3.14 one place to the right.

The circumference of the circle is approximately 31.4 cm.

Self Check 1

Find the circumference of the circle shown below. Give the exact answer and an approximation.

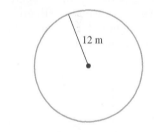

Now Try **Problem 25**

Using Your CALCULATOR   Calculating Revolutions of a Tire

When the $\boxed{\pi}$ key on a scientific calculator is pressed (on some models, the $\boxed{\text{2nd}}$ key must be pressed first), an approximation of π is displayed. To illustrate how to use this key, consider the following problem. How many times does the tire shown to the right revolve when a car makes a 25-mile trip?

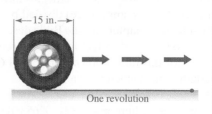
One revolution

We first find the circumference of the tire. From the figure, we see that the diameter of the tire is 15 inches. Since the circumference of a circle is the product of π and the length of its diameter, the tire's circumference is $\pi \cdot 15$ inches, or 15π inches. (Normally, we rewrite a product such as $\pi \cdot 15$ so that π is the second factor.)

We then change the 25 miles to inches using two unit conversion factors.

$$\frac{25 \text{ miles}}{1} \cdot \frac{5{,}280 \text{ feet}}{1 \text{ mile}} \cdot \frac{12 \text{ inches}}{1 \text{ foot}} = 25 \cdot 5{,}280 \cdot 12 \text{ inches}$$

The units of miles and feet can be removed.

The length of the trip is $25 \cdot 5{,}280 \cdot 12$ inches.

Finally, we divide the length of the trip by the circumference of the tire to get

$$\frac{\text{The number of}}{\text{revolutions of the tire}} = \frac{25 \cdot 5{,}280 \cdot 12}{15\pi}$$

We can use a scientific calculator to make this calculation.

$\boxed{(}\, 25 \,\boxed{\times}\, 5280 \,\boxed{\times}\, 12 \,\boxed{)}\, \boxed{\div}\, \boxed{(}\, 15 \,\boxed{\times}\, \boxed{\pi}\, \boxed{)}\, \boxed{=}$ $\boxed{\text{33613.52398}}$

The tire makes about 33,614 revolutions.

Self Check 2

Find the perimeter of the figure shown below. Round to the nearest hundredth. (Assume the arc is a semicircle.)

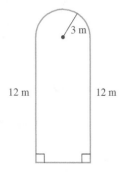

3 m

12 m   12 m

EXAMPLE 2   *Architecture* A Norman window is constructed by adding a semicircular window to the top of a rectangular window. Find the perimeter of the Norman window shown here.

Strategy We will find the perimeter of the rectangular part and the circumference of the circular part of the window and add the results.

8 ft   8 ft

WHY The window is a combination of a rectangle and a semicircle.

6 ft

Solution The perimeter of the rectangular part is

$$P_{\text{rectangular part}} = 8 + 6 + 8 = 22 \quad \text{Add only 3 sides of the rectangle.}$$

The perimeter of the semicircle is one-half of the circumference of a circle that has a 6-foot diameter.

$$P_{\text{semicircle}} = \frac{1}{2}C \qquad \text{This is the formula for the circumference of a semicircle.}$$

$$P_{\text{semicircle}} = \frac{1}{2}\pi D \qquad \text{Since we know the diameter, replace } C \text{ with } \pi D. \text{ We could also have replaced } C \text{ with } 2\pi r.$$

$$= \frac{1}{2}\pi(6) \qquad \text{Substitute 6 for D, the diameter.}$$

$$\approx 9.424777961 \qquad \text{Use a calculator to do the multiplication.}$$

Now Try Problem 29

The total perimeter is the sum of the two parts.

$$P_{\text{total}} = P_{\text{rectangular part}} + P_{\text{semicircle}}$$
$$P_{\text{total}} \approx 22 + 9.424777961$$
$$\approx 31.424777961$$

To the nearest hundredth, the perimeter of the window is 31.42 feet.

3 Find the area of a circle.

If we divide the circle shown in figure (a) into an even number of pie-shaped pieces and then rearrange them as shown in figure (b), we have a figure that looks like a parallelogram. The figure has a base b that is one-half the circumference of the circle, and its height h is about the same length as a radius of the circle.

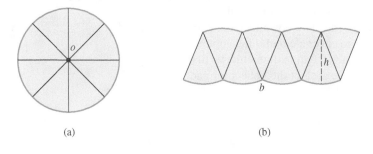

(a)   (b)

If we divide the circle into more and more pie-shaped pieces, the figure will look more and more like a parallelogram, and we can find its area by using the formula for the area of a parallelogram.

$$A = bh$$
$$A = \frac{1}{2}Cr \qquad \text{Substitute } \frac{1}{2} \text{ of the circumference for } b, \text{ the length of the base of the "parallelogram." Substitute } r \text{ for the height of the "parallelogram."}$$
$$= \frac{1}{2}(2\pi r)r \qquad \text{Substitute } 2\pi r \text{ for } C.$$
$$= \pi r^2 \qquad \text{Simplify: } \frac{1}{2} \cdot 2 = 1 \text{ and } r \cdot r = r^2.$$

This result gives the following formula.

Area of a Circle

The area of a circle with radius r is given by the formula

$$A = \pi r^2$$

EXAMPLE 3   Find the area of the circle shown on the right. Give the exact answer and an approximation to the nearest tenth.

Strategy We will find the radius of the circle, substitute that value for r in the formula $A = \pi r^2$, and evaluate the right side.

WHY The variable A represents the unknown area of the circle.

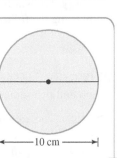

$\leftarrow$—10 cm—$\rightarrow$

Self Check 3

Find the area of a circle with a diameter of 12 feet. Give the exact answer and an approximation to the nearest tenth.

Now Try Problem 33

Solution Since the length of the diameter is 10 centimeters and the length of a diameter is twice the length of a radius, the length of the radius is 5 centimeters.

$$A = \pi r^2 \qquad \text{This is the formula for the area of a circle.}$$

$$A = \pi(5)^2 \qquad \text{Substitute 5 for } r, \text{ the radius of the circle. The notation } \pi r^2 \text{ means } \pi \cdot r^2.$$

$$= \pi(25) \qquad \text{Evaluate the exponential expression.}$$

$$= 25\pi \qquad \text{Write the product so that } \pi \text{ is the last factor.}$$

The exact area of the circle is 25π cm^2. We can use a calculator to approximate the area.

$$A \approx 78.53981634 \qquad \text{Use a calculator to do the multiplication: } 25 \cdot \pi.$$

To the nearest tenth, the area is 78.5 cm^2.

Using Your CALCULATOR   Painting a Helicopter Landing Pad

Orange paint is available in gallon containers at $19 each, and each gallon will cover 375 ft^2. To calculate how much the paint will cost to cover a circular helicopter landing pad 60 feet in diameter, we first calculate the area of the helicopter pad.

$$A = \pi r^2 \qquad \text{This is the formula for the area of a circle.}$$

$$A = \pi(30)^2 \qquad \text{Substitute one-half of 60 for } r, \text{ the radius of the circular pad.}$$

$$= 30^2\pi \qquad \text{Write the product so that } \pi \text{ is the last factor.}$$

The area of the pad is exactly $30^2\pi$ ft^2. Since each gallon of paint will cover 375 ft^2, we can find the number of gallons of paint needed by dividing $30^2\pi$ by 375.

$$\text{Number of gallons needed} = \frac{30^2\pi}{375}$$

We can use a scientific calculator to make this calculation.

$$30 \boxed{x^2} \boxed{\times} \boxed{\pi} \boxed{=} \boxed{\div} 375 \boxed{=} \qquad\qquad \boxed{\mathsf{7.539822369}}$$

Because paint comes only in full gallons, the painter will need to purchase 8 gallons. The cost of the paint will be 8($19), or $152.

Self Check 4

Find the area of the shaded figure below. Round to the nearest hundredth.

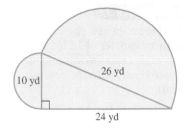

EXAMPLE 4   Find the area of the shaded figure on the right. Round to the nearest hundredth.

Strategy We will find the area of the entire shaded figure using the following approach:

$$A_{\text{total}} = A_{\text{triangle}} + A_{\text{smaller semicircle}} + A_{\text{larger semicircle}}$$

WHY The shaded figure is a combination of a triangular region and two semicircular regions.

Solution The area of the triangle is

$$A_{\text{triangle}} = \frac{1}{2}bh = \frac{1}{2}(6)(8) = \frac{1}{2}(48) = 24$$

Since the formula for the area of a circle is $A = \pi r^2$, the formula for the area of a semicircle is $A = \frac{1}{2}\pi r^2$. Thus, the area enclosed by the smaller semicircle is

$$A_{\text{smaller semicircle}} = \frac{1}{2}\pi r^2 = \frac{1}{2}\pi(4)^2 = \frac{1}{2}\pi(16) = 8\pi$$

The area enclosed by the larger semicircle is

$$A_{\text{larger semicircle}} = \frac{1}{2}\pi r^2 = \frac{1}{2}\pi(5)^2 = \frac{1}{2}\pi(25) = 12.5\pi$$

The total area is the sum of the three results:

$$A_{\text{total}} = 24 + 8\pi + 12.5\pi \approx 88.4026494 \qquad \text{Use a calculator to perform the operations.}$$

To the nearest hundredth, the area of the shaded figure is 88.40 in.^{2}.

Now Try **Problem 37**

$$
\begin{array}{r}
12.5 \\
2\overline{)25.0} \\
-2 \\
\hline
05 \\
-4 \\
\hline
10 \\
-10 \\
\hline
0
\end{array}
$$

ANSWERS TO SELF CHECKS

1. 24π m ≈ 75.4 m   **2.** 39.42 m   **3.** 36π ft$^2 \approx 113.1$ ft^2 **4.** 424.73 yd^2

SECTION 2.12   STUDY SET

VOCABULARY

Fill in the blanks.

1. A segment drawn from the center of a circle to a point on the circle is called a _____.

2. A segment joining two points on a circle is called a _____.

3. A _____ is a chord that passes through the center of a circle.

4. An arc that is one-half of a complete circle is a _____.

5. The distance around a circle is called its _____.

6. The surface enclosed by a circle is called its _____.

7. A diameter of a circle is _____ as long as a radius.

8. Suppose the exact circumference of a circle is 3π feet. When we write $C \approx 9.42$ feet, we are giving an _____ of the circumference.

CONCEPTS

Refer to the figure below, where point 0 is the center of the circle.

9. Name each radius.

10. Name a diameter.

11. Name each chord.

12. Name each minor arc.

13. Name each semicircle.

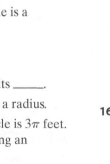

14. Name major arc $\overgroup{ABD}$ in another way.

15. Tell which concept applies, circumference or area.
    a. The cooking surface for a circular barbeque grill
    b. The distance run by a hamster on an exercise wheel
    c. The amount of room on a circular dance floor
    d. The length of plastic pipe needed to make a Hula Hoop
    e. The distance a point on the tip of a ceiling fan blade travels
    f. The amount of glass covering the face of a circular clock
    g. One revolution on a Ferris wheel ride

16. a. If you know the radius of a circle, how can you find its diameter?
    b. If you know the diameter of a circle, how can you find its radius?

17. a. What are the two formulas that can be used to find the circumference of a circle?
    b. What is the formula for the area of a circle?

18. a. If C is the circumference of a circle and D is its diameter, then $\frac{C}{D} = $ ▢.
    b. If D is the diameter of a circle and r is its radius, then $D = $ ▢ r.

19. When evaluating $\pi(6)^2$, what operation should be performed first?

20. a. Which type of measurement listed below is circumference related to?

weight   time   area   perimeter   volume

b. Which units listed below are acceptable when finding circumference?

ft² in.³ sec meters pounds yd

Fill in the blanks.

21. The symbol $\overset{\frown}{AB}$ is read as "____ ____."

22. To the nearest hundredth, the value of π is _____.

23. a. In the expression $2\pi r$, what operations are indicated?

b. In the expression πr^2, what operations are indicated?

24. Write each expression in better form. Leave π in your answer.

a. $\pi(8)$ **b.** $2\pi(7)$ **c.** $\pi \cdot \dfrac{25}{3}$

GUIDED PRACTICE

The answers to the problems in this Study Set may vary slightly, depending on which approximation of π is used.

Find the circumference of the circle shown below. Give the exact answer and an approximation to the nearest tenth. See Example 1.

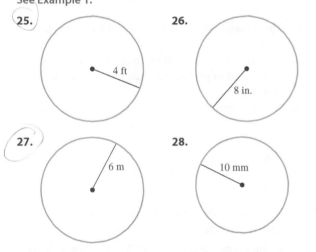

25.   **26.**

4 ft   8 in.

27.   **28.**

6 m   10 mm

Find the perimeter of each figure. Assume each arc is a semicircle. Round to the nearest hundredth. See Example 2.

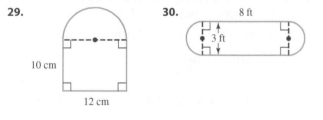

29.   **30.**   8 ft

3 ft

10 cm

12 cm

31.   **32.**   18 in.

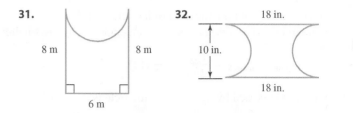

8 m   8 m   10 in.

6 m   18 in.

Find the area of each circle given the following information. Give the exact answer and an approximation to the nearest tenth. See Example 3.

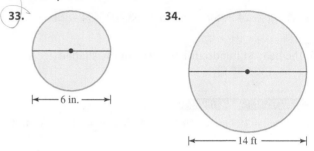

33.   **34.**

6 in.

14 ft

35. Find the area of a circle with diameter 18 inches.

36. Find the area of a circle with diameter 20 meters.

Find the total area of each figure. Assume each arc is a semicircle. Round to the nearest tenth. See Example 4.

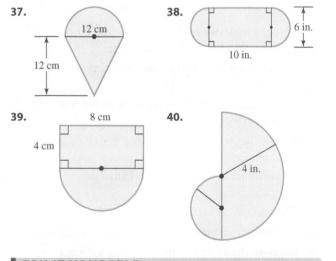

37.   **38.**   6 in.

12 cm   10 in.

12 cm

39.   8 cm   **40.**

4 cm   4 in.

TRY IT YOURSELF

Find the area of each shaded region. Round to the nearest tenth.

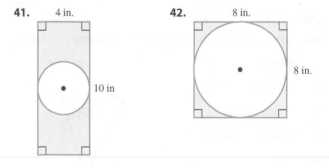

41.   4 in.   **42.**   8 in.

10 in   8 in.

43.

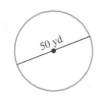

r = 4 in.
h = 9 in.
13 in.

44.

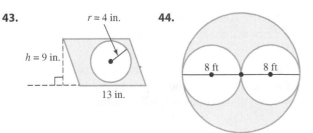

8 ft   8 ft

(Hint: For a parallelogram, $A = bh$.)

45. Find the circumference of the circle shown below. Give the exact answer and an approximation to the nearest hundredth.

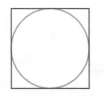

50 yd

46. Find the circumference of the semicircle shown below. Give the exact answer and an approximation to the nearest hundredth.

25 cm

47. Find the circumference of the circle shown below if the square has sides of length 6 inches. Give the exact answer and an approximation to the nearest tenth.

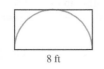

48. Find the circumference of the semicircle shown below if the length of the rectangle in which it is enclosed is 8 feet. Give the exact answer and an approximation to the nearest tenth.

8 ft

49. Find the area of the circle shown below if the square has sides of length 9 millimeters. Give the exact answer and an approximation to the nearest tenth.

50. Find the area of the shaded semicircular region shown below. Give the exact answer and an approximation to the nearest tenth.

⟵ 6.5 mi ⟶

CONCEPT EXTENSIONS

51. Which has the greater area, a circle with radius 8 in. or a circle with diameter 17 in.?

52. a. If you double the radius of a circle, how much larger does its circumference become?

b. If you double the radius of a circle, how much larger does its area become?

53. What is the radius of a circle whose area is 49π ft²?

54. Three semicircles are drawn on a right triangle with sides of length 6 in., 8 in., and 10 in., as shown below.

a. Find the area of each semicircle. You may leave π in each answer.

b. What is the mathematical relationship between the areas of the three semicircles?

c. What important geometric theorem comes to mind?

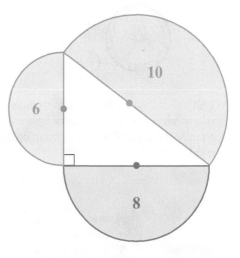

10

6

8

APPLICATIONS

55. Suppose the two "legs" of the compass shown below are adjusted so that the distance between the pointed ends is 1 inch. Then a circle is drawn.

   a. What will the radius of the circle be?

   b. What will the diameter of the circle be?

   c. What will the circumference of the circle be? Give an exact answer and an approximation to the nearest hundredth.

   d. What will the area of the circle be? Give an exact answer and an approximation to the nearest hundredth.

56. Suppose we find the distance around a can and the distance across the can using a measuring tape, as shown to the right. Then we make a comparison, in the form of a ratio:

$$\frac{\text{The distance around the can}}{\text{The distance across the top of the can}}$$

After we do the indicated division, the result will be close to what number?

When appropriate, give the exact answer and an approximation to the nearest hundredth. Answers may vary slightly, depending on which approximation of π is used.

57. WHEELCHAIRS Find the diameter of the rear wheel and the radius of the front wheel.

12.5 in.   5 in.

58. SKATEBOARDING A half-pipe ramp is in the shape of a semicircle with a radius of 8 feet. To the nearest tenth of a foot, what is the length of the arc that the rider travels on the ramp?

8 ft

Plywood

59. LAKES Round Lake has a circular shoreline that is 2 miles in diameter. Find the area of the lake.

60. HELICOPTERS Refer to the figure below. How far does a point on the tip of a rotor blade travel when it makes one complete revolution?

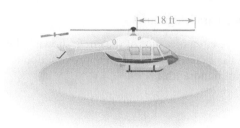

←—18 ft—→

61. GIANT SEQUOIA The largest sequoia tree is the General Sherman Tree in Sequoia National Park in California. In fact, it is considered to be the largest living thing in the world. According to the *Guinness Book of World Records*, it has a diameter of 32.66 feet, measured $4\frac{1}{2}$ feet above the ground. What is the circumference of the tree at that height?

62. TRAMPOLINE See the figure below. The distance from the center of the trampoline to the edge of its steel frame is 7 feet. The protective padding covering the springs is 18 inches wide. Find the area of the circular jumping surface of the trampoline, in square feet.

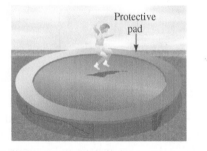

Protective pad

63. JOGGING Joan wants to jog 10 miles on a circular track $\frac{1}{4}$ mile in diameter. How many times must she circle the track? Round to the nearest lap.

64. CARPETING A state capitol building has a circular floor 100 feet in diameter. The legislature wishes to have the floor carpeted. The lowest bid is $83 per square yard, including installation. How much must the legislature spend for the carpeting project? Round to the nearest dollar.

65. ARCHERY The diameter of a standard archery target used in the Olympics is 48.8 inches. Find the area of the target. Round to the nearest square inch.

66. BULLS-EYE See Exercise 65. The diameter of the center yellow ring of a standard archery target is 4.8 inches. What is the area of the bulls-eye? Round to the nearest tenth of a square inch.

67. HORSES A horse trots in a circle around its trainer at the end of a 28-foot-long rope. Find the area of the circle that is swept out. Round to the nearest square foot.

68. YO-YOS How far does a yo-yo travel during one revolution of the "around the world" trick if the length of the string is 21 inches?

69. COOKING If the fish shown in the illustration is 18 inches long, what is the area of the grill? Round to the nearest square inch.

70. TEEPEES The teepees constructed by the Blackfoot Indians were cone-shaped tents about 10 feet high and about 15 feet across at the ground. Estimate the amount of floor space of a teepee with these dimensions, to the nearest square foot.

71. IGLOOS During long journeys, some Canadian Eskimos built winter houses of snow blocks stacked in the dome shape shown. Estimate the amount of floor space of an igloo having an interior height of 5.5 feet to the nearest square foot.

72. LANDSCAPE DESIGN See the figure below. How many square feet of lawn does not get watered by the four sprinklers at the center of each circle?

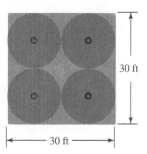

30 ft

30 ft

73. COMPARING PRICES A large 14-inch diameter cheese pizza sells for $13 and a personal-size 7-inch diameter cheese pizza sells for $6.

   a. Find the area of the large pizza. Then divide its cost, $13, by the area. (Round to the nearest hundredth.) This is the cost per square inch of a large pizza.

   b. Find the area of the personal-size pizza. Then divide its cost, $7, by the area. (Round to the nearest hundredth.) This is the cost per square inch of a personal-size pizza.

   c. Use your answer to determine which pizza is the better buy.

74. POOL COVERS The diameter of a circular swimming pool is 20 feet.

   a. Find the surface area of the pool. Round your answer up, to the nearest square foot.

   b The solar cloth from which the cover is to be made comes in bolts that are 8-feet wide. How many linear feet of cloth off of the bolt should be purchased to cover the pool? Round up, to the nearest foot.

   c. To keep it in place, the cover needs to have an elastic border. How many feet of elastic should be purchased? Round up, to the nearest foot.

▌WRITING

75. Explain what is meant by the circumference of a circle.

76. Explain what is meant by the area of a circle.

77. Explain the meaning of π.

78. Explain what it means for a car to have a small *turning radius*.

Objectives

1. Multiply decimals by powers of 10 greater than 1.
2. Multiply decimals by powers of 10 less than 1.
3. Convert from scientific notation to standard notation.
4. Write numbers in scientific notation.

SECTION 2.13
Scientific Notation

ARE YOU READY?

The following problems review some basic skills that are needed when working with scientific notation.

1. Evaluate: 10^2
2. Multiply: $1,000 \cdot 4.528$
3. Evaluate: 10^6
4. Multiply: $0.01 \cdot 6.22$

Scientists often deal with extremely large and extremely small numbers. Two examples are shown below.

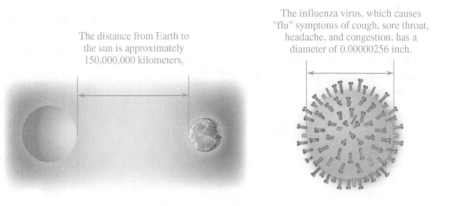

The distance from Earth to the sun is approximately 150,000,000 kilometers,

The influenza virus, which causes "flu" symptoms of cough, sore throat, headache, and congestion, has a diameter of 0.00000256 inch.

The large number of zeros in 150,000,000 and 0.00000256 makes them difficult to read and hard to remember. In this section, we will discuss a notation that will make such numbers easier to use. To write numbers in that notation, you need to be familiar with powers of 10.

1 Multiply decimals by powers of 10 greater than 1.

The numbers 10, 100, and 1,000, on are called **powers of ten** because they are the results when we evaluate 10^1, 10^2, and 10^3. In Section 2.9: Multiplying Decimals, we developed a rule to quickly find the product when multiplying a decimal by a power of 10 that is greater than 1.

> **Multiplying a Decimal by 10, 100, 1,000 and So On**
>
> To find the product of a decimal and 10, 100, 1,000, and so on, move the decimal point to the right the same number of places as there are zeros in the power of 10.

Several examples of the use of this rule are shown below. We quickly find the product of 8.675 and 10, 100, and 1,000, by moving the decimal point the correct number of places to the right.

One zero in 10	Two zeros in 100	Three zeros in 1,000
$8.675 \cdot 10 = 86.75$	$8.675 \cdot 100 = 867.5$	$8.675 \cdot 1,000 = 8675$
It moves 1 place to the right.	It moves 2 places to the right.	It moves 3 places to the right.

If we replace 10, 100, and 1,000 in the previous examples with their equivalent exponential expressions ($10^1, 10^2, 10^3$), we see that the exponent gives the number of places to move the decimal point to the right to quickly find the product.

The exponent is 1.

$8.675 \cdot 10^1 = 86.75$

It moves 1 place
to the right.

The exponent is 2.

$8.675 \cdot 10^2 = 867.5$

It moves 2 places
to the right.

The exponent is 3.

$8.675 \cdot 10^3 = 8675$

It moves 3 places
to the right.

2 Multiply decimals by powers of 10 less than 1.

So far, we have only considered powers of 10 that have positive integer exponents (1, 2, 3, 4, 5, and so on). It is also possible for a power of 10 to have a zero exponent or a negative integer exponent. To understand what zero and negative exponents mean, examine the following pattern.

$10^4 = 10,000$

$10^3 = 1000$

$10^2 = 100$

$10^1 = 10$

Divide by 10.

Divide by 10.

Divide by 10.

For Positive integer exponents,
each time that we decrease
the exponent by 1, the value of
the exponential expression is
divided by 10.

$10^0 = 1$ For the pattern to continue, we define $10^0 = 1$.

$10^{-1} = \dfrac{1}{10}$ For the pattern to continue, we define $10^{-1} = \dfrac{1}{10} = \dfrac{1}{10}$.

$10^{-2} = \dfrac{1}{100}$ For the pattern to continue, we define $10^{-2} = \dfrac{1}{10^2} = \dfrac{1}{100}$.

$10^{-3} = \dfrac{1}{1,000}$ For the pattern to continue, we define $10^{-3} = \dfrac{1}{10^3} = \dfrac{1}{1,000}$.

The observations from the pattern above illustrate the following definitions.

Zero Exponent

$10^0 = 1$ Read as "10 to the zero power equals 1."

Negative Exponents

For any integer n,

$10^{-n} = \dfrac{1}{10^n}$ Read as "10 to the negative nth power equals 1 over 10 to the nth power."

In words, 10^{-n} is the reciprocal of 10^n.

When we evaluate powers of 10 that have negative integer exponents, we can express the result in fraction form or in its equivalent decimal form. For example:

$10^{-1} = \dfrac{1}{10^1} = \dfrac{1}{10} = 0.1$ $10^{-2} = \dfrac{1}{10^2} = \dfrac{1}{100} = 0.01$ $10^{-3} = \dfrac{1}{10^3} = \dfrac{1}{1,000} = 0.001$

In Section 2.9: Multiplying Decimals, we developed a rule to quickly find the product when multiplying a decimal by a power of 10 that is less than 1.

Multiplying a Decimal by 0.1, 0.01, 0.001, and So On

To find the product of a decimal and 0.1, 0.01, 0.001, and so on, move the decimal point to the left the same number of decimal places as there are in the power of 10.

Several examples of the use of this rule are shown below. We quickly find the product of 5.19 and 0.1, 0.01, and 0.01, by moving the decimal point the correct number of places to the left.

Multiply: $5.19 \cdot 0.1$

$$\begin{array}{r} 5.19 \\ \times \quad 0.1 \\ \hline 0.519 \end{array}$$

Multiply: $5.19 \cdot 0.01$

$$\begin{array}{r} 5.19 \\ \times \quad 0.01 \\ \hline 0.0519 \end{array}$$

Multiply: $5.19 \cdot 0.001$

$$\begin{array}{r} 5.19 \\ \times \quad 0.001 \\ \hline 0.00519 \end{array}$$

If we replace 0.1, 0.01, and 0.001 in the examples above with their equivalent exponential expressions ($10^{-1}, 10^{-2}, 10^{-3}$), we see that the exponent gives the number of places to move the decimal point to the left to quickly find the product.

The exponent is -1.

$5.19 \cdot 10^{-1} = 0.519$

It moves 1 place to the left.

The exponent is -2.

$5.19 \cdot 10^{-2} = 0.0519$

It moves 2 places to the left.

The exponent is v3.

$5.19 \cdot 10^{-3} = 0.00519$

It moves 3 places to the left.

3 ## Convert from scientific notation to standard notation.

Scientific notation

A positive number is written in scientific notation when it is written in the form $N \times 10^n$, where N is a number greater than or equal to 1 and less than 10 and n is an integer.

To write numbers in scientific notation, you need to be familiar with **powers of 10,** like those listed in the table below.

Power of 10	10^4	10^3	10^2	10^1	10^0	10^{-1}	10^{-2}	10^{-3}	10^{-4}
Value	10,000	1,000	100	10	1	$\frac{1}{10} = 0.1$	$\frac{1}{100} = 0.01$	$\frac{1}{1,000} = 0.001$	$\frac{1}{10,000} = 0.0001$

Three examples of numbers written in scientific notation are shown below. Note that each of them is the product of a decimal number (between 1 and 10) and a power of 10.

An integer exponent
↓
3.67×10^2 2.158×10^{-3} 4.0×10^{57}

A decimal that is at least 1, but less than 10

The Language of Mathematics The $\times$ sign for multiplication is usually used to write scientific notation. However, some books use a raised dot $\cdot$ instead.

A number written in scientific notation can be converted to standard notation by performing the indicated multiplication. For example, to convert 3.67×10^2, we recall that multiplying a decimal by 100 moves the decimal point 2 places to the right.

$$3.67 \times 10^2 = 3.67 \times 100 = 3\,6\,7.$$

To convert 2.158×10^{-3} to standard notation, we recall that multiplying a decimal by 0.001 moves the decimal point 3 places to the left.

$$2.158 \times 10^{-3} = 2.158 \times 0.001 = \frac{2.158}{1,000} = 0.0\,0\,2\,1\,5\,8$$

In 3.67×10^2 and 2.158×10^{-3}, the exponent gives the number of decimal places that the decimal point moves, and the sign of the exponent indicates the direction in which it moves. Applying this observation to several other examples, we have

$5.32 \times 10^6 = 5\,3\,2\,0\,0\,0\,0.$ *Move the decimal point 6 places to the right.*

$1.95 \times 10^{-5} = 0.0\,0\,0\,0\,1\,9\,5$ *Move the decimal point $|-5| = 5$ places to the left.*

$9.7 \times 10^0 = 9.7$ *There is no movement of the decimal point.*

The following procedure summarizes our observations.

Converting from Scientific to Standard Notation

1. If the exponent is positive, move the decimal point the same number of places to the right as the exponent.

2. If the exponent is negative, move the decimal point the same number of places to the left as the absolute value of the exponent.

EXAMPLE 1   Convert to standard notation: **a.** 3.467×10^5
b. 8.9×10^{-4}

Strategy In each case, we need to identify the exponent on the power of 10 and consider its sign.

WHY The exponent gives the number of decimal places that we should move the decimal point. The sign of the exponent indicates whether it should be moved to the right or the left.

Solution

a. Since the exponent in 10^5 is 5, the decimal point moves 5 places to the right.

$3\,4\,6\,7\,0\,0.$ *To move 5 places to the right, two placeholder zeros must be written.*

Thus, $3.467 \times 10^5 = 346,700$.

b. Since the exponent in 10^{-4} is -4, the decimal point moves 4 places to the left.

$0.0\,0\,0\,8\,9$ *To move 4 places to the left, three placeholder zeros must be written.*

Thus, $8.9 \times 10^{-4} = 0.00089$.

Self Check 1
Convert to standard notation:
a. 4.88×10^6
b. 9.8×10^{-3}

Now Try **Problems 15 and 17**

4   Write Numbers in Scientific Notation.

To write a number in scientific notation ($N \times 10^n$) we first determine N and then n.

EXAMPLE 2   Write each number in scientific notation: **a.** 150,000,000
b. 0.00000256

Strategy We will write each number as the product of a number between 1 and 10 and a power of 10.

WHY Numbers written in scientific notation have the form $N \times 10^n$.

Solution

a. We must write 150,000,000 (the distance in kilometers from the Earth to the sun) as the product of a number between 1 and 10 and a power of 10. We note that 1.5 lies between 1 and 10. To obtain 150,000,000, we must move the deci-mal point in 1.5 exactly 8 places to the right.

$$1.5\,0\,0\,0\,0\,0\,0\,0$$

This will happen if we multiply 1.5 by 10^8. Therefore,

$$150{,}000{,}000 = 1.5 \times 10^8 \quad \text{This is the distance (in kilometers) from the Earth to the sun.}$$

b. We must write 0.00000256 (the diameter in inches of a flu virus) as the product of a number between 1 and 10 and a power of 10. We note that 2.56 lies between 1 and 10. To obtain 0.00000256, the decimal point in 2.56 must be moved 6 places to the left.

$$0\,0\,0\,0\,0\,0\,2.56$$

This will happen if we multiply 2.56 by 10^{-6}. Therefore,

$$0.00000256 = 2.56 \times 10^{-6} \quad \text{This is the diameter (in inches) of a flu virus.}$$

The results from Example 2 illustrate the following forms to use when converting numbers from standard to scientific notation.

For real numbers between 0 and 1:    $\times 10^{\text{negative integer}}$
For real numbers at least 1, but less than 10:   ▨ $\times 10^0$
For real numbers greater than or equal to 10:   ▨ $\times 10^{\text{positive integer}}$

SECTION 2.13   STUDY SET

▌VOCABULARY

Fill in the blanks.

1. 4.84×10^5 is written in _____ notation. 484,000 is written in _____ notation.

2. 10^3, 10^{50}, and 10^{-4} are _____ of 10.

▌CONCEPTS

Fill in the blanks.

3. When we multiply a decimal by 10^5, the decimal point moves 5 places to the _____. When we multiply a decimal by 10^{-7}, the decimal point moves 7 places to the ____.

4. Describe the procedure for converting a number from scientific notation to standard form.

    a. If the exponent on the base of 10 is positive, move the decimal point the same number of places to the _____ as the exponent.

    b. If the exponent on the base of 10 is negative, move the decimal point the same number of places to the _____ as the absolute value of the exponent.

5. **a.** When a real number greater than or equal to 10 is written in scientific notation, the exponent on 10 is a _____ integer.

    b. When a real number between 0 and 1 is written in scientific notation, the exponent on 10 is a _____ integer.

6. The arrows show the movement of a decimal point. By what power of 10 was each decimal multiplied?

    a. 0.000000556

    b. 8,041,000,000.

Fill in the blanks to write each number in scientific notation.

7. **a.** $7{,}700 = \boxed{} \times 10^3$ **b.** $500{,}000 = \boxed{} \times 10^5$

    c. $114{,}000{,}000 = 1.14 \times 10^{\boxed{}}$

8. **a.** $0.0082 = \boxed{} \times 10^{-3}$

    b. $0.0000001 = \boxed{} \times 10^{-7}$

    c. $0.00003457 = 3.457 \times 10^{\boxed{}}$

9. Complete the table.

Standard form	Decimal	Exponent for power of 10	Scientific Notation
2,840,000	2.84	6	
909,400,000	9.094		
16,000,000,000,000			
	6.411		6.411×10^5

10. Complete the table.

Standard form	Decimal	Exponent for power of 10	Scientific Notation
0.00081	8.1	−4	
0.0000746	7.46		
0.0000000002919			
	4.605		4.605×10^{-7}

NOTATION

11. Fill in the blanks. A positive number is written in scientific notation when it is written in the form $N \times 10^n$, where N is a number greater than or equal to ___ and less than ___ and n is an _____.

12. Express each power of 10 in fraction form and decimal form.

    a. 10^{-3} **b.** 10^{-6}

GUIDED PRACTICE

Convert each number to standard notation. **See Example 1.**

13. 2.3×10^2 14. 3.75×10^4

15. 8.12×10^5 16. 1.2×10^3

17. 1.15×10^{-3} 18. 4.9×10^{-2}

19. 9.76×10^{-4} 20. 7.63×10^{-5}

21. 6.001×10^6 22. 9.998×10^5

23. 2.718×10^0 24. 3.14×10^0

25. 6.789×10^{-2} 26. 4.321×10^{-1}

27. 2.0×10^{-5} 28. 7.0×10^{-6}

Write each number in scientific notation. **See Example 2.**

29. 23,000   30. 4,750

31. 1,700,000   32. 290,000

33. 0.062   34. 0.00073

35. 0.0000051   36. 0.04

37. 5,000,000,000   38. 7,000,000

39. 0.0000003   40. 0.0001

41. 909,000,000   42. 7,007,000,000

43. 0.0345   44. 0.000000567

45. 9   46. 2

47. 11   48. 55

49. 1,718,000,000,000,000,000

50. 44,180,000,000,000,000,000

51. 0.0000000000000123

52. 0.0000000000000000555

CONCEPT EXTENSIONS

53. Arrange the following numbers in order from least to greatest. Do not convert them to standard notation.
7.81×10^7 7.81×10^{-3} 7.81×10^1 7.81×10^{-5} 7.81×10^4

54. Fill in the blanks.

    a. If $1{,}000 = 10^3$, then $\dfrac{1}{1{,}000} = 10^{\boxed{}}$.

    b. If $\dfrac{1}{10{,}000{,}000} = 10^{-7}$, then $10{,}000{,}000 = 10^{\boxed{}}$.

55. **a.** What is the reciprocal of 10^0?

    b. What is the opposite of 10^0?

    c. What is the additive inverse of 10^0?

56. **a.** Explain why 23.91×10^{15} is not written in scientific notation.

    b. Write 23.91×10^{15} in scientific notation.

APPLICATIONS

57. ASTRONOMY The distance from Earth to Alpha Centauri (the nearest star outside our solar system) is about 25,700,000,000,000 miles. Express this number in scientific notation.

58. SPEED OF SOUND The speed of sound in air is 33,100 centimeters per second. Express this number in scientific notation.

59. GEOGRAPHY The largest ocean in the world is the Pacific Ocean, which covers 6.38×10^7 square miles. Express this number in standard notation.

60. ATOMS The number of atoms in 1 gram of iron is approximately 1.08×10^{22}. Express this number in standard notation.

61. LENGTH OF A METER One meter is approximately 0.00622 mile. Use scientific notation to express this number.

62. ANGSTROM One angstrom is 1.0×10^{-7} millimeter. Express this number in standard notation.

63. WAVELENGTHS Transmitters, vacuum tubes, and lights emit energy that can be modeled as a wave, as shown. Examples of the most common types of electromagnetic waves are given in the table. List the wavelengths in order from shortest to longest.

This distance between the two crests of the wave is called the wavelength.

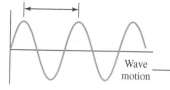

Wave motion

Type	Use	Wavelength (m)
visible light	lighting	9.3×10^{-6}
infrared	photography	3.7×10^{-5}
x-ray	medical	2.3×10^{-11}
radio wave	communication	3.0×10^2
gamma ray	treating cancer	8.9×10^{-14}
microwave	cooking	1.1×10^{-2}
ultraviolet	sun lamp	6.1×10^{-8}

64. WATER According to the U.S. Geological Survey, the total water supply of the world is 366,000,000,000,000,000,000 gallons. Write this number in scientific notation.

65. EARTH, SUN, MOON The surface area of Earth is 1.97×10^8 square miles, the surface area of the sun is 1.09×10^{17} square miles, and the surface area of the moon is 1.46×10^7 square miles. Convert each number to standard notation.

66. SAND The mass of one grain of beach sand is approximately 0.00000000045 ounce. Write this number in scientific notation.

67. MOLECULES The mass of a water molecule is approximately 0.00000000000000000000001056 ounce. Write this number in scientific notation.

68. FIVE-CARD POKER The odds against being dealt the hand shown in the illustration are about 2.6×10^6 to 1. Express the odds using standard notation.

69. ENERGY See the graph below. Express each of the following using scientific notation.
  a. U.S. energy consumption (94 quadrillion, 600 trillion Btu)
  b. U.S. energy production (72 quadrillion, 900 trillion Btu)
  c. The difference in 2009 consumption and production

2009 U.S. Energy Consumption and Production
(petroleum, natural gas, coal, hydroelectric, nuclear, geothermal, solar, wind)

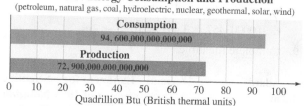

Source: Energy Information Administration, United States Department of Energy

70. ASTRONOMY The American Physical Society recently honored first-year graduate student Gwen Bell for coming up with what it considers the most accurate estimate of the mass of the Milky Way. In pounds, her estimate is a 3 with 42 zeros after it. Express this number in scientific notation.

71. NATIONAL DEBT As of January 2011, the U.S. national debt was approximately $13,950,000,000,000. The estimated population of the United States at that time was approximately 310,000,000. Write the amount of the debt in scientific notation. (Source: www.census .gov; www.usdebtclock.org).

72. POWER OF 10 In the United States, we use Latin prefixes in front of "illion" to name extremely large numbers. Write each number in scientific notation.

One million: 1,000,000

One billion: 1,000,000,000

One trillion: 1,000,000,000,000

One quadrillion: 1,000,000,000,000,000

One quintillion: 1,000,000,000,000,000,000

73. THE MILITARY The graph shows the number of U.S. troops for several years. Estimate each of the following and express your answers in scientific and standard notation.

  a. The number of troops in 1993

  b. The largest numbers of troops during these years

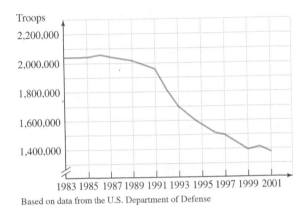

Troops

Based on data from the U.S. Department of Defense

74. ATOMS A hydrogen atom is so small that a single drop of water contains more than a million million billion hydrogen atoms. Express this number in scientific notation.

WRITING

75. In what situations would scientific notation be more convenient than standard notation?

76. To multiply a number by a power of 10, we move the decimal point. Which way, and how far? Explain.

77. 2.3×10^{-3} contains a negative sign but represents a positive number. Explain.

78. Is this a true statement? $2.0 \times 10^3 = 2 \times 10^3$ Explain.

MODULE 2 TEST

1. Fill in the blanks.

  a. For the fraction $\frac{6}{7}$, the _____ is 6 and the _____ is 7.

  b. Two fractions are _____ if they represent the same number.

  c. A fraction is in _____ form when the numerator and denominator have no common factors other than 1.

  d. To _____ a fraction, we remove common factors of the numerator and denominator.

  e. The _____ of $\frac{4}{5}$ is $\frac{5}{4}$.

  f. A _____ number, such as $1\frac{9}{16}$, is the sum of a whole number and a proper fraction.

2. See the illustration below.

  a. What fractional part of the plant is above ground?

  b. What fractional part of the plant is below ground?

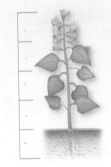

3. Each region outlined in black represents one whole. Write an improper fraction and a mixed number to represent the shaded portion.

4. Graph $2\frac{4}{5}$, $-\frac{2}{5}$, $-1\frac{1}{7}$, and $\frac{7}{6}$ on a number line.

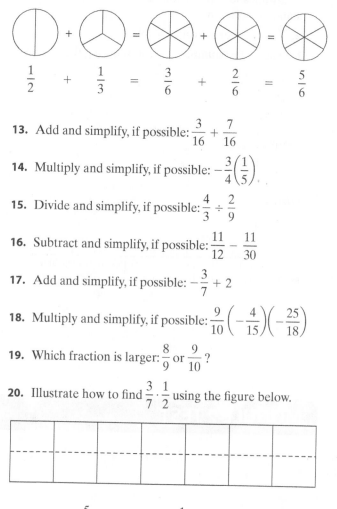

5. Are $\frac{1}{3}$ and $\frac{5}{15}$ equivalent?

6. Express $\frac{7}{8}$ as an equivalent fraction with denominator 24.

7. Simplify each fraction, if possible.

   a. $\frac{0}{15}$ **b.** $\frac{9}{0}$

8. Simplify each fraction.

   a. $\frac{27}{36}$ **b.** $\frac{72}{180}$

9. Explain how the fraction $\frac{42}{56}$ was simplified in each case below.

   a. $\frac{42}{56} = \frac{2 \cdot 3 \cdot 7}{2 \cdot 2 \cdot 2 \cdot 7} = \frac{3}{4}$

   b. $\frac{42}{56} = \frac{3 \cdot 14}{4 \cdot 14} = \frac{3}{4}$

10. What two equivalent fractions are shown below?

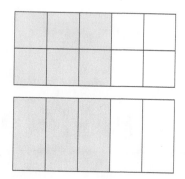

11. What subtraction problem is shown below?

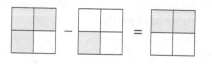

12. Use the figures below to illustrate how to find the sum.

$$\frac{1}{2} \quad + \quad \frac{1}{3} \quad = \quad \frac{3}{6} \quad + \quad \frac{2}{6} \quad = \quad \frac{5}{6}$$

13. Add and simplify, if possible: $\frac{3}{16} + \frac{7}{16}$

14. Multiply and simplify, if possible: $-\frac{3}{4}\left(\frac{1}{5}\right)$

15. Divide and simplify, if possible: $\frac{4}{3} \div \frac{2}{9}$

16. Subtract and simplify, if possible: $\frac{11}{12} - \frac{11}{30}$

17. Add and simplify, if possible: $-\frac{3}{7} + 2$

18. Multiply and simplify, if possible: $\frac{9}{10}\left(-\frac{4}{15}\right)\left(-\frac{25}{18}\right)$

19. Which fraction is larger: $\frac{8}{9}$ or $\frac{9}{10}$?

20. Illustrate how to find $\frac{3}{7} \cdot \frac{1}{2}$ using the figure below.

21. a. When $\frac{5}{16}$ is multiplied by $\frac{1}{2}$, why is the result smaller than both fraction?

   b. Explain why 5 divided by $\frac{1}{2}$ is larger than 5.

22. COFFEE DRINKERS Two-fifths of 100 adults surveyed said they started their morning with a cup of coffee. Of the 100, how many would this be?

23. THE INTERNET The graph on the next page shows the fraction of the total number of Internet searches that were made using various sites in January 2009.

What fraction of the all the searches were done using Google, Yahoo, or Microsoft sites?

Online Search Share
January 2009

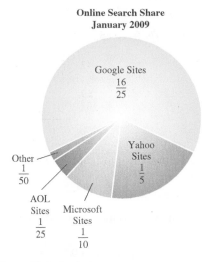

Google Sites $\frac{16}{25}$

Yahoo Sites $\frac{1}{5}$

Other $\frac{1}{50}$

AOL Sites $\frac{1}{25}$

Microsoft Sites $\frac{1}{10}$

Source: Marketingcharts.com

24. **a.** Write $\frac{55}{6}$ as a mixed number.

   b. Write $1\frac{18}{21}$ as an improper fraction.

25. Find the sum of $157\frac{3}{10}$ and $103\frac{13}{15}$. Simplify the result.

26. Subtract and simplify, if possible: $67\frac{1}{4} - 29\frac{5}{6}$

27. Divide and simplify, if possible: $6\frac{1}{4} \div 3\frac{3}{4}$

28. BOXING Two of the greatest heavyweight boxers of all time are Muhammad Ali and George Foreman. Refer to the "Tale of the Tape" comparison shown below.

   a. Which fighter weighed more? How much more?

   b. Which fighter had the larger waist measurement? How much larger?

   c. Which fighter had the larger forearm measurement? How much larger?

Tale of the Tape		
Muhammad Ali		**George Foreman**
6-3	Height	6-4
210½ lb	Weight	250 lb
82 in.	Reach	79 in.
43 in.	Chest (Normal)	48 in.
45½ in.	Chest (Expanded)	50 in.
34 in.	Waist	39½ in.
12½ in.	Fist	13½ in.
15 in.	Forearm	14¾ in.

Source: The International Boxing Hall of Fame

29. TAPE MEASURES Use the information shown in the illustration below to determine the inside length of the drawer.

30. SPORTS CONTRACTS A basketball player signed a nine-year contract for $13\frac{1}{2}$ million. How much is this per year?

31. SEWING When cutting material for a $10\frac{1}{2}$-inch-wide placemat, a seamstress allows $\frac{5}{8}$ inch at each end for a hem, as shown below. How wide should the material be cut to make a placemat?

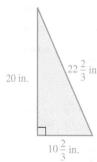

$10\frac{1}{2}$ in.

?

32. Find the perimeter and the area of the triangle shown below.

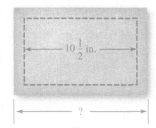

20 in.

$22\frac{2}{3}$ in.

$10\frac{2}{3}$ in.

33. NUTRITION A box of Tic Tacs contains 40 of the $1\frac{1}{2}$-calorie breath mints. How many calories are there in a box of Tic Tacs?

34. COOKING How many servings are there in an 8-pound roast, if the suggested serving size is $\frac{2}{3}$ pound?

35. **a.** Find a fraction and a mixed number whose product is 1.
    b. Find two fractions with different denominators such that their sum is greater than $\frac{2}{3}$
    c. Find two different mixed numbers whose sum is 3.

36. Explain what is meant when we say, "The product of any number and its reciprocal is 1." Give an example.

37. Graph $-3\frac{1}{4}$, 0.75, -1.5, $-\frac{9}{8}$, 3.8, and 2 on a number line.

```
←――|――|――|――|――|――|――|――|――|――|――|――→
   -5  -4  -3  -2  -1   0   1   2   3   4   5
```

38. Express the amount of the square region that is shaded using a fraction and a decimal.

39. Consider the decimal number: 629.471

   a. What is the place value of the digit 1?

   b. Which digit tells the number of tenths?

   c. Which digit tells the number of hundreds?

   d. What is the place value of the digit 2?

40. WATER PURITY A county health department sampled the pollution content of tap water in five cities, with the results shown. Rank the cities in order, from dirtiest tap water to cleanest.

City	Pollution, parts per million
Monroe	0.0909
Covington	0.0899
Paston	0.0901
Cadia	0.0890
Selway	0.1001

41. Write *four thousand five hundred nineteen and twenty-seven ten-thousandths* in standard form.

42. Write each decimal in
   • expanded form
   • words
   • as a fraction or mixed number. (You do not have to simplify the fraction.)

   a. SKATEBOARDING Gary Hardwick of Carlsbad, California, set the skateboard speed record of 62.55 mph in 1998. (Source: skateboardballbearings.com)

   b. MONEY A dime weighs 0.08013 ounce.

43. Round each decimal number to the indicated place value.

   a. 461.728, nearest tenth

   b. 2,733.0495, nearest thousandth

   c. -1.9833732, nearest millionth

44. Round $0.648209 to the nearest cent.

Perform each operation.

45. $4.56 + 2 + 0.896 + 3.3$

46. Subtract 39.079 from 45.2

47 $(0.32)^2$

48. $\dfrac{0.1368}{0.24}$

49. $-6.7(-2.1)$

50. $\begin{array}{r} 8.7 \\ \times\ 0.004 \\ \hline \end{array}$

51. $11\overline{)13}$

52. $-2.4 - (-1.6)$

53. Divide. Round the quotient to the nearest hundredth:
   $$\frac{12.146}{-5.3}$$

54. **a.** Estimate the product using front-end rounding: $34 \cdot 6.83$

   b. Estimate the quotient: $3{,}907.2 \div 19.3$

55. Perform each operation in your head.

   a. $567.909 \div 1{,}000$

   b. $0.00458 \cdot 100$

56. Write 61.4 billion in standard notation.

57. EARTHQUAKE DAMAGE After an earthquake, geologists found that the ground on the west side of the fault line had dropped 0.834 inch. The next week, a strong aftershock caused the same area to sink 0.192 inch deeper. How far did the ground on the west side of the fault drop because of the earthquake and the aftershock?

58. NEW YORK CITY Refer to the illustration on the right. Central Park, which lies in the middle of Manhattan, is the city's best-known park. If it is 2.5 miles long and 0.5 mile wide, what is its area?

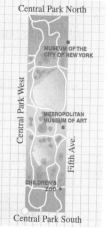

59. TELEPHONE BOOKS To print a telephone book, 565 sheets of paper were used. If the book is 2.26 inches thick, what is the thickness of each sheet of paper?

60. ACCOUNTING At an ice-skating complex, receipts on Friday were $130.25 for indoor skating and $162.25 for outdoor skating. On Saturday, the corresponding amounts were $140.50 and $175.75. On which day, Friday or Saturday, were the receipts higher? How much higher?

61. CHEMISTRY In a lab experiment, a chemist mixed three compounds together to form a mixture weighing 4.37 g. Later, she discovered that she had forgotten to record the weight of compound C in her notes. Find the weight of compound C used in the experiment.

	Weight
Compound A	1.86 g
Compound B	2.09 g
Compound C	?
Mixture total	4.37 g

62. WEIGHT OF WATER One gallon of water weighs 8.33 pounds. How much does the water in a $2\frac{1}{2}$-gallon jug weigh?

63. GUITAR DESIGN Find the missing dimension on the vintage 1962 Stratocaster body shown below.

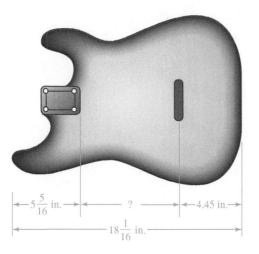

$5\frac{5}{16}$ in. — ? — 4.45 in.

$18\frac{1}{16}$ in.

64. Write each fraction as a decimal.

a. $\dfrac{17}{50}$ b. $\dfrac{5}{12}$

Evaluate each expression.

65. $4.1 - (3.2)(0.4)^2$

66. $\left(\dfrac{2}{5}\right)^2 + 6\left|-6.2 - 3\dfrac{1}{4}\right|$

67. $\dfrac{2}{3} + 0.7$ (Work in terms of fractions.)

68. Graph $\frac{3}{8}$, $\frac{2}{3}$, and $-\frac{4}{5}$ on a number line. Label each point using the decimal equivalent of the fraction.

$-1 \quad 0 \quad 1$

69. SALADS A shopper purchased $\frac{3}{4}$ pound of potato salad, priced at $5.60 per pound, and $\frac{1}{3}$ pound of coleslaw, selling for $4.35 per pound. Find the total cost of these items.

70. Write each number in decimal form.

a. $-\dfrac{27}{25}$ b. $2\dfrac{9}{16}$

71. Place an $<$, $>$, or an $=$ symbol in the box to make a true statement.

a. $-6.78 \quad\square\quad -6.79$

b. $0.3 \quad\square\quad \dfrac{3}{8}$

c. $\dfrac{4}{9} \quad\square\quad 0.\overline{4}$

d. $0.45 \quad\square\quad 0.\overline{45}$

72. Although the decimal 3.2999 contains more digits than 3.3, it is smaller than 3.3. Explain why this is so.

73. COOKING Suppose you have a bag of sugar and you need to measure out $\frac{1}{6}$ cup of it to make a cookie recipe. However, you only have measuring cups labeled 1 cup, 0.5 cup, $\frac{1}{3}$ cup, and 0.25 cup. Explain how to use them to obtain the needed $\frac{1}{6}$ cup of sugar.

74. Fill in the blank: If C is the circumference of a circle and D is the length of its diameter, then $\dfrac{C}{D} = \square$.

In Problems 25–27, when appropriate, give the exact answer and an approximation to the nearest tenth.

75. Find the circumference of a circle with a diameter of 21 feet

76. Find the perimeter of the figure shown below. Assume that the arcs are semicircles.

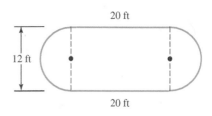

20 ft

12 ft

20 ft

77. HISTORY Stonehenge is a prehistoric monument in England, believed to have been built by the Druids. The site, 30 meters in diameter, consists of a circular arrangement of stones, as shown below. What area does the monument cover?

78. Find the area of the shaded region shown below, which is created using two semicircles. Round to the nearest hundredth.

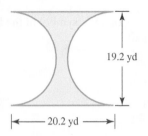

19.2 yd

20.2 yd

79. SEWING A circular tablecloth is going to be made from fabric that sells for $8.99 a square yard. Estimate the cost of the fabric if the tablecloth has diameter 7 feet. Assume no waste. (Hint: There are 9 square feet in one square yard.)

80. COMPARISON SHOPPING Which pizza is the better buy:

- An 8-inch diameter cheese pizza for $9
- A 15-inch diameter cheese pizza for $14

81. a. Explain why $3{,}000 = 3 \times 10^3$.

b. Explain why $0.003 = 3 \times 10^{-3}$.

82. What is the value of 10^0?

83. ELECTRICITY One ampere (amp) corresponds to the flow of 6,250,000,000,000,000,000 electrons per second past any point in a direct current (DC) circuit. Write this number in scientific notation.

84. Write 9.3×10^{-5} in standard notation.

85. Write 0.0000000043 in scientific notation.

86. WORLD OIL According to estimates in the *World Fact Book*, there were 1.35×10^{12} barrels of crude oil reserves in the ground at the start of the year 2010. Write this number in standard notation.

87. Express each power of 10 in fraction form and decimal form.

a. 10^{-5} **b.** 10^{-7}

88. Fill in the blanks.

a. $10^{} = 100{,}000$ **b.** $10^{} = 0.0001$

Module 2 Answers

Applications Introduction: Fractions Section 2.1 (page 4)

1. $\frac{3}{4}$ 2. $\frac{9}{10},\frac{1}{10}$ 3. $\frac{5}{8}$ 4. $\frac{1}{7}$ 5. $\frac{1}{8}$ 6. $\frac{1}{4}$ 7. $\frac{7}{8}$ 8. $\frac{9}{10}$ 9. $\frac{3}{8}$
10. $\frac{13}{32},\frac{2}{32}$ 11. $\frac{3}{10},\frac{4}{10}$ 12. $\frac{1}{5}$ 13. $\frac{1}{16},\frac{1}{64}$ 14. $\frac{1}{4}$ 15. $\frac{3}{4}$ 16. $\frac{1}{100}$
17. $\frac{7}{500}$ 18. $\frac{1}{4}$ 19. $\frac{22}{7},\frac{355}{113}$ 20. $\frac{3}{16},\frac{7}{8}$ 21. $\frac{1}{2},\frac{1}{200}$ 22. $\frac{1}{3}$ 23. $\frac{1}{2},\frac{1}{8}$
24. $\frac{1}{5}$

Are You Ready? Section 2.1 (page 6)

1. 1 2. 150 3. Yes 4. a. 2 b. 5 5. a. 4 b. 12 6. 8

Study Set Section 2.1 (page 16)

1. fraction 3. proper, improper 5. number 7. building
9. prime 11. a. equivalent fractions: $\frac{2}{6}=\frac{1}{3}$ b. $\frac{4}{12}=\frac{1}{3}$
13. a. improper fraction b. proper fraction c. proper fraction d. improper fraction 15. 5 17. numerators
19. $\frac{-7}{8}=-\frac{7}{8}$ 21. 3, 1, 3, 18 23. a. numerator: 4; denominator: 5 b. numerator: 7; denominator: 8
c. numerator: 17; denominator: 10 d. numerator: 29; denominator: 21 25. a. $\frac{3}{4},\frac{1}{4}$ b. $\frac{2}{3},\frac{1}{3}$ c. $\frac{5}{8},\frac{3}{8}$ d. $\frac{7}{12},\frac{5}{12}$
27.

$$-\frac{1}{3} \qquad \frac{3}{4}$$
number line from −1 to 1

29.

$$-\frac{4}{5} \qquad \frac{7}{9}$$
number line from −1 to 1

31. a. 4 b. 1 c. 0 d. undefined 33. $\frac{35}{40}$ 35. $\frac{12}{27}$ 37. $\frac{45}{54}$
39. $\frac{4}{14}$ 41. $\frac{15}{30}$ 43. $\frac{22}{32}$ 45. $\frac{35}{28}$ 47. $\frac{48}{45}$ 49. $\frac{36}{9}$ 51. $\frac{48}{8}$ 53. $\frac{15}{5}$
55. $\frac{28}{2}$ 57. $3\cdot5\cdot5$ 59. $3\cdot3\cdot3\cdot3$ 61. $3\cdot3\cdot13$
63. $2\cdot2\cdot5\cdot11$ 65. a. no b. yes 67. a. yes b. no 69. $\frac{2}{3}$
71. $\frac{4}{5}$ 73. $\frac{1}{3}$ 75. $\frac{1}{24}$ 77. $\frac{3}{8}$ 79. in simplest form 81. in simplest form 83. $\frac{10}{11}$ 85. $\frac{5}{9}$ 87. $\frac{6}{7}$ 89. $\frac{5}{2}$ 91. $\frac{8}{7}$ 93. $-\frac{7}{6}$
95. $-\frac{1}{17}$ 97. not equivalent 99. equivalent
101. a.

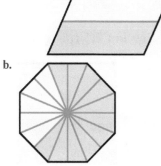

b.

c.

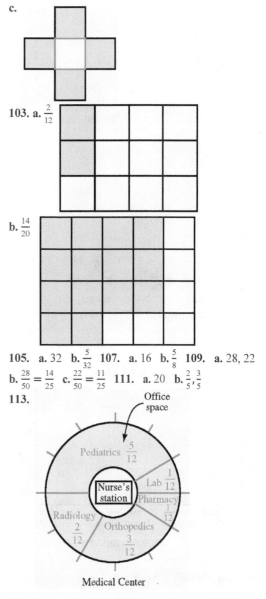

103. a. $\frac{2}{12}$

b. $\frac{14}{20}$

105. a. 32 b. $\frac{5}{32}$ 107. a. 16 b. $\frac{5}{8}$ 109. a. 28, 22
b. $\frac{28}{50}=\frac{14}{25}$ c. $\frac{22}{50}=\frac{11}{25}$ 111. a. 20 b. $\frac{2}{5},\frac{3}{5}$
113.

Medical Center

121. the months of April, May, and June of 2008

Are You Ready? Section 2.2 (page 22)

1. a. $\frac{3}{4}$ b. $\frac{1}{9}$ 2. $3\cdot5\cdot5$ 3. a. 36 b. 64 4. a. positive b. negative

Study Set Section 2.2 (page 31)

1. multiplication 3. simplify 5. area 7. numerators, denominators, simplify 9. a. negative b. positive
c. positive d. negative 11. base, height, $\frac{1}{2}bh$ 13. a. $\frac{4}{1}$
b. $-\frac{3}{1}$ 15. $\frac{7}{15}$, 2, 3, 5, 5, 24 17. $\frac{1}{8}$ 19. $\frac{1}{45}$ 21. $\frac{14}{27}$ 23. $\frac{24}{77}$

25. $-\frac{4}{15}$ **27.** $-\frac{35}{72}$ **29.** $\frac{9}{8}$ **31.** $\frac{5}{2}$ **33.** $\frac{1}{2}$ **35.** $\frac{1}{7}$ **37.** $\frac{1}{10}$ **39.** $\frac{2}{15}$
41. **a.** $\frac{9}{25}$ **b.** $\frac{9}{25}$ **43.** **a.** $-\frac{1}{36}$ **b.** $-\frac{1}{216}$ **45.** $\frac{15}{32}$ **47.** 9
49. $\frac{5}{32}$ in.^{2} **51.** $\frac{81}{256}$ in.^{2} **53.** 15 ft^2 **55.** 63 in.^{2} **57.** 6 m^2
59. 60 ft^2

61.

·	$\frac{1}{2}$	$\frac{1}{3}$	$\frac{1}{4}$	$\frac{1}{5}$	$\frac{1}{6}$
$\frac{1}{2}$	$\frac{1}{4}$	$\frac{1}{6}$	$\frac{1}{8}$	$\frac{1}{10}$	$\frac{1}{12}$
$\frac{1}{3}$	$\frac{1}{6}$	$\frac{1}{9}$	$\frac{1}{12}$	$\frac{1}{15}$	$\frac{1}{18}$
$\frac{1}{4}$	$\frac{1}{8}$	$\frac{1}{12}$	$\frac{1}{16}$	$\frac{1}{20}$	$\frac{1}{24}$
$\frac{1}{5}$	$\frac{1}{10}$	$\frac{1}{15}$	$\frac{1}{20}$	$\frac{1}{25}$	$\frac{1}{30}$
$\frac{1}{6}$	$\frac{1}{12}$	$\frac{1}{18}$	$\frac{1}{24}$	$\frac{1}{30}$	$\frac{1}{36}$

63. $-\frac{1}{5}$ **65.** $\frac{21}{128}$ **67.** $\frac{1}{30}$ **69.** -15 **71.** $-\frac{27}{64}$ **73.** 1 **75.** $\frac{8}{3}$
77. $-\frac{3}{2}$ **79.** $\frac{2}{9}$ **81.** $-\frac{25}{81}$ **83.** $\frac{2}{3}$ **85.** $\frac{5}{6}$ **87.** $\frac{77}{60}$ **89.** $\frac{1}{2}$
91. **a.** (answers may vary) **b.** (answers may vary)
93. **a.** (answers may vary) **b.** (answers may vary)
95. 60 votes **97.** 18 in., 6 in., and 2 in. **99.** $\frac{3}{8}$ cup sugar
cup, $\frac{1}{6}$ molasses

101.

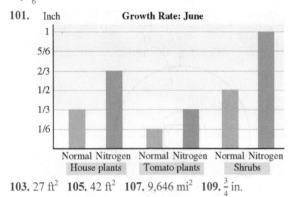

Growth Rate: June

103. 27 ft^2 **105.** 42 ft^2 **107.** 9,646 mi^2 **109.** $\frac{3}{4}$ in.

Are You Ready? Section 2.3 (page 36)

1. $\frac{4}{9}$ **2.** $\frac{9}{35}$ **3.** **a.** -16 **b.** 2 **4.** **a.** positive **b.** negative

Section 2.3 Study Set (page 42)

1. reciprocal **3.** quotient **5.** **a.** multiply, reciprocal
b.   **7.** **a.** negative **b.** positive

$$\frac{1}{2} \div \frac{2}{3} = \frac{1}{2} \cdot \frac{3}{2}$$

9. **a.** 1 **b.** 1 **11.** 27, 27, 8, 9; 2, 4, 4, 9, 3 **13.** **a.** $\frac{7}{6}$
b. $-\frac{8}{15}$ **c.** $\frac{1}{10}$ **15.** **a.** $\frac{8}{11}$ **b.** -14 **c.** $-\frac{1}{63}$ **17.** $\frac{3}{16}$ **19.** $\frac{14}{23}$ **21.** $\frac{35}{8}$

23. $\frac{3}{4}$ **25.** 45 **27.** 320 **29.** -4 **31.** $-\frac{7}{2}$ **33.** $\frac{4}{55}$ **35.** $\frac{3}{23}$ **37.** 50
39. $\frac{5}{6}$ **41.** $\frac{2}{3}$ **43.** 1 **45.** $-\frac{5}{8}$ **47.** 36 **49.** $\frac{2}{15}$ **51.** $\frac{1}{192}$ **53.** $-\frac{27}{8}$
55. $-\frac{15}{2}$ **57.** $\frac{27}{16}$ **59.** $-\frac{1}{64}$ **61.** $\frac{3}{14}$ **63.** $\frac{8}{15}$ **65.** $\frac{13}{32}$ **67.** $\frac{2}{9}$ **69.** -6
71. $\frac{11}{6}$ **73.** $\frac{15}{28}$ **75.** $-\frac{5}{2}$ **77.** **a.** (answers may vary)
b. (answers may vary)
79.

$$-1 \quad\quad -\frac{5}{8} \quad\quad 0 \quad\quad \frac{7}{9} \quad\quad 1$$

81. **b.** $3 \div \frac{1}{10}$ **c.** 30 **83.** 4 applications **85.** 6 cups
87. **a.** 30 days **b.** 15 mi **c.** 25 days **d.** route 2 **89.** **a.** 16
b. $\frac{3}{4}$ in. **c.** $\frac{1}{120}$ in **91.** 7,855 sections

Are You Ready? Section 2.4 (page 45)

1. -4 **2.** $2 \cdot 2 \cdot 2 \cdot 5 \cdot 7$ **3.** 9, 15, 27 **4.** $\frac{5}{12}$ **5.** $\frac{9}{16}, \frac{7}{16}$ **6.** $\frac{21}{40}$

Study Set Section 2.4 (page 56)

1. common **3.** build, $\frac{2}{2}$ **5.** multiples **7.** numerators,
common, Simplify **9.** larger **11.** $\frac{9}{9}$ **13.** 9, 18, 27, 36, 45,
54, 63, 72, 81, 90 **15.** **a.** once **b.** twice **c.** three times
17. $2 \cdot 2 \cdot 3 \cdot 3 \cdot 5 = 180$ **21.** 7, 7, 14, 35, 14, 5, 19 **23.** $\frac{5}{9}$
25. $\frac{1}{2}$ **27.** $\frac{4}{15}$ **29.** $\frac{2}{5}$ **31.** $-\frac{3}{5}$ **33.** $-\frac{5}{21}$ **35.** $\frac{3}{8}$ **37.** $\frac{7}{11}$ **39.** $\frac{10}{21}$
41. $\frac{9}{10}$ **43.** $\frac{1}{20}$ **45.** $\frac{13}{28}$ **47.** $\frac{1}{4}$ **49.** $\frac{1}{2}$ **51.** $-\frac{13}{9}$ **53.** $-\frac{3}{4}$ **55.** $\frac{19}{24}$
57. $\frac{31}{36}$ **59.** $\frac{24}{35}$ **61.** $\frac{9}{20}$ **63.** $\frac{3}{8}$ **65.** $\frac{4}{5}$ **67.** $\frac{11}{12}$ **69.** $\frac{7}{6}$ **71.** $\frac{2}{3}$ **73.** $\frac{11}{10}$
75. $\frac{1}{3}$ **77.** $\frac{2}{5}$ **79.** $-\frac{11}{20}$ **81.** $-\frac{3}{16}$ **83.** $\frac{1}{4}$ **85.** $\frac{5}{12}$ **87.** $\frac{341}{400}$ **89.** $\frac{9}{20}$
91. $\frac{20}{103}$ **93.** $-\frac{23}{4}$ **95.** $\frac{17}{54}$ **97.** $-\frac{1}{50}$ **99.** $\frac{5}{36}$ **101.** $-\frac{17}{60}$
103. **a.** $\frac{55}{63}$ **b.** $\frac{1}{63}$ **c.** $\frac{4}{21}$ **d.** $\frac{28}{27}$ **105.** $\frac{7}{10}$ ft **107.** **a.** (answers
may vary) **b.** (answers may vary) **c.** (answers may vary)
d. (answers may vary) **109.** **a.** $\frac{7}{32}$ in. **b.** $\frac{3}{32}$ in. **111.** $\frac{11}{16}$ in.
113. **a.** $\frac{3}{8}$ **b.** $\frac{2}{6} = \frac{1}{3}$ **c.** $\frac{17}{24}$ of a pizza was left **d.** no
115. $\frac{1}{16}$ lb, undercharge **117.** $\frac{7}{10}$ of the full-time students
study 2 or more hours a day. **119.** no **121.** **a.** RR: right
rear **b.** LR: left rear

Applications Introduction: Improper Fractions and Mixed Numbers Section 2.5 (page 62)

1. **b.** $2\frac{4}{5}$ **2.** **b.** $-3\frac{1}{4}$

Are You Ready? Section 2.5 (page 63)

1. 2 R 1 **2.** 30 **3.**

$$-4 \quad -3 \quad -2 \quad -1 \quad 0 \quad 1 \quad 2 \quad 3 \quad 4$$

4. 6 **5.** $\frac{3}{2}$ **6.** $A = \frac{1}{2}bh$

Study Set Section 2.5 (page 71)

1. mixed **3.** improper **5.** **a.** $5\frac{1}{3}$° **b.** $-6\frac{7}{8}$ in.

7. 1. Multiply 2. Add 3. denominator **9.** $-\frac{4}{5}, -\frac{2}{5}, \frac{1}{5}$

11. improper **13.** not reasonable: $4\frac{1}{5} \cdot 2\frac{5}{7} \approx 4 \cdot 3 = 12$

15. a. and, sixteenths **b.** negative, two **17.** 8, 4, 8, 4, 4, 4, 6, 6

19. $\frac{19}{8}, 2\frac{3}{8}$ **21.** $\frac{34}{25}, 1\frac{9}{25}$ **23.** $\frac{13}{2}$ **25.** $\frac{104}{5}$ **27.** $-\frac{68}{9}$

29. $-\frac{26}{3}$ **31.** $3\frac{1}{4}$ **33.** $5\frac{3}{5}$ **35.** $4\frac{2}{3}$ **37.** $10\frac{1}{2}$ **39.** 4 **41.** 2

43. $-8\frac{2}{7}$ **45.** $-3\frac{1}{3}$

47.

$-2\frac{8}{9}$ $-\frac{1}{2}$ $1\frac{2}{3}$ $\frac{16}{5}=3\frac{1}{5}$

$-5\ -4\ -3\ -2\ -1\ \ 0\ \ 1\ \ 2\ \ 3\ \ 4\ \ 5$

49.

$-\frac{10}{3}=-3\frac{1}{3}$ $-\frac{98}{99}$ $\frac{3}{2}=1\frac{1}{2}$ $3\frac{1}{7}$

$-5\ -4\ -3\ -2\ -1\ \ 0\ \ 1\ \ 2\ \ 3\ \ 4\ \ 5$

51. $8\frac{1}{6}$ **53.** $7\frac{2}{5}$ **55.** 8 **57.** -10 **59.** $\frac{4}{9}$ **61.** $6\frac{9}{10}$ **63.** $2\frac{1}{3}$

65. $1\frac{10}{21}$ **67.** $-13\frac{3}{4}$ **69.** $-\frac{9}{10}$ **71.** $\frac{25}{9}=2\frac{7}{9}$ **73.** $2\frac{1}{2}$ **75.** 12 **77.** 14

79. -2 **81.** $-8\frac{1}{3}$ **83.** $\frac{35}{72}$ **85.** $\frac{5}{16}$ **87.** $-1\frac{1}{4}$ **89.** $-\frac{64}{27}=-2\frac{10}{27}$

91. b. $4\frac{1}{3}$ **95. a.** $3\frac{2}{3}$ **b.** $\frac{11}{3}$ **97.** $2\frac{1}{2}$ **99. a.** $2\frac{2}{3}$

b. $-1\frac{1}{3}$ **101.** size 14, slim cut **103.** $76\frac{9}{16}$ in.² **105.** $42\frac{5}{8}$ in.²

107. 64 calories **109.** $357¢ = \$3.57$ **111.** $1\frac{1}{4}$ cups

113. 600 people **115.** $8\frac{1}{2}$ furlongs

Applications Introduction: Estimation with Mixed Numbers Section 2.6 (page 77)

1. about 60 in. **2.** about 5 mi **3.** about 8 in. **4.** about 76 lb

Are You Ready? Section 2.6 (page 78)

1. $\frac{41}{12}$ **2.** $1\frac{3}{16}$ **3.** $\frac{41}{63}$ **4.** $\frac{27}{24}$ **5.** 172 **6.** 365

Study Set Section 2.6 (page 87)

1. mixed **3.** fractions, whole **5.** carry **7. a.** $76\frac{3}{4}$ **b.** $76+\frac{3}{4}$

9. a. 12 **b.** 30 **c.** 18 **d.** 24 **11.** 21, 5, 5, 35, 31, 35

13. $3\frac{7}{12}$ **15.** $6\frac{11}{15}$ **17.** $-2\frac{3}{8}$ **19.** $-3\frac{1}{6}$ **21.** $376\frac{17}{21}$ **23.** $714\frac{19}{20}$

25. $59\frac{28}{45}$ **27.** $132\frac{29}{33}$ **29.** $121\frac{9}{10}$ **31.** $147\frac{8}{9}$ **33.** $102\frac{13}{24}$

35. $129\frac{28}{45}$ **37.** $10\frac{1}{4}$ **39.** $13\frac{8}{15}$ **41.** $31\frac{14}{33}$ **43.** $71\frac{43}{56}$ **45.** $579\frac{4}{15}$

47. $62\frac{23}{32}$ **49.** $11\frac{1}{30}$ **51.** $5\frac{11}{30}$ **53.** $9\frac{3}{10}$ **55.** $3\frac{7}{8}$ **57.** $5\frac{2}{3}$

59. $10\frac{7}{16}$ **61.** $397\frac{5}{12}$ **63.** $-1\frac{11}{24}$ **65.** $7\frac{1}{2}$ **67.** $-5\frac{1}{4}$ **69.** $6\frac{1}{3}$

71. $53\frac{5}{12}$ **73.** $2\frac{1}{2}$ **75.** $-5\frac{7}{8}$ **77.** $3\frac{5}{8}$ **79.** $4\frac{1}{3}$ **81.** $461\frac{1}{8}$ **83.** $\frac{1}{4}$

85. a. $5\frac{23}{25}$ **b.** $2\frac{7}{24}$ **c.** $7\frac{9}{16}$ **d.** $2\frac{1}{4}$ **87.** $2\frac{5}{8}$ in. **89.** $4\frac{3}{8}$

91. $5\frac{1}{4}$ hr **93.** $7\frac{1}{6}$ cups **95.** $20\frac{1}{16}$ lb **97.** $108\frac{1}{2}$ in. **99.** $2\frac{3}{4}$ mi

101. $48\frac{1}{2}$ ft **103. a.** 20¢ **b.** 20¢ **105.** $3\frac{1}{4}$ in.

Are You Ready? Section 2.7 (page 91)

1. a. 7 **b.** 5 **c.** 9 **2. a.** seven-tenths **b.** forty-one hundredths **c.** two hundred thirteen thousandths **3.** $\frac{3}{10}$ **4.** $\frac{19}{100}$

Study Set Section 2.7 (page 101)

1. point **3.** expanded

5.

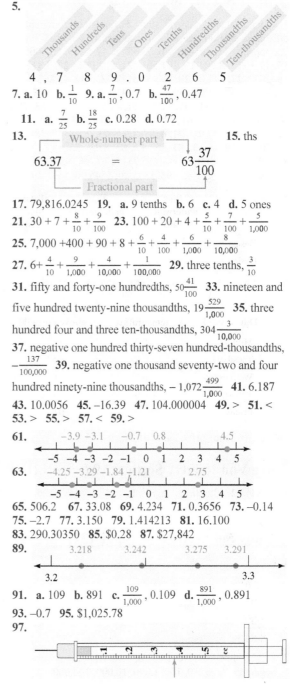

Thousands Hundreds Tens Ones Tenths Hundredths Thousandths Ten-thousandths

4 , 7 8 9 . 0 2 6 5

7. a. 10 **b.** $\frac{1}{10}$ **9. a.** $\frac{7}{10}$, 0.7 **b.** $\frac{47}{100}$, 0.47

11. a. $\frac{7}{25}$ **b.** $\frac{18}{25}$ **c.** 0.28 **d.** 0.72

13. Whole-number part Fractional part 63.37 $=$ $63\frac{37}{100}$ **15.** ths

17. 79,816.0245 **19. a.** 9 tenths **b.** 6 **c.** 4 **d.** 5 ones

21. $30+7+\frac{8}{10}+\frac{9}{100}$ **23.** $100+20+4+\frac{5}{10}+\frac{7}{100}+\frac{5}{1,000}$

25. $7,000+400+90+8+\frac{6}{10}+\frac{4}{100}+\frac{6}{1,000}+\frac{8}{10,000}$

27. $6+\frac{4}{10}+\frac{9}{1,000}+\frac{4}{10,000}+\frac{1}{100,000}$ **29.** three tenths, $\frac{3}{10}$

31. fifty and forty-one hundredths, $50\frac{41}{100}$ **33.** nineteen and five hundred twenty-nine thousandths, $19\frac{529}{1,000}$ **35.** three hundred four and three ten-thousandths, $304\frac{3}{10,000}$

37. negative one hundred thirty-seven hundred-thousandths, $-\frac{137}{100,000}$ **39.** negative one thousand seventy-two and four hundred ninety-nine thousandths, $-1,072\frac{499}{1,000}$ **41.** 6.187

43. 10.0056 **45.** -16.39 **47.** 104.000004 **49.** > **51.** <

53. > **55.** > **57.** < **59.** >

61.

-3.9 -3.1 -0.7 0.8 4.5

$-5\ -4\ -3\ -2\ -1\ \ 0\ \ 1\ \ 2\ \ 3\ \ 4\ \ 5$

63.

-4.25 -3.29 -1.84 -1.21 2.75

$-5\ -4\ -3\ -2\ -1\ \ 0\ \ 1\ \ 2\ \ 3\ \ 4\ \ 5$

65. 506.2 **67.** 33.08 **69.** 4.234 **71.** 0.3656 **73.** -0.14

75. -2.7 **77.** 3.150 **79.** 1.414213 **81.** 16.100

83. 290.30350 **85.** $0.28 **87.** $27,842

89.

3.218   3.242   3.275   3.291

3.2   3.3

91. a. 109 **b.** 891 **c.** $\frac{109}{1,000}$, 0.109 **d.** $\frac{891}{1,000}$, 0.891

93. -0.7 **95.** $1,025.78

97.

99. two-thousandths, $\frac{2}{1,000} = \frac{1}{500}$ **101.** $0.16, $1.02, $1.20, $0.00, $0.10 **103.** candlemaking, crafts, hobbies, folk dolls, modern art **105.** Cylinder 2, Cylinder 4 **107.** bacterium, plant cell, animal cell, asbestos fiber **109. a.** Q3, 2007; $2.75 **b.** Q4, 2006; –$2.05

Are You Ready? Section 2.8 (page 107)

1. 12,678 **2.** 1,607 **3.** 8,147 **4.** 48,760 **5. a.** –9 **b.** –27 **c.** 27 **d.** –27 **6.** 4,000

Study Set Section 2.8 (page 116)

1. addend, addend, addend, sum **3.** minuend, subtrahend, difference **5.** estimate **7.** It is not correct: $15.2 + 12.5 \neq 28.7$ **9.** opposite **11. a.** –1.2 **b.** 13.55 **c.** –7.4 **13.** 00, .000 **15.** 39.9 **17.** 8.59 **19.** 101.561 **21.** 202.991 **23.** 3.31 **25.** 2.75 **27.** 341.7 **29.** 703.5 **31.** 7.235 **33.** 43.863 **35.** –14.7 **37.** –18.8 **39.** –14.68 **41.** –6.15 **43.** –66.7 **45.** –45.3 **47.** 6.81 **49.** 17.82 **51.** –4.5 **53.** –3.4 **55.** 790 **57.** 610 **59.** 4,300 **61.** 12,400 **63.** –10.9 **65.** 38.29 **67.** 55.00 **69.** 47.91 **71.** 658.04007 **73.** 0.19 **75.** 288.46 **77.** 70.29 **79.** –14.3 **81.** –57.47 **83.** 8.03 **85.** 15.2 **87.** 4.977 **89.** 2.598 **91. a.** 185.75 **b.** 10.795 **93. a.** 410 **b.** greater than **c.** 1.82 **95.** $815.80, $545.00, $531.49

97.

	Pipe underwater (mi)	Pipe underground (mi)	Total pipe (mi)
Design 1	1.74	2.32	4.06
Design 2	2.90	0	2.90

99. 2.375 in. **101.** 42.39 sec **103.** $523.19, $498.19

105.

Day of week	Patient's A.M. temperature	Amount above normal
Monday	99.7°	1.1°
Tuesday	101.1°	2.5°
Wednesday	98.6°	0°
Thursday	100.0°	1.4°
Friday	99.5°	0.9°

107. about 21 mi **109. a.** $101.94 **b.** $55.80

Are You Ready? Section 2.9 (page 121)

1. 66,834 **2.** 63,000 **3. a.** 81 **b.** 144 **4.** –44 **5.** 26 **6.** 351.7

Study Set Section 2.9 (page 131)

1.

3.4 ←	factor
× 2.6 ←	factor
204 ←	partial product
680 ←	partial product
8.84 ←	product

3. a. 2.28 **b.** 14.499 **c.** 14.0 **d.** 0.00026 **5. a.** positive **b.** negative **7. a.** 10, 100, 1,000, 10,000, 100,000

b. 0.1, 0.01, 0.001, 0.0001, 0.00001 **9.** 29.76 **11.** 49.84 **13.** 0.0081 **15.** 0.0522 **17.** 1,127.7 **19.** 2,338.4 **21.** 684 **23.** 410 **25.** 6.4759 **27.** 0.00115 **29.** 14,200,000 **31.** 98,200,000,000 **33.** 1,421,000,000,000 **35.** 657,100,000,000 **37.** –13.68 **39.** 5.28 **41.** 448,300 **43.** –678,231 **45.** 11.56 **47.** 0.0009 **49.** 3.16 **51.** 68.66 **53.** 119.70 **55.** 38.16 **57.** 14.6 **59.** 15.7 **61.** 250 **63.** 66.69 **65.** 420 **67.** 0.0021 **69.** –0.1848 **71.** 0.84 **73.** 0.00072 **75.** 12.32 **77.** –17.48 **79.** 0.0049 **81.** 14.24 **83.** 8.6265 **85.** –57.2467 **87.** –22.39 **89.** –3.872 **91.** 24.48 **93.** –0.8649

95.

Decimal	Its square
0.1	0.01
0.2	0.04
0.3	0.09
0.4	0.16
0.5	0.25
0.6	0.36
0.7	0.49
0.8	0.64
0.9	0.81

97. 43.79804 **99. a.** 17.39 **b.** less than **c.** 0.0196 **101.** 1.9 in. **103.** about $80,000 **105.** $95.20, $123.75 **107.** 0.000000136 in., 0.0000000136 in., 0.00000004 in. **109. a.** 2.1 mi **b.** 3.5 mi **c.** 5.6 mi **111.** $102.65 **113. a.** 19,600,000 acres **b.** 6,500,000,000 **c.** 3,026,000,000,000 miles **115. a.** 192 ft^2 **b.** 223.125 ft^2 **c.** 31.125 ft^2

117. a.

Ticket type	Price	Number sold	Receipts
Floor	$12.50	1,000	$12,500
Balcony	$15.75	100	$1,575

b. $14,075 **119.** 136.4 lb **121.** 0.84 in.

Are You Ready? Section 2.10 (page 136)

1. 218 **2.** 704 **3.** 25 **4.** 3 **5.** –3 **6.** 54.09

Study Set Section 2.10 (page 147)

1.

	3.17 ← quotient
divisor → 5)15.85	← dividend

3. a. 5.26 **b.** 0.008 **5. a.** 13)106.6 **b.** 371)1669.5 **7.** $\frac{10}{10}$ **9.** thousandths **11. a.** left **b.** right **13.** moving the decimal points in the divisor and dividend 2 places to the right **15.** 2.1 **17.** 9.2 **19.** 4.27 **21.** 8.65 **23.** 3.35 **25.** 4.56 **27.** 0.46 **29.** 0.39 **31.** 19.72 **33.** 24.41 **35.** $280 \div 70 = 28 \div 7 = 4$ **37.** $400 \div 8 = 50$ **39.** $4,000 \div 50 = 400 \div 5 = 80$ **41.** $15,000 \div 5 = 3,000$ **43.** 4.5178 **45.** 0.003009 **47.** 12.5 **49.** 545,200 **51.** –8.62 **53.** 4.04 **55.** 20,325.7 **57.** –0.00003

59. −5.162 **61.** 0.1 **63.** 3.5 **65.** 58.5 **67.** 2.66 **69.** 7.504
71. 0.0045 **73.** 0.321 **75.** −1.5 **77.** −122.02 **79.** −2.4
81. 9.75 **83.** 789,150 **85.** 0.6 **87.** 13.60 **89.** 0.0348
91. 1,027.19 **93.** 0.15625 **95.** 6.5 **97. a.** 56.3 **b.** 563
c. 0.0563 **d.** 0.0563 **99.** 280 **101.** 2,000,000 **103.** 500
squeezes **105.** 11 hr, 6 P.M. **107.** 1,453.4 million
109. 0.231 sec

Are You Ready? Section 2.11 (page 151)

1. 21, 7 **2.** $\frac{75}{100}$ **3.** 6, $\frac{5}{9}$ **4.** <

Study Set Section 2.11 (page 162)

1. equivalent, **3.** terminating **5.** ÷ **7.** zeros **9.** repeating
11. a. 0.38 **b.** 0.212 **13. a.** $\frac{7}{10}$ **b.** $\frac{77}{100}$ **15.** 0.5
17. 0.875 **19.** 0.55 **21.** 2.6 **23.** 0.5625 **25.** −0.53125
27. 0.6 **29.** 0.225 **31.** 0.76 **33.** 0.002 **35.** 3.75
37. 12.6875 **39.** $0.\overline{1}$ **41.** $0.58\overline{3}$ **43.** $0.0\overline{7}$ **45.** $0.01\overline{6}$
47. $-0.\overline{45}$ **49.** $-0.\overline{60}$ **51.** 0.23 **53.** 0.49 **55.** 1.85
57. −1.08 **59.** 0.152 **61.** 0.370

63.

65.

67. < **69.** > **71.** = **73.** < **75.** 6.25, $\frac{19}{3}$, $6\frac{1}{2}$
77. $-\frac{8}{9}$, $-\frac{6}{7}$, $-0.\overline{81}$ **79.** $\frac{37}{90}$ **81.** $\frac{19}{60}$ **83.** $\frac{3}{22}$ **85.** 1
87. 0.57 **89.** 5.27 **91.** 0.35 **93.** −0.48 **95.** −2.55
97. 0.068 **99.** 7.305 **101.** 0.075 **103. a.** 12.5 ft **b.** $9\frac{5}{8}$ ft^2
105. a. $0.\overline{7}$, $0.\overline{07}$, $0.\overline{007}$ **b.** $0.\overline{0007}$
107. 0.0625, 0.375, 0.5625, 0.9375 **109.** $\frac{3}{40}$ in. **111.** 23.4 sec,
23.8 sec, 24.2 sec, 32.6 sec **113.** 93.6 in.^{2} **115.** $7.02

Are You Ready? Section 2.12 (page 167)

1. formula **2.** perimeter, area **3.** square **4.** $\frac{1}{2}bh$

Study Set Section 2.12 (page 173)

1. radius **3.** diameter **5.** circumference **7.** twice
9. $\overline{OA}, \overline{OC}, \overline{OB}$ **11.** $\overline{DA}, \overline{DC}, \overline{AC}$ **13.** $\overset{\frown}{ABC}, \overset{\frown}{ADC}$
15. a. area **b.** circumference **c.** area **d.** circumference
e. circumference **f.** area **g.** circumference
17. a. $C = \pi D$, $C = 2\pi r$ **b.** $A = \pi r^2$ **19.** square 6
21. arc AB **23. a.** multiplication:2 • π • r **b.** raising to a
power and multiplication: $\pi \cdot r^2$ **25.** 8π ft ≈ 25.1 ft
27. 12 π m ≈ 37.7 m **29.** 50.85 cm **31.** 31.42 m
33. 9π in.^{2} ≈ 28.3 in.^{2} **35.** 81π in.^{2} ≈ 254.5 in.^{2}
37. 128.5 cm^2 **39.** 57.1 cm^2 **41.** 27.4 in.^{2} **43.** 66.7 in.^{2}
45. 50π yd ≈ 157.08 yd **47.** 6π in. ≈ 18.8 in.
49. 20.25π mm^2 ≈ 63.6 mm^2 **51.** a circle with diameter 17 in.
53. 7 ft **55. a.** 1 in. **b.** 2 in. **c.** 2π in. ≈ 6.28 in.
d. π in.^{2} ≈ 3.14 in.^{2} **57.** 25 in., 2.5 in. **59.** π mi^2 ≈ 3.14 mi^2

61. 32.66π ft ≈ 102.60 ft **63.** 13 times
65. 595.36 π in^2 1,870 in.^{2} **67.** 784π ft^2 ≈ 2,463 ft^2
69. 81π in.^{2} ≈ 254 in.^{2} **71.** 30.25π ft^2 ≈ 95 ft^2
73. a. $0.08 per square inch **b.** $0.18 per square inch
c. the large pizza

Are You Ready? Section 2.13 (page 178)

1. 100 **2.** 4,528 **3.** 1,000,000 **4.** 0.0622

Study Set Section 2.13 (page 182)

1. scientific, standard **3.** right, left **5. a.** positive
b. negative **7. a.** 7.7 **b.** 5.0 **c.** 8

9.

Standard form	Decimal	Exponent for power of 10	Scientific Notation
2,840,000	2.84	6	2.84×10^6
909,400,000	9.094	8	9.094×10^8
16,000,000,000,000	1.6	13	1.6×10^{13}
641,100	6.411	5	6.411×10^5

11. 1, 10, integer **13.** 230 **15.** 812,000 **17.** 0.00115
19. 0.000976 **21.** 6,001,000 **23.** 2.718 **25.** 0.06789
27. 0.00002 **29.** 2.3×10^4 **31.** 1.7×10^6 **33.** 6.2×10^{-2}
35. 5.1×10^{-6} **37.** 5.0×10^9 **39.** 3.0×10^{-7} **41.** 9.09×10^8
43. 3.45×10^{-2} **45.** 9.0×10^0 **47.** 1.1×10^1 **49.** 1.718×10^{18}
51. 1.23×10^{-14} **53.** 7.81×10^{-5}, 7.81×10^{-3}, 7.81×10^1,
7.81×10^4, 7.81×10^7 **55. a.** 1 **b.** −1 **c.** −1
57. 2.57×10^{13} mi **59.** 63,800,000 mi^2 **61.** 6.22×10^{-3} mi
63. g, x, u, v, i, m, r **65.** 197,000,000 mi^2;
109,000,000,000,000,000 mi^2;14,600,000 mi^2
67. 1.056×10^{-24} oz **69. a.** 9.46×10^{16} Btu
b. 7.29×10^{16} Btu **c.** 2.17×10^{16} Btu
71. 1.395×10^{13} dollars **73. a.** 1.7×10^6, 1,700,000
b. 1986: 2.05×10^6, 2,050,000

Module 2 Test (page 185)

1. a. numerator, denominator **b.** equivalent **c.** simplest
d. simplify **e.** reciprocal **f.** mixed **2. a.** $\frac{4}{5}$ **b.** $\frac{1}{5}$
3. $\frac{13}{6} = 2\frac{1}{6}$ **4.** $-1\frac{1}{7} -\frac{2}{5} \quad \frac{7}{6} = 1\frac{1}{6} \quad 2\frac{4}{5}$ **5.** yes

6. $\frac{21}{24}$ **7. a.** 0 **b.** undefined **8. a.** $\frac{3}{4}$ **b.** $\frac{2}{5}$ **9. a.** The
numerator and denominator were prime factored, and pairs
of factors common to the numerator and denominator were
removed. **b.** The numerator and denominator have a
common factor of 14. It was removed from the numerator
and denominator. **10.** $\frac{6}{10}, \frac{3}{5}$ **11.** $\frac{3}{4} - \frac{1}{4} = \frac{1}{2}$ **13.** $\frac{5}{8}$ **14.** $-\frac{3}{20}$
15. 6 **16.** $\frac{11}{20}$ **17.** $\frac{11}{7}$ **18.** $\frac{1}{3}$ **19.** $\frac{9}{10}$ **20.** $\frac{3}{14}$
21. a. Multiplying two proper fractions is like finding a
part of a part, so the result is smaller than either of the
answers. **b.** Division of 5 by $\frac{1}{2}$ is equivalent to
multiplication of 5 by the reciprocal of $\frac{1}{2}$, which is 2.
22. 40 **23.** $\frac{47}{50}$ **24. a.** $9\frac{1}{6}$ **b.** $\frac{39}{21}$ **25.** $261\frac{1}{6}$ **26.** $37\frac{5}{12}$

27. $1\frac{2}{3}$ **28. a.** Foreman, $39\frac{1}{2}$ lb   **b.** Foreman, $5\frac{1}{2}$ in.

c. Ali, $\frac{1}{4}$ in.   **29.** $11\frac{1}{8}$ in.   **30.** $1\frac{1}{2}$ million   **31.** $11\frac{3}{4}$ in.

32. perimeter: $53\frac{1}{3}$ in., area: $106\frac{2}{3}$ in.^{2} **33.** 60 calories

34. 12 servings   **35. a.** (answers may vary)   **b.** (answers may vary)   **c.** (answers may vary)   **36.** When we multiply a number, such as $\frac{3}{4}$, and its reciprocal, $\frac{4}{3}$, the result is 1: $\frac{3}{4} \cdot \frac{4}{3} = 1$.

37.

38. $\frac{79}{100}$, 0.79   **39. a.** 1 thousandth   **b.** 4   **c.** 6   **d.** 2 tens

40. Selway, Monroe, Paston, Covington, Cadia

41. 4,519.0027   **42. a.** $60 + 2 + \frac{5}{10} + \frac{5}{100}$, sixty-two and fifty-five hundredths, $62\frac{55}{100}$ **b.** $\frac{8}{100} + \frac{1}{10,000} + \frac{3}{100,000}$, eight thousand thirteen hundred-thousandths , $\frac{8,013}{100,000}$

43. a. 461.7   **b.** 2,733.050   **c.** −1.983373   **44.** $0.65

45. 10.756   **46.** 6.121   **47.** 0.1024   **48.** 0.57   **49.** 14.07

50. 0.0348   **51.** $1.\overline{18}$ **52.** −0.8   **53.** −2.29   **54. a.** 210

b. $4,000 \div 20 = 400 \div 2 = 200$ **55. a.** 0.567909   **b.** 0.458

56. 61,400,000,000   **57.** 1.026 in.   **58.** 1.25 mi^2 **59.** 0.004 in.

60. Saturday, $23.75   **61.** 0.42 g   **62.** 20.825 lb   **63.** 8.3 in.

64. a. 0.34   **b.** $0.41\overline{6}$ **65.** 3.588   **66.** 56.86   **67.** $\frac{41}{30}$

68.

69. $5.65   **70. a.** −1.08

b. 2.5625   **71. a.** >   **b.** <   **c.** =   **d.** <   **74.** π

75. 21π ft $\approx$ 66.0 ft   **76.** $(40 + 12\pi)$ft $\approx$ 77.7 ft

77. 225π m^2 $\approx$ 706.9 m^2 **78.** 98.31 yd^2 **79.** about $39

80. The 15-inch diameter cheese pizza is the better buy.

81. a. $3 \times 10^3 = 3 \times 1,000 = 3,000$

b. $3 \times 10^{-3} = 3 \times 0.001 = 0.003$ **82.** 1   **83.** 6.25×10^{18}

84. 0.000093   **85.** 4.3×10^{-9} **86.** 1,350,000,000,000

87. a. $\frac{1}{100,000}$; 0.00001   **b.** $\frac{1}{10,000,000}$; 0.0000001

88. a. 5   **b.** −4